"As denominations tear themselves apart over issues of marriage and sexual ethics, we urgently need better and more hermeneutically reflective conversations about what the Bible means. Bringing Gadamer and practical theology together in this timely study, Seán McGuire helps us see what's really going on beneath the surface of our disagreements."

—**ANDREW JUDD**, deputy principal, Ridley College

"What might it look like for church leaders, when navigating ecclesial disagreement, to clearly articulate the main influences that have shaped their understanding? Taking the well-known Wesleyan Quadrilateral as a starting point, Seán McGuire exemplifies an approach to talking about theological reflection that can help church leaders to speak more clearly and talk past one another less frequently. In the aftermath of postmodernism, this kind of practical meta-theology is badly needed."

—**CHRISTOPHER LAND**, associate professor of New Testament and linguistics, McMaster Divinity College

"In this timely book, Seán McGuire offers a deep dive into the complexities of why Christians interpret the same Bible passages differently. Through an innovative combination of metamodernism and a revised Wesleyan quadrilateral, he methodically develops an analytical framework to help readers uncover roots of interpretative difference. With a practical theology sensibility, McGuire offers much food for thought both in his analysis and constructive proposals for transformative reading of the Scriptures."

—**ANDREW P. ROGERS**, associate professor of practical theology, University of Roehampton

"*Biblical Hermeneutics in the Metamodern Mood* is an invaluable resource for helping followers of Jesus see scriptural interpretation with fresh eyes. With wisdom and acumen, Seán McGuire enables readers to critically reflect on both their own hermeneutic while fostering a kind of thoughtful curiosity about interpretive lenses employed by others. In a time of increasing division, this book equips readers to engage with the sacred text in a way that is both faithful to their own context—body, time, place, communities, and traditions—and open to diverse perspectives."

—DWIGHT J. FRIESEN, professor of practical theology,
The Seattle School of Theology & Psychology

# Biblical Hermeneutics
# in the Metamodern Mood

# Biblical Hermeneutics in the Metamodern Mood

*Understanding Differences in Interpretation and Theological Integration in Practice*

SEÁN M. W. MCGUIRE

PICKWICK *Publications* · Eugene, Oregon

BIBLICAL HERMENEUTICS IN THE METAMODERN MOOD
Understanding Differences in Interpretation and Theological Integration in Practice

Pickwick Publications
An Imprint of Wipf and Stock Publishers
199 W. 8th Ave., Suite 3
Eugene, OR 97401

www.wipfandstock.com

PAPERBACK ISBN: 979-8-3852-0902-6
HARDCOVER ISBN: 979-8-3852-0903-3
EBOOK ISBN: 979-8-3852-0904-0

*Cataloguing-in-Publication data:*

Names: McGuire, Seán M. W., author.

Title: Biblical hermeneutics in the metamodern world : understanding differences in interpretation and theological integration in practice / Seán M. W. McGuire.

Description: Eugene, OR : Pickwick Publications, 2024 | Includes bibliographical references and index.

Identifiers: ISBN 979-8-3852-0902-6 (paperback) | ISBN 979-8-3852-0903-3 (hardcover) | ISBN 979-8-3852-0904-0 (ebook)

Subjects: LCSH: Bible—Hermeneutics. | Postmodernism.

Classification: BS476 .M34 2024 (paperback) | BS476 .M34 (ebook)

VERSION NUMBER 07/16/24

May these words of my mouth
and this meditation of my heart
be pleasing in your sight,
LORD, my Rock and my Redeemer

—PSALM 19:14

# Contents

# Contents

# List of Figures and Tables

# Acknowledgments

THIS BOOK REPRESENTS A revision of my doctoral dissertation, which was defended in March 2023 at McMaster Divinity College in Hamilton, ON. The seed of the project was planted while I was writing documents in preparation for ordination between September 2018 and April 2019. I owe of debt of gratitude to my ordination supervisor, Rev. Glenn Cordery, whose encouragement and curiosity led me to articulate my thoughts about theological reflection, and who pushed me to consider pursuing doctoral study when it became clear that my ordination paper had grown to be roughly forty pages too long.

While many know her primarily as a brilliant New Testament scholar, I have the privilege of calling Cynthia Long Westfall a mentor, congregant, and close friend. Her wisdom and pastoral disposition helped me to understand academic work as an aspect of my calling as a Pastor-Scholar. I would not have considered completing this project without her initial input and continued encouragement throughout its development. Likewise, I am grateful to my doctoral supervisor Christopher D. Land, whose belief in this project, and in me, helped pull me through the inevitable darker days of doctoral work. The fingerprints of our conversations about metamodernism and hermeneutics, during which iron certainly sharpened iron, are found throughout this work. His friendship has been a gift from the Lord, and has made me a better pastor, scholar, and interpreter.

Many others provided direction and encouragement as I completed this project: my secondary supervisor, Gord Heath; my external examiner, Andrew Rogers; and the chair of my defence committee, Wendy Porter. Each of the above offered insightful feedback that improved my work immensely, and each encouraged me to share my research in seminars and publication. Furthermore, Michael Knowles, Dwight Friesen, and Andrew Judd graciously gave of their time to talk about hermeneutics, Gadamer, and the metamodern tension, and gave feedback and encouragement for which I am grateful.

Truly, there are too many people to thank in detail. However, it would be remiss of me not to specially recognize the following: my extended family for their ongoing encouragement—especially my parents, Patrick and Michele, for their constant encouragement, and in-laws Rod and Laurie for letting me take over their basement and office to use for writing retreats. I would also like to thank Francis Pang, Lee Beach, Lane Fusilier, Andy Groen, Merv Budd, and Allan Heidman for their friendship, mentorship, and encouragement. I made life-long friends while studying at McMaster Divinity College. Throughout the program my thinking was sharpened by Beth Gould Nolson, Dale Sanger, David Long, Greg Sinclair, Shawn Lazar, Paul Lucas, Ambrose Thomson, and many others. Our regular Zoom meetings, ongoing Facebook chat, phone calls, and GA Office discussions provided much needed encouragement, food for thought, laughter, and sharing of our struggles which made researching and writing significantly more enjoyable—because we were doing it together.

I would also not have made it far without the encouragement and prayers of the saints at Wentworth Baptist Church (Hamilton, ON). I am especially indebted to the Board of Deacons who have sought to care for and support me by caring for my family with prayers, meals, and child care during the busiest seasons. They have kept my eyes on the ultimate goal of serving Christ and being a doctor both *of* and *for* the Church. In particular, the wisdom, encouragement, and support from Angela Shimizu, Tracy Upham, Ryder Wishart, Mary and Doug Peters, and Kelvin and Jan Mutter were a continued source of strength and grounding during the development of this project. Mary passed away before the completion of this project, but the fruit of our discussions over the years are peppered throughout this work. We miss her every day.

When I first brought up the idea pursuing a vocation as a Pastor-Scholar, my wife's immediate response was to affirm this calling and tell me "It's obvious that the Lord is telling you to do this." Jessica, your discernment, faith that the Lord would provide for us (which He has, abundantly), encouragement in my calling, help while editing, and sacrifices—as we welcomed multiple children into the world while I finished course work and then my thesis, all while a pandemic raged—are what made completing this project possible. *I love you, Habibti.*

# 1

---

# Introduction

IN A SERIES OF sermons preached in the early 2010s at a Canadian Baptists of Ontario and Quebec (CBOQ) affiliated church, an LGBTQ inclusive theological position was offered, arguing that Paul, in his letters, was wrong about the sinfulness of homosexual sexual activity. By the time I entered vocational ministry in 2014, these sermons had proven to be the starting point for a renewed theological conflict regarding homosexuality and gay marriage in the denomination[1]—heated debates that have been slowly, but steadily, crescendoing ever since. Like in other denominations, these debates have had well-intentioned believers of different convictions arguing for their theological suppositions to either be maintained or become permissible within the policies and doctrinal standards of the denomination. In the ensuing years this conversation has only intensified and grown in tension in churches and denominations throughout the West, and indeed

---

1. Baptist churches are autonomous, making the designation of "denomination" problematic because the word suggests an ecclesiological hierarchy that does not exist between Baptist churches. While many Baptists do refer to their associative organizations as denominations, other churches, and the CBOQ organization itself, refers to it either as a "family of churches" or by using the term "convention," both of which are meant to signify that churches remain autonomous while freely associating with one another. However, this family of churches, as well as other Baptist groups, function in ways similar to other protestant denominations, such that referring to the CBOQ as a denomination is not out of line. For the sake of clarity and wider applicability, throughout this work I will be referring to the CBOQ as a denomination but ask that readers keep the above nuance of Baptist polity in mind.

the world, as the "traditional" understanding of marriage and human sexuality is increasingly abandoned in secularized cultures. At its essence, the debate—like countless others in the church—has largely centered on significant differences in interpretive practices. But what are these differences exactly, and how can we begin to talk about them in order to work through difficult topics of conversation, such as the above, together?

In this volume, I will use the above situation as an illustrative example to explore and develop an approach to understanding one's hermeneutic (that is, one's approach to interpretation) that will complexify the nature of biblical interpretive practice in the contemporary age. Utilizing the proposed approach, the project will reveal how one's hermeneutics is affected by the prioritization of certain theological reflection sources, with different priorities prompting particular interpretive conclusions. By showing the multivalent nature of interpretation, readers will be equipped to think through how they come to their conclusions and how those conclusions shape faithful application or embodiment of the gospel.

Because application (in the sense of *praxis*) is an element of understanding, the practice being studied in this project is more complex than simply biblical interpretation. Indeed, the practice of biblical interpretation is, fundamentally, a component of the practice of discipleship. As such, biblical interpretive practice has congruence with paradigms of theological reflection because, as I will argue, these paradigms are a necessary element of interpretive practice. It is through the practice of biblical interpretation that Christians come to understand what Peter Jensen refers to as Scripture's "authentic interpretation of human experience,"[2] and through theological reflection that Scripture-informed understanding shapes how Christians live. Consequently, when Christians read (that is, interpret) Scripture, they do so, in part, to bring their experiences into conformity with the revelation of God in the Bible in order to participate in the *missio Dei*, the ongoing and Spirit-empowered mission of God.[3] This participation is, in many ways, predicated on understanding developed through interpretive practices, for obedience to Christ is dependent on our reflexive understanding such that it is a "thoughtful obedience."[4] By clarifying interpretive practice, as this project aims to do, believers can be equipped to faithfully follow Christ.

---

2. Jensen, *Revelation*, 41.

3. Collins, *Reordering Reflection*, 16.

4. O'Donovan, *Crisis*, 69, 77.

Thus, this project's aim can be expanded to include equipping believers in understanding their interpretive practice so that they are encouraged by their renewed understanding toward greater faithfulness to God and fidelity to Scripture, which, in turn, acts as an encouragement for believers to live as citizens of God's in-breaking kingdom. This means the practice being studied is not simply biblical interpretation but *biblical interpretation as an act of discipleship*—a practice that shapes believers into increasingly faithful and obedient followers of Jesus Christ.

## SELF-REFLECTION ON (THE IMPORTANCE OF) PREUNDERSTANDINGS

While the initial situation giving rise to this project is the ongoing debates about biblical interpretation related to homosexuality, this debate should *not* be understood as the topic of the study. Rather, the debate serves as a sort of case study for understanding interpretive practice, providing a discourse that I apply my theoretical approach to understanding interpretive practice. Thus, it is important to note at the onset that the project's aim is not to be apologetic for a particular interpretive conclusion on the topic of homosexuality nor to make an argument against or for LGBT-affirming interpretations. Rather, the aim is to better understand the underlying elements that lead different persons and churches towards their varied interpretive conclusions.

As an ordained minister with the CBOQ, my theology of marriage conforms to that of my family of churches, which is the so-called "traditional" view. I have chosen to maintain the categorical poles of "traditional" and "affirming" for discussing the sexuality debate throughout the project because they, for better or worse, are the poles used to describe the debate in my research data and within evangelicalism more broadly. Simply stated, the "traditional" position is the belief that sex-difference is an essential part of what marriage is, which is most profoundly expressed in the act of sex; the "affirming" position is the belief that marriage is a covenant between two consenting adults, regardless of sex difference.[5]

I recognize the above places me at risk of allowing prejudgments to negatively guide my reflections on the research topic. Indeed, judgments will necessarily be made in the course of the research about whether I think one way of interpretation is better or worse than others, according to my

5. Sprinkle, *People*, 23.

theological and theory-driven convictions and presuppositions. However, such a confession also opens the possibility for engaging the research with greater humility, as it invites ongoing reflexivity, on my part, to ensure I am fairly representing and articulating the position of those with whom I disagree. This invitation extends further, to readers of the project, to reflect on their presuppositions, such that we will each come to better understand how we interpret Scripture in practice.

Through self-reflection on our practice, we become better equipped to engage in critical dialogue about the conclusions we come to, and better understand our assumptions and the decisions that lead us to our differing convictions. Indeed, as Stanley Porter comments, if church leaders (pastors, professors, and others), who are both interpreters and hermeneutical guides for others, "were more sensitive to the models that are used in interpretation, as well as the paradigms they presume, we would clarify and advance discussion and debate significantly by at least being aware of the presuppositions of other interpreters."[6] It is my hope that this volume will help church leaders, and indeed informed laity, better understand the hidden elements of their interpretive practice, and therefore the interpretive practice of others, so that constructive dialogue across difference with regards to biblical interpretation can occur. For, as Oliver O'Donovan incisively argued regarding the homosexuality debate in the Anglican communion, disagreement—especially sharp disagreement—is an opportunity to grow in faithfulness, as "the very attempt to reach a resolution transforms our experience of the disagreement. . . . [T]hey are openings for those who share a common faith to explore and resolve important tensions within the context of communion."[7]

The importance of reflexivity for this project is thus difficult to overstate for two reasons. First, theologically informed insight into situation requires an openness to being wrong, to our preunderstandings being challenged, and therefore to our being changed. Reflexivity creates a context for all this to happen.[8] By taking a reflexive posture, researchers are meant to recognize the contextual nature of their inquiry and at least become aware

6. Porter, *Interpretation for Preaching*, 8–9.

7. O'Donovan, *Crisis*, 32.

8. As Jean-Yves Lacoste commented, "Preunderstanding without honest admission of non-understanding will hardly invite more than the most meagre discoveries" ("More Haste," 272).

of, or recognize, the limits (and role) of their subjectivity.[9] It is for this reason that reflexivity is now considered essential for practical theological inquiries. As Andrew Rogers comments, "reflexivity has now become a fundamental aspect of practical theology. It features in practical theology programme criteria, in most introductions to the subject and is lauded as a sign of high quality practical theological work."[10] Second, the volatility with which the topic of sexual ethics is treated in the church and contemporary culture requires clear, self-critical thinking. It has been my experience that people tend to speak past one another on this topic because of a variety of hermeneutical issues at play in the conversation's background. For the church, this includes how we understand revelation and specific biblical texts, and how this understanding is applied in situations. Indeed, by applying the text of Scripture, the Bible's meaning is understood and *substantiated*, making application an important aspect of one's hermeneutical process.[11] This being the case, it is no wonder Western culture has moved away from Scripture as a trustworthy document, for its application in many people's lives has been devastating. Rather than speaking the truth in love, the church has become more known for yelling truth about love at people, utilizing the Bible as a weapon to enforce its will. The above tension is highly visible in church discussions on homosexuality, where a handful of verses are referred to as "clobber-texts" because of how they have been used against people. It is generally agreed by both traditional and affirming interpreters, for lack of better terms, that these passages include: Lev 18:22; 20:13; 1 Cor 6:9–11; 1 Tim 1:10; and Rom 1:18—2:1. Other passages regularly commented on include: Gen 9:20–27; 19:1–28; Judg 19:22–25; and Jude 7. Without reflexivity on whether I am falling into the trope of using passages to clobber people—especially through uncharitable readings of what others have said regarding their interpretive practice—meaningful and productive discussion about interpretation will not be possible.

Further to the bias above, the research scope will be limited by context. Both I and the source data I have gathered can be broadly described as evangelical, with priority given to Canadian Baptist sources. Thus, the research will not discuss the wide range of interpretive practice within the church universal. Indeed, my evangelical perspective and source data may leave much to be desired for non-evangelical readers, even if the research

9. Rogers, "Looking into the Mirror," 464–65.

10. Rogers, "Looking into the Mirror," 464.

11. Westphal, *Whose Community?*, 108–10; Ehrensperger, *Dynamics of Power*, 188.

outcomes set the stage for a wider ecumenical dialogue. My aim is to be *descriptive* so that the project sufficiently and accurately elucidates interpretive practice. By locating the research within Canada's evangelical tradition, I describe what is (as I see it) but do not presume that the reader should or must also be Canadian, evangelical, or hold baptistic convictions to learn from the research. On the contrary, locating the research in these traditions is to make key assumptions clear so that the implications of the research can be more easily contextualized.

A further clarification is required regarding my theological bias, as the term *evangelical* has become increasingly misunderstood over the past decade. Reflecting on evangelicalism in the United States, political scientist Ryan Burge has argued that *evangelical* is quickly becoming a synonym for *Republican Party*, making the term increasingly politicized.[12] However, I believe the term still has utility because of the difference in use of this term between American and British evangelicals. To be sure, the Canadian Baptist tradition is a complex mix of British and American sensibilities, such that there is a wide spectrum of thought regarding what evangelicalism is within Canada. But evangelicals in the CBOQ, and indeed in much of Canada, share an underlying theological self-understanding of, and hope for, evangelicalism that is more akin to British sensibilities, which is significantly less politicized and has largely lacked the "culture war" ethos that continues to mark American evangelical self-understanding.[13]

Central to evangelical's theological self-understanding is the helpful summary by David Bebbington, who utilizes a quadripartite framework to describe evangelicalism. According to Bebbington, evangelicals embrace (i) biblicism, the affirmation of the authority of Scripture; (ii) crucicenterism, the affirmation of the centrality of the cross for understanding the Christian faith; (iii) conversionism, the affirmation of the importance of a personal experience of God by the gospel; and (iv) activism, the conviction that faith is both private and public, and, as such, the gospel must be shared with non-believers.[14] It is with these elements in mind that I understand and identify with the evangelical tradition.[15]

12. Burge, *Nones*, 16.

13. Reimer, *Caught in the Current*, 6–7, 12–13.

14. Bebbington, *Evangelicalism in Modern Britain*, 5–17.

15. For discussion on evangelical practical theology, see Morris and Cameron, *Evangelicals*, 3–7.

## PRACTICAL (EMPIRICAL) THEOLOGY

The primary disciplinary context this project is situated in is practical theology. The field of practical theology is a highly diverse and somewhat contested area of study.[16] Explaining why, Bonnie Miller-McLemore has suggested that practical theology can be described as a discipline, activity, method, and curricular area, which makes discussing practical theology fraught with complications.[17] Indeed, Miller-McLemore's description offers a window into why practical theology may be considered contested, as these four "areas" of practical theological inquiry are not dissociated from one another but are argued to be in constant flux and conversation. Furthermore, the field's foci has shifted over the past decades away from being "applied theology," with a focus on practical training for pastors and clinicians, and towards theological reflection on faithful practice in varied contexts.[18] Graham et al. further comments, "As a result . . . Christian ministry may be understood less in terms of the application of specific expertise and more about facilitating the vocation of all Christians through processes of understanding, analysing, and reflecting."[19] Thus, practical theology has moved away from imposing theology onto practice towards reflecting on practice theologically—a subtle but critical shift in the field.

The above raises an interesting issue regarding language, as within Canadian and American strands of evangelicalism the ends of biblical interpretation are widely referred to as "applying," or "the application of," Scripture. However, such language can be confusing in the field of practical theology because of its contentious history emerging in opposition to applied theology, opening the possibility of a contextual misunderstanding of this phrase. Indeed, what is colloquially meant by "application" in the North American context is essentially similar to what practical theologians aim for, which is *faithful response*. As Andrew Abernethy discusses, faithful response and application are not mutually exclusive terms, and indeed have a similar end in mind: "to respond to the voice of the living God who speaks through the Word today."[20] The language of application implies a gap between Scripture and contemporary readers—not least of which

16. Farley, "Situations," 1.

17. Miller-McLemore, "Introduction," 5.

18. Graham et al., *Theological Reflection*, 2; Graham, Review of *Practical Theology*, 493.

19. Graham et al., *Theological Reflection*, 6.

20. Abernethy, *Savouring Scripture*, 145.

being the time that has passed between Scripture's composition and our reception of it—which is why one does theological reflection in situations in the first place. Due to this, I will continue to use the language of application. However, it is important readers note from the outset that my use of the phrase "application" should not be understood to suggest an imposition of "hints and helps" on practice but as the ends of the reflective process, expressed necessarily in action; reflection brought to completion through faithful response to the living God.

Because of all of the complexity briefly described in the preceding paragraphs, defining how one understands practical theology can help locate a given project within a wider research conversation. While some in the field would argue for a definition of practical theology that is as widely applicable as possible, the current project's work will be distinctly and confessionally Christian. Therefore, taking cues from Dorothy Bass, I define (Christian) practical theology as *the church's critically reflexive theological inquiry on the nature and embodiment of Christian practices.*[21] Put more simply, practical theology is the reflective study of the what and how of Christian practices, so that those practices can be more faithfully practiced. Indeed, I share the conviction of Helen Collins who writes, "*How* we think about the relationship between God, God's Word, and our lives is as important as *what* we think, and the two shape each other."[22] Thus, the theological inquiry this project represents is a response to God's revelation and continued work in the church and world; a critical reflection on the intersection of theologies of Scripture and practices of interpretation in order to understand the complexities of this practice.

Because practical theology is focused on understanding and improving faithful practice, it has a number of distinctive features that shape each of the areas that Miller-McLemore described. First, practical theology is *critically reflexive.* By this phrase, I mean that practical theology engages in critical self-reflection on the intersection of theology and practice. In practical theology, this point is often related to the phrase "interpreting situations," which Edward Farley argues is to be a practice that is "self conscious, self-critical, and disciplined."[23] By focusing on interpreting situations,

---

21. Bass, "Ways of Life," 30. This definition does not disqualify non-Christian forms of practical theology, but rather clarifies that the theological perspective of the project will be Christian.

22. Collins, *Reordering Reflection,* 6.

23. Farley, "Situations," 10.

practical theology invites one to investigate specific moments to discover God at work—and do so carefully and critically, bringing the situation into conversation with Scripture and one's tradition(s). As Swinton and Mowat argue, "the text of human experience in general and the experience of the church, in particular, holds interpretive significance for theological development."[24] Therefore the critical reflexivity of practical theology is dialogical, particularly with other theological disciplines, including (but not limited to) systematic theology, biblical studies, and church history.[25]

Second, practical theology's aim is *theological inquiry*—a response to God's revelation, focusing on how practice is a source for knowledge of God because God continues to work through the church and in the world. Broadly described, the inquiry of practical theology is theological reflection on situations or experiences whereby one begins to reflect on God's work in their midst by asking, "what am I experiencing and why is this so?"[26] The concept of theological reflection, which is central to this project, will be further elucidated in chapter 2.

Finally, the theological inquiry of practical theology is honed in *on the nature and embodiment of Christian practices*. Practical theology is concerned with understanding and articulating the complexities of practice, including questions and needs, as they arise in situations.[27] Because of this concern, which is reflection on experience,[28] practical theologians have been drawn towards using the research methods of the social sciences to investigate present-day practice and uncover tensions, issues, or curiosities that reveal places where the church's practice can be better understood and, therefore, more faithfully practiced. Indeed, Swinton and Mowat's evaluation is certainly correct: "the social sciences have thus been vital and fruitful dialogue partners in the ongoing process of theological reflection."[29] The social sciences have been critical in shaping practical theology in the early decades of the twenty-first century.

---

24. Swinton and Mowat, *Qualitative Research*, 15.

25. Swinton and Mowat, *Qualitative Research*, 16.

26. Byrne, "Practice-Led Theology," 200.

27. Swinton and Mowat, *Qualitative Research*, 13, 20, 23.

28. Cartledge (*Mediations*, 51) names various practical theological understandings of experience, which includes "specific incidents or events," passively "going through life," and "common human experience," each of which can be the ground from which practical theological inquiry sprouts.

29. Swinton and Mowat, *Qualitative Research*, xii.

Due to the field's use of social scientific methods, it is appropriate—and indeed has been argued, perhaps most famously by Johannes van der Ven—to say that practical theology is empirical theology.[30] In other words, practical theological research observes and measures practices and experiences, and by doing so collects *theological* data that can be analyzed to develop renewed social and theological understandings.[31] Data gathering and analysis can be either quantitative or qualitative, with qualitative methodologies growing in popularity in the field of practical theology in recent decades.[32] This growth is due to the varied aims of the two research approaches. The quantitative research approach seeks to count and measure in order to derive understanding, via numeric simplification, and develop predictions, while qualitative research instead seeks to observe, describe, and interpret experiences in order to map patterns and make inferences to answer a research question.[33] Because I am aiming to describe and interpret *interpretive practice*, the qualitative research approach is more suitable for this project.

While empirical theological research into the practice of biblical interpretation has been performed by many others, the focus of this project sets it apart from similar work in the field. In order to describe this difference in foci more effectively, and therefore situate this project within an ongoing conversation, a brief review of key research in practical theology regarding biblical interpretive practice is necessary. Broadly speaking, these can be divided into two areas: the use of Scripture in practical theological research and the study of ordinary hermeneutics.

## Using the Bible in Practice Theology

How the Bible is utilized in practical theology is a topic that, like the discipline itself, is often murky and debated. Indeed, Paul Ballard has argued the use of Scripture in practical theology is a complex and under-researched aspect of the field requiring further attention.[34] While Ballard does outline approaches to the use of Scripture over the course of the discipline's

---

30. Ven, *Practical Theology*.

31. Francis et al., *Empirical Theology*, xiii; Beaudoin, "Practice Matter Theologically," 25; Roest, *Collaborative Practical Theology*, 117.

32. For discussion on qualitative versus quantitative research in practical theology, see: Swinton and Mowat, *Qualitative Research*, 42–49.

33. Village, *Bible and Lay People*, 7.

34. Ballard, "Use of Scripture," 164, 170–71.

development, researchers such as Zoë Bennett[35] have more recently offered constructive proposals for how the field might approach its use of Scripture in the future. However, one research paper looms large over the discipline on this topic, Mark Cartledge's "The Use of Scripture in Practical Theology." This study reviewed the use of Scripture in academic works of practical theology and concluded "the practical theological academy, for the most part, is content to sit loose to an engagement with Scripture."[36] Although Cartledge overviews various ways that practical theologians have described the use of Scripture, and himself developed a topology of ways practical theologians use Scripture, he does not prescribe how, why, or *how the field ought to understand* its use of the Bible moving forward. Indeed, the topology Cartledge presents does not, in my mind, engender practical theologians to better utilizing the Scriptures in their theological research, even as there is emerging evidence that explicit biblical engagement has begun improving in the years since his paper was published.[37] I will engage explicitly with Cartledge's work and broader topic of the use of the Bible in practical theology in chapter 6.

## Ordinary Hermeneutics

Ordinary hermeneutics is a description of the hermeneutical practices of Christians who do not have specialized training in academic biblical scholarship.[38] There has been much interest in this aspect of the practice of biblical interpretation in practical theology, as Bible reading is something that most Christians do to some extent. And even still, studies continue to show that Bible engagement among "ordinary" readers is in a free-fall. Case in point, a 2013 study by *Faith Today* revealed that 75 percent of Canadians who self-identify as Christian seldom to never read the Bible.[39] It is no wonder, then, why there would be research interest in the topic of ordinary hermeneutics.

In *The Bible and Lay People*, Andrew Village explored the relationship Christians laity, untrained in academic biblical scholarship, have with the Bible. Using data collected via analytical survey, Village investigated a range of what he describes as 'interpretative possibilities' and 'extra-biblical

---

35. Bennett, *Using the Bible*.
36. Cartledge, "Use of Scripture," 281.
37. Rogers, "Looking into the Mirror," 463–64.
38. Village, *Bible and Lay People*, 1.
39. Hiemstra, *Engagement*, 10.

variables' in order to develop predictions regarding how those variables affect biblical interpretation.[40] Indeed, the predictions Village develops are both interesting and useful for understanding the relationship laity have with the Bible across various traditions and the underling factors that shape varied interpretive practices.

Likewise, in *Congregational Hermeneutics*, Andrew Rogers researched the biblical interpretive practices of congregations to describe how Christians actually read the Bible and to suggest how they *should* read the Bible.[41] In essence, Rogers argues that churches should be helping Christians to shape what he describes as hermeneutical virtues: preunderstandings which inform—and are the goal of—biblical interpretation.[42] These virtues are: honesty, faithfulness, openness, courage, humility, confidence, and community.[43] Both of the above studies offer valuable practical theological research into the practice of biblical interpretation that inform the church in how it could improve this practice.

There is also a body of research into the use of the Bible in small group settings. James Bielo's study on evangelical Bible study groups focused on the importance of Bible studies on evangelical church culture, and how that culture in turn shapes evangelical Christian's practice of Bible reading.[44] Hans de Wit has proposed a cross-cultural approach for groups of varied ethnic, educational, and socioeconomic backgrounds to come together to interpret Scripture.[45] More recently, Anna Clare Creedon has researched whether small group Bible studies are able to promote what she calls 'transformative biblical engagement,' whereby Bible study in community promotes one to "more fully resemble Jesus Christ and glorify God by the power of the Holy Spirit."[46] Concluding that yes, small groups can facilitate this transformation—that is, they can help believers be shaped into Christlikeness—Creedon argues that ongoing reflection on the roles of experts, challenge, and use of materials in small group contexts is necessary, as these

40. Village, *Bible and Lay People*, 11, 159–62.

41. Rogers, *Congregational Hermeneutics*, 2.

42. Rogers, *Congregational Hermeneutics*, 36.

43. Rogers, *Congregational Hermeneutics*, 177.

44. Bielo, *Words upon the Word*, 4–5, 156–57.

45. Wit, *Empirical Hermeneutics;* see also Powell, *What Do They Hear?*

46. Creedon, *Small Groups*, 34.

elements are all contributors to the transformation of participants, as well as potential hinderances to transformation occurring.[47]

Given this brief overview of recent works, the concerns of each of these studies differ from mine in a subtle but important way, in that I am only tangentially interested in the interpretive practices of ordinary readers. While Village and Rogers, in particular, focus, in some sense, on the understanding and development of *preunderstanding* amongst ordinary readers, and other texts focus on how cultures, contexts, expectations, and expertise (or lack thereof) inform interpretation, I am more interested in describing differences in interpretive practice. By doing this, I hope to help interpreters better understand and describe their interpretive practice for themselves. Because of this, rather than studying ordinary readers, my project utilizes communications from critical readers to audiences of ordinary readers, so that I can observe and describe the tensions within the interpretive practices being exemplified for Christians, and therefore name those tensions in such a way as to provide clarity for what is going on hermeneutically under the surface of significant debates in the church. As such, this project aims to observe the "what" of the practice of biblical interpretation and exemplify, via description, the "how" of this practice, in order to offer new insight that will improve the practice in the future.

## RESEARCH PARADIGMS AND CORE CONCEPTS

As a multi-disciplinary work, this project utilizes several methodologies and paradigms: practice-led research, hermeneutic theory, cultural studies, and doctrines of Scripture. These inform the methods of investigation and reflection used and developed throughout the project in a dialogical sense, as they work together to form a paradigm that informs both the practice being studied and the disciplines within which the project finds its footing.

## Practice-Led Research

Practice-led research is a research paradigm that frames and organizes research in a way that is initiated, informed, quickened, and shaped by practice. It recognizes that practice is generative for knowledge production, taking seriously Charles Taylor's assertion that "If understanding makes the

---

47. Creedon, *Small Groups*, 168.

practice possible, it is also true that it is the practice that largely carries the understanding."[48] This approach to research began in the 1970s, when British researchers in Art and Design disciplines began crafting "practice-led" doctoral-level programs that could facilitate merging creative and professional practice with structured and rigorous academic inquiry.[49] For the present project, the research inquiry initiates in discussions regarding the practice of biblical interpretation and will be informed and shaped by this context and practice. Indeed, the project emerges from discussions, discernments, and my writing a portion of my ordination statement on the sexuality debate, and the realization that more was going on under the surface of our interpretations than was being recognized.

By beginning in practice, the practice-led research paradigm orients research towards the theory undergirding a practice, in this case the practice of interpretation as an act of discipleship, such that, after research and reflection, new knowledge can be articulated and applied to the practice—on the level of *theory*.[50] This both gives a theoretical framework that structures the present research and makes reflection a vital aspect of the paradigm, for it is reflecting on practice that leads to the theoretical roots of a practice where new knowledge can be articulated. Indeed, the very point of research is not to explain one's subjective self for others but, as Andrew McNamara argues, to "explain something of significance and broader relevance to a research community."[51]

These two crucial factors of practice-led research—practice informing theory and reflexivity—make this research paradigm uniquely fitted for research inquiries in the discipline of practical theology. This is because practical theology is concerned with understanding and articulating the complexities of how practices are shaped by and shape humanity, in both practical and theological terms.[52] In other words, practical theology assumes that practice informs theory—an assumption shared with practice-led research—and thus approaches theological reflection with this insight at the forefront of an inquiry. Furthermore, the necessarily reflexive nature of practice-led research finds natural correspondence with practical theology. Reflexivity is a deliberately interrogative self-reflection carried out in each

48. Taylor, *Social Imaginaries*, 25.
49. Gray, "Inquiry through Practice," 2–3; Biggs and Büchler, "Rigor," 63.
50. Gray, "Ground Up," 14.
51. McNamara, "Six Rules," 6.
52. Bass, "Ways of Life," 29.

stage of the research process. As Swinton and Mowat argue, "reflexivity is a mode of knowing that accepts the impossibility of the researcher standing outside of the research field and seeks to incorporate that knowledge creatively and effectively."[53] Thus, of all possible research paradigms, practice-led research seems uniquely suited for practical theological inquiry. Likewise, reflexivity is a core component of qualitative research methods, making such methods necessary for productive practice-led practical theological research. At this juncture, is may be clearer why I began this chapter with a contextual self-reflection, as doing so was an important step towards grounding the project in a reflexive posture.

## The Emergence of Metamodernism

A core assumption made from the outset of this project is about contemporary culture's nature: that Western culture is not gripped by modernism, nor postmodernism, but *metamodernism*. Metamodernism is a term coined by Timotheus Velmeulen and Robin van den Akker to describe the cultural mood or sensibility that has been emerging in the West since the turn of the millennium. As a cultural mood, metamodernism negotiates between modernism and postmodernism—both of which are latent within Western culture—and thus is best characterized as a condition of cultural in-betweenness.[54] Taking its name from the Greek word *metaxis*, meaning "with, between, and beyond," metamodernism is an oscillation between the cultural sensibilities of the modern and postmodern that aims to move *beyond* those sensibilities.[55] In this sense, metamodernism can be understood as the prolegomena of a new epoch bursting with reconstructive potential.

As Velmeulen and van den Akker explain, "ontologically, metamodernism oscillates between the modern and the postmodern. . . . Indeed, by oscillating to and fro, the metamodern negotiates between the modern and the postmodern."[56] This negotiation is, in some regard, an attempt to hold the best of both modernism and postmodernism in tension, while also taking account of their flaws, in order to move towards a more coherent

---

53. Swinton and Mowat, *Qualitative Research*, 57; Schreier, *Qualitative in Practice*, 23.

54. Velmeulen and van den Akker, "Metamodernism," para. 1, 16–17; Velmeulen and van den Akker, "Utopia," 56.

55. Bargár, "Transforming Sensibility," 5.

56. Velmeulen and van den Akker, "Metamodernism," para. 15.

social imaginary.[57] Jason Ānanda Josephson Storm describes this in terms of sublation, such that metamodernism negotiates between the modern and postmodern so that both can be negated and therefore overcome.[58] As Pavol Bargár observes, this means that "metamodernism takes the project of *construction* from modernism and that of *deconstruction* from postmodernism to come up with its own *reconstruction*."[59] It is, therefore, necessary to offer a preliminary clarification regarding modernism and postmodernism, which will be elaborated on throughout the project, as these inform how one understands the metamodern mood.

To be sure, because of their character as widespread cultural movements whose influence is found in everything from literature to theology to architecture to fashion, defining modernism and postmodernism is fraught with issues. Moreover, modernism and postmodernism are often defined in opposition to one another, which means they are often used as generalizations that act as shorthand for referencing a number of competing cultural developments, and the disagreements between these developments—even when disagreement is muted. For example, postmodernism was perhaps most famously described by Jean-Francois Lyotard as being marked by an "incredulity to meta-narratives."[60] However, it is doubtful that postmodern philosophers and theorists were ever, truly, dismissive of metanarrative. Indeed, as Storm rightly articulates, "much of the postmodern canon was even rooted in its own pessimistic grand narratives about the fallenness of Being, colonialism, the death of God, or disenchantment."[61] One of the implications of this is that any definition or description of modernism and postmodernism is, at best, qualified, as no one definition can perfectly describe these cultural moods (nor the epochs of modernity or postmodernity). I suspect this is why metamodern scholarship has, so far, sought to describe markers or the cultural codes of these moods in terms of oppositional distinctions.[62] To define or describe these terms is to set

57. I and other metamodern theorists who utilize this term are borrowing Charles Taylor's notion of the social imaginary as a descriptor for the values, symbols, institutions, and myths (or narratives, micro- and meta-) which shape how we think of ourselves as social beings. Taylor, *Social Imaginaries*, 23–25.

58. Storm, *Metamodernism*, 18.

59. Bargár, "Transforming Sensibility," 5.

60. Lyotard, *Postmodern Condition*, xxiv.

61. Storm, *Metamodernism*, 18.

62. This work will take on this character of metamodern scholarship later in the project. Cf. Velmeulen and van den Akker, "Metamodernism," para. 12; Andersen, *Metamodernity*, 55, 84; Gerrie, *Borderless Fashion*, 15.

boundaries regarding how one provisionally understands them, which, in turn, develops a context for how these concepts can then be used in service towards the reconstructive telos of metamodernism.

Placing a date to the emergence of modernism has proven difficult because, as with postmodernism and now metamodernism, these cultural moods do not exert themselves in a widespread way within a cultural context until decades after their emergence as intellectual projects. Thus, naming a starting point is more naming what one considers an inflection point in the development of a cultural mood; a point when cultural elements came together in a way that created ripples eventually felt broadly throughout a given culture. Before naming the inflection point of modernism, it is important to name the beginning of modernity, as modernity was (as the two names suggest) the context in which modernism arose.

The birth of moder*nity* is, in my view, marked by the death of René Descartes in 1650 AD, as Descartes' intellectual project moved the starting point of knowledge from divine revelation (in the premodern epoch) to individuality—summed up in his now famous phrase, "I think therefore I am." This new perspective towards epistemology became a central pillar of the Enlightenment, leading to the development of the scientific method and approaching history with a hubris of progress, and the belief that rational investigation would eventually alleviate the world's ills. However, the development of moder*nism* is better marked by the death of Friedrich Schleiermacher in 1834, whose hermeneutical and philosophical ideas are considered, by some, to be modernism's starting point.[63] The hermeneutics of Schleiermacher will be discussed in the following chapter. Immanuel Kant is also a candidate for this distinction, as his thought was certainly, as Paul Tillich describes, "decisive for the theology of the nineteenth century."[64] While Kant was critical to the development of the Enlightenment, I believe Schleiermacher had a more direct influence on the development of modernism as a distinct cultural mood, thus why I have outlined this cultural history as I have. However, in many respects this is a discretionary point, as these inflection points are simply meant to be a taxonomy that aims to help one grasp—imperfectly and conditionally—the development of these cultural movements. Moreover, it has been argued that modernism emerged in 1910, in large part because of the suggestion of such by Virginia Wolfe.[65]

63. Murphy, "Modernism and Schleiermacher," 377, 382–85.

64. Tillich, *Perspectives*, 64.

65. McHale, "Introduction," 85.

However, 1910 seems to rather be the approximate time when modernism began exerting itself more widely in the public domain, beginning by 1907 with the pontifical publication of *Pascendi dominici gregis* denouncing the errors of modernism.[66]

While the Enlightenment and modernism certainly led to massive leaps in knowledge, technology, and human flourishing, with a corresponding cultural focus on utopianism, ecumenicalism, and relentless progress, it also led to the War to End All War (World War I) and then a war to end the world (World War II). Yet, it seems, modernist optimism did not completely die out with the development of the nuclear bomb. Instead, further war—in Korea, then Vietnam—fortified a deep suspicion and critique of the structures of culture, particularly of unlimited optimism, power, and the limits of knowledge. Thus, postmodernism emerged. While dating the "start" of postmodernism is highly debated,[67] the events of the mid-1950s—namely the end of the First Indochian War and the start of the Vietnam War—seem, to me, to be an important inflection point from which postmodernism began to take shape, particularly among French philosophers. However, postmodernism does not seem to have taken full shape until the latter half of the so-called "long sixties."[68]

Using the brief historico-cultural sketch above, differences between modernism and postmodernism can be understood to have emerged as layers of responses to what came before—modernism to the *premodern*, postmodernism to the modern *and* premodern—which is why the terms are often used as shorthand for oppositional disagreement (for example, modernist optimism and postmodernism suspicion, sincerity and irony, naïveté and knowing, and others).[69] These differences will continue to be illuminated in greater detail throughout this work. Importantly for the purposes of this project, divergent underlying assumptions regarding the relationship between authors and readers characterize modernism and postmodernism. Indeed, many of the marks of modernism and postmodernism can be found in the realms of hermeneutics and literary criticism. For the premodern, the assumption was that the relationship between author and reader was marked by what Peter Faulkner described as an expectation

---

66. Pius X, *Pascendi Dominici Gregis* (Encyclical of Pope Pius X on the Doctrines of the Modernists).

67. See McHale, "Introduction," 86–92.

68. McHale, "Introduction," 91.

69. Velmeulen and van den Akker, "Metamodernism," para. 17.

of shared experience derived from a shared understanding about the nature of literature, such that a "writer could assume a community of attitudes, a shared sense of reality" with their readership.[70] Modernism responded by realizing the complexity of experience was infinite, leading to a self-consciousness regarding historical locatedness—and the distance between author and interpreter. Postmodernism responded, in turn, by focusing on the reader as recipient, viewing literature as essentially independent of an author and their intention. These subtle shifts in response gave rise to all number of implications, many of which will be discussed in relation to the dataset of this study. But it stands to reason that metamodernity is, likewise, marked by an oscillation between the modernist and postmodernist notions related to author and reader, such that their relationship can be reconstructed in some sense.[71]

Therefore, central to my proposal is an integration of author-, text-, and reader-centered hermeneutical approaches with the insights of metamodernism. As has been widely acknowledged in hermeneutic literature, texts can either be read centered on the author's intentions or on the reader's reception, which may be generally classified as author- or reader-centeredness, respectively.[72] With texts, the text mediates the author and reader, thus allowing for a third category—text-centered reading—to develop. These hermeneutical categories, when partnered with recognition of the metamodern mood, provide a framework for understanding the history of contemporary hermeneutics. Some metamodern theorists have noted that metamodernism is, in terms of literature, marked by a melting of author, text, and reader, such that the "surface" level of a texts meaning can be "dissolved" and depth therefore recognized, making, as Huber and Funk comment, the hermeneutical act immersive and marked by a renewed "depthiness."[73] It is a sense of this hermeneutical depthiness that this project seeks to develop.

The metamodern development and its applicability to practical theology was anticipated by Ray Anderson. In *The Shape of Practical Theology*, Anderson comments that postmodernism's critique of metanarratives does not have the tools to answer the critique—an issue metamodernism

70. Faulkner, *Modernism*, 1.

71. In recent years there has been a movement towards including the premodern in the metamodern tension, though there are complications in doing this, especially hermeneutically. I will reflect on this difficulty in later chapters. See van den Akker and Velmeulen, "Periodising the 2000s," 9; Andersen, *Metamodernity*, 17.

72. Putman, *When Doctrine Divides*, 40.

73. Huber and Funk, "Reconstructing Depth," 156; Vermeulen, "Depth," 149.

answers by returning to metanarrative for organizing micro-narratives.[74] Further, Anderson describes his context at the turn of the twenty-first century as being marked by "modern and postmodern thought [that vie] for allegiance," which is a succinct description of the metamodern mood's emergence.[75] Thus, the project's metamodernism-informed framework will form the basis of a theological reflection paradigm that will elucidate how theological sources function authoritatively in practice, especially in relation to one another. By utilizing the framework in this way, the project will break new ground both in terms of the application of Gadamerian hermeneutics in relation to metamodernism and develop a paradigm for critical and cautious theological reflection.

## Metamodernism and Metamodernity

While Velmeulen and van den Akker's seminal articulation of the metamodern mood is the foundation for much of the metamodern-oriented scholarship produced today, there is not one notion of metamodernism but a plethora of *metamodernisms* from various theorists, each of which seek to either describe the contemporary milieu or develop a distinctly metamodern philosophy.[76] Indeed, such diversity should be expected for a cultural mood of oscillation, as each theorist is, in some sense, located in oscillation themselves—which is true of me as well. My aim will be to utilize my methodologies to describe the poles of oscillation as pertains to interpretation (and, I will argue, this includes theological reflection), thus enabling a more robust reflection about what metamodern interpretive practice looks like. By situating interpretations of Scripture within the *tension of metaxis*, between modernism and postmodernism, the project will develop a new way to describe contemporary interpretive practice.

One of the complications that arises in relation to metamodern*ism* is that this cultural theory is only one element of what is now being termed metamodern*ity*. While metamodernism describes the oscillation between

74. Anderson, *Shape*, 20–21. See also Corsa, "Grand Narratives," 252.

75. Anderson, *Shape*, 20–21.

76. Corsa, "Grand Narratives," 251–52; Clasquin-Johnson, "Metamodern Academic Study," 2; Storm, *Metamodernism*, 16. Storm, in particular, states his work is fundamentally philosophical in nature, with a goal of helping readers know "how to disintegrate concepts, how to practice deconstructive vigilance, and then how to achieve a new kind of reconstructive capability." Storm, *Metamodernism*, 276.

the latent sensibilities of modernism and postmodernism, metamodernity describes the constructive integration of values and systems of meaning of (seemingly) all past cultures. Thus, rather than just modernism and postmodernism's integration, which metamodernism seeks to describe, metamodernity includes the premodern and what Lene Rachel Andersen terms 'indigenous' imaginaries.[77] Describing metamodernity, Andersen notes that the cultural codes—that is, the social imaginaries—that were operative in stone age, premodern, modern, and postmodern cultures are all operative, to some extent, in contemporary culture, such that each must be taken account of in order to develop a new sense of possibility, values, and approaches to understanding.[78] Thus, metamodernism does not seem to go far enough in describing the state of the world, as it is today, on a cultural level.[79]

However, even in describing metamodernity, Andersen places heavy emphasis of modernity and postmodernity as the dominant cultural codes in contemporary society, and expects modernity (and, through it, modernism), to continue to exert significant influence far after postmodernity has faded. This points to the already noted dialogical feature of cultural development, in that each cultural epoch develops in response to the previous: modernity to the premodern, postmodernity to the modern *and* premodern. Metamodernity is, therefore, a response to premodern, modern, *and* postmodern sensibilities. But postmodern theorists have been noted to have an affinity with premodern thought, with some even arguing that the postmodern project could eventually revert to a type of premodern sensibility (that lacks the divine as ultimate referent).[80] As such, discerning what is authentically premodern and what is, more properly, a postmodernism-informed return to a form of premodern sensibilities is difficult to ascertain. This is further complicated by fundamentalism, which can act as a conceptual trojan horse within and in relation to culture, making cultural exegesis more difficult than it may otherwise seem—especially in the church.

Suffice to say, while metamodernity and metamodernism seem to accurately describe something of contemporary culture, the underlying complexity—even just between modernity and postmodernity in relation

---

77. Andersen, *Metamodernity*, 23–24.

78. Andersen, *Metamodernity*, 56.

79. Andersen, *Metamodernity*, 82.

80. On the affinity between the premodern and postmodern, see Holsinger, *Premodern Condition*; Clark, *History, Theory, Text*.

to fundamentalism, as we will find—is such that utilizing metamodern*ity* widely throughout the project would add a layer of complexity that would risk making the volume useless for most readers. However, this being the case, readers should note that because metamodernity is a complex interplay of cultural sensibilities, finding concepts and ideas related to the premodern should be *expected* in the metamodern mood, even as the foundation of such ideas (be they authentic or developed in response to, and therefore fundamentally tethered to, modernism and postmodernism) remains unclear. Throughout the project, I will thus use the term metamodern (and metamodernity) with the trifold premodern-modern-postmodern view in mind but will focus more significant attention on the oscillation between the modern and postmodern which metamodernism describes, while noting when premodern concepts come to the fore.

## Hermeneutic Theory

The project has a further core assumption that, in my experience, the majority of evangelicals do not know how they interpret Scripture so much as they know that they do it and, most often, refer to their *conclusions* as "interpretations." As Donald Thorsen argues, everyone has a way they theologically reason that is often left unexamined because of a focus on "finding solutions to immediate problems."[81] However, conflating interpretive conclusions with the interpretive process is a misunderstanding of what interpretation is, which is compounded by a focus on the outcome of interpretation rather than careful reflection on interpretation itself. Indeed, philosophical hermeneutics has revealed the complexity of interpretation, and that any conclusion we arrive at is fundamentally informed by previous interpretive practice, cumulatively, through the development of filter-like prejudices—which has so far in this project been referred to as preunderstandings—that we utilize, revise, and refine each time we interpret.[82] This complexity often goes unrecognized, at least in any meaningful sense,

---

81. Thorsen, *Quadrilateral*, 11.

82. By utilizing the term "interpretive paradigm," I am attempting to develop distance from the temptation to create a set process for interpretation (e.g., "Do interpretation in this specific way and you will end with this specific result"). Hermeneutics, as a practice and as a discipline, is more open-ended, being driven by sensing that is guided by our prejudices—understood in the etymological sense as prejudgments, assumptions, preconceptions, pre-commitments, emotions, and convictions. See Gadamer, *Truth and Method*, 283.

when evangelicals interpret Scripture, so this is an area where my research can shed some light. To help do this, the philosophical hermeneutics of Hans-Georg Gadamer will be utilized as the theory at the foundation of my research, which will offer a conceptual framework for understanding what happens during interpretation.

Indeed, hermeneutics is, generally speaking, the interpretation *of interpretation*, what Porter and Malcolm describe as "an attempt to reflect at a more abstract level on how productive human understanding takes place."[83] Hermeneutics is not itself the practice of interpretation, even though "hermeneutics" and "interpretation" tend to be misunderstood as synonyms at the popular level. Instead, hermeneutics is the investigation into how interpretive paradigms function in the development of understanding, which is why hermeneutic theory is a natural fit for this research project. Therefore, when applied to biblical interpretation, hermeneutic theory can help reveal how one understands the Bible by describing the complex interplays at work in the process of their understanding. In this project, hermeneutic theory will uncover what is happening during the practice of interpretation, particularly in relation to theological reflection.

Utilizing hermeneutic theory will mean the research will take on characteristics of philosophical hermeneutics—especially that of Gadamer. Gadamerian hermeneutics has particular congruence with the practice-led research paradigm and practical theology, both of which would find agreement (in their disciplinary contexts) with Gadamer's assertion that hermeneutics "must arise from practice itself and . . . be related back to practice."[84] Or as Don Browning pointed out, Gadamer's hermeneutic implies a "practice–theory–practice model of understanding" that forms the foundation of practical theology as a discipline.[85]

Furthermore, I believe the hermeneutics of Gadamer to be particularly well suited for the metamodern mood. Indeed, within the metamodern conversation, there has been a lack of discussion regarding hermeneutics, and of Gadamer in particular. As pointed out by Wouter Hanegraaff in his review article of *Metamodernism: The Future of Theory* by Jason Ānanda

83. Porter and Malcolm, *Future*, x. Porter (*Interpretation for Preaching*, 3) has further defined hermeneutics as "discussion of the principles of understanding found in various models used to interpret a written text." This definition has some utility, as it draws out the dialogical and paradigmatic nature of hermeneutics. These elements of hermeneutics will be elaborated on later in this volume.

84. Gadamer, *Reader*, 231.

85. Browning, *Fundamental*, 39.

Josephson Storm, not only does Storm not engage Gadamer's thought, he also seems to misunderstand the hermeneutical circle and in doing so reveals "the deeply depressing poststructuralist/deconstructionist key assumption that . . . interpretation, communication, translation, or understanding are all 'impossibilities.'"[86] And yet, if Gadamer's thought was utilized, Storm—and metamodern scholars in general—would find the conceptual tools needed to answer a critical call of metamodernism, which is to bring "our hidden values to the surface in such a way that they help to further intellectual progress."[87] In part, this is the aim of the present project, related specifically to the interpretation of Scripture.

Moreover, the metamodern conversation has been recently characterized by an increased awareness of how culture has never stopped developing, and indeed how humans continue to seek flourishing, which requires at least a functional historical imagination. On this point Gadamer proves particularly helpful, as Gadamer's hermeneutic vision is energized by how history effects (and makes possible) human understanding. Indeed, it is within Gadamer's work that metamodern scholars can find a hermeneutic phenomenological guide who can provide a language for understanding *understanding* that "allows us to come to terms with the gap between what we thought we knew and the things we experience in our daily lives."[88]

The above being the case, there are specific characteristics of Gadamerian hermeneutics this project will take on. First, hermeneutics—and therefore hermeneutic research—is dialogical, seeking an encounter with the other, in some sense, as the horizon of the researcher and the researched fuse as the research process unfolds.[89] Understanding does not come from dissociating from a situation but by being embedded in it alongside others while also "transposing ourselves" into the tradition that informs the present situation.[90] Consequently, this means that this project focuses on the particular nature of the situation from which the research arises so that it can reach meaningful conclusions applicable both in and beyond that context. Thus, the complexity of the conflict must be accounted for

---

86. Hanegraaff, "Provincializing American Theory," 511.

87. Storm, *Metamodernism*, 96. Storm goes on to comment, "What we need—rather than suppressing our values—is to bring them to the surface and make them work for us, because only if they are acknowledged can we address them honestly and openly" (*Metamodernism*, 96).

88. Van den Akker and Velmeulen, "Periodising the 2000s," 3.

89. Brown, "Hermeneutic Theory," 114.

90. Gadamer, *Truth and Method*, 315–17.

via reflexivity throughout the project. Secondly, hermeneutic research must attend to research data carefully in order for the practice (of research) to be driven by the subject at hand.[91] This means being responsive, reflexive, and inquisitive during the research, particularly regarding how to handle source materials, doing so with accuracy and charity,[92] and being drawn into the dialogical element of hermeneutic theory and the fusion of horizons from which understanding develops.[93]

## Theological Perspective

There are several doctrinal assumptions that form the theological foundation of this project. The first is that Christian theology is an act of discipleship. Theology is the attempt to think about, reflect on, and articulate faith in God *rightly* in order to know God more fully even as we are fully known, and live faithfully according to this relational knowledge.[94] But one's ability to theologize is informed by assumed, functional theologies, giving shape to how they think and speak of God. Knowing that we have a functional theology is important, even if we cannot articulate precisely what it is, because naming its existence clarifies things about the interpretive process and all the moving parts that shuffle interpreters towards particular conclusions.[95]

Indeed, if functional theologies—as well as other assumptions and presuppositions—were left unrecognized, and particularly for academic researchers if these are left unnamed and untested, Johnson rightly comments that "we are likely to be shaped not only by Scripture but also by our ideals and the predominant currents of our age."[96] Thus, recognizing these theologies allows for deeper reflection and envisioning regarding what faithfully responding to God's Word looks like in a given context.[97] One's theology is essential to this, and it is paramount for the sake of knowledge of God and

91. Moules et al., *Conducting Hermeneutic*, 62–63.

92. Gadamer, *Truth and Method*, 383.

93. Gadamer, *Truth and Method*, 386.

94. Johnson, *Discipleship*, 16; McGuire, "Equipped," 52–53; Rogers, "Looking into the Mirror," 479.

95. Johnson, *Discipleship*, 18; Cameron et al., *Talking about God*, 53–54; Packiam, *Worship*, 21, 24; Toren and Hoare, "Evangelicals," 78–79, 88.

96. Johnson, *Discipleship*, 33. These assumptions include emotions and intuition, as well as the cultural presumptions that come from being born in a specific time and place.

97. Whitehead, "Practical Play," 44; Bass, "Ways of Life," 33.

a believer's discipleship as a follower of Christ to be as accurate as possible in who they say God is, so that they can live faithfully in response to this God—to whom they are covenanted.

Secondly, a theological doctrine at the core of this project is the authority of Scripture, which is informed by the doctrine of Scripture's inspiration (which, in turn, is related to the Lordship of Christ). Christ's Lordship, and therefore Christ's authority over believers, is extended via the Bible through the doctrine of Scripture's inspiration by the Holy Spirit. It is not the text that is authoritative, per se, but the God who authored the text (thus why it is not simply a text but *Scripture*), and, evangelicals believe, God's authority is mediated primarily textually today.[98] The confession that the Spirit inspired the Bible forms part of the foundation for why the Bible ought to be considered authoritative and normative, even today.

The theologies of Scripture's authority and inspiration come together in the doctrine of revelation. This doctrine holds that Scripture is *special* revelation, a divine self-disclosure focused on the person and work of Christ and that communicates God's covenant. Because it is a self-disclosure, the doctrine of Scripture as revelation implies the text's inspiration (otherwise the text could not claim a definitive revelatory character) and a personal posture towards authority—for God's self-disclosure is, by definition, personal, both in Scripture and, importantly, in the incarnation. Related to the topic of the present study, how Scripture is understood *as revelation* has been redefined concurrently with the author–text–reader movements within hermeneutics—away from the inspiration of the text and towards the inspiration of the reader, emphasizing immanence in a divine–human encounter as revealing God over the "static" text of the Scriptures.[99] Indeed, Scripture can be considered both inspired and authoritative because of the knowledge it shares, which is a relational knowledge of God through Christ.

The implications of the above insights are significant. First, they connect obedience to Scripture with obedience to Christ, for it is only through Christ that covenant loyalty is due.[100] Second, scriptural authority is kingdom-oriented because its authority is, as Jensen reminds us, the "personal authority of the Lord over the people who he has saved."[101] Thus, interpreting Scripture it is not just an abstract search for truth but a relational action

---

98. Jensen, *Revelation*, 49, 82. Porter, *Interpretation for Preaching*, 25–26.

99. Jensen, *Revelation*, 18.

100. Jensen, *Revelation*, 150–52.

101. Jensen, *Revelation*, 154.

of listening for God's invitation to live faithfully as the Lord's people. Finally, because the gospel's covenantal nature calls people to obedience and repentance, we can expect how scriptural authority—and, indeed, how theological reflection—functions will include aspects of both. These implications form a preliminary theological framework for the project and will be implemented throughout the project's methodology and later analytical constructs.


## RESEARCH DESIGN

As tools of the aforementioned research paradigms that form the project's methodology, the project utilizes various methods for data gathering and analysis, chosen for how they correspond to the project's underlying theories. With the interpretive debate regarding sexuality being used as a test subject, data was gathered from publicly available sources. Analytical constructs drawn from my methodology, which are discussed in chapter 3, were used for analyzing this data by employing a form of qualitative content analysis.


## Hermeneutic Content Analysis

Content analysis is a data analysis method that breaks down texts into smaller units of meaning and categorizes them so that meaningful inferences can be made to generate new insights and knowledge.[102] This method began in mass communication research but is now utilized throughout social studies to analyze textual data, which Heidi Julien describes as "including interview transcripts, recorded observations, narratives, responses to open-ended questionnaire items, speeches . . . and media such as drawings, photographs, and video."[103] While content analysis has most often been utilized for quantitative studies, there is growing interest in utilizing the method in qualitative studies, as qualitative research has a particular concern for data interpretation.[104]

The qualitative approach to content analysis has multiple benefits, many of which intersect with hermeneutic theory and the aims of the practice-led research paradigm. These benefits, according to Jamie Baxter, include "a

102. Baxter, "Content," 391; Krippendorff, *Content Analysis*, 18.
103. Julien, "Content Analysis," 120.
104. Schreier, *Qualitative in Practice*, vii, 21; Baxter, "Content," 392–93.

focus on theory development," flexibility, recognition of the place of authors and readers in understanding a message (text), the use of multiple content types, recognizing "hidden meaning" in texts (e.g., inferences), and the identification of concepts and their presence or absence within a dataset.[105] Margrit Schreier also offers a description of the method that finds a similar correspondence. For her, the method (like other qualitative methods) is concerned with situations, reflexivity, flexibility, interpretation, and "the messy features that make up real-life contexts" (what she terms "naturalistic")[106]— all of which are concerns shared by hermeneutics, metamodernism,[107] the practice-led research paradigm, and practical theology.

When performing content analysis, researchers analyze the meaning (content) of texts, looking to break textual data down into clusters to develop a stable correlation between the research question and the texts being researched. According to the framework developed by Klaus Krippendorff, content analysis proper happens when the texts are analyzed, aided by what Krippendorff terms "analytical constructs" from which meaningful inferences are developed that answer the research question and be validated by the research's inciting evidence/situation.[108] The analytical construct "operationalizes" the research context by mapping correlations between the texts and the research question, such that meaningful inferences can be uncovered.[109] This mapping utilizes what is termed "coding," categorizing units of meaning within texts (words, sentences, paragraphs, etc.) to develop overarching themes and inferences.[110]

I have termed my use of qualitative content analysis as *hermeneutical* content analysis to make clear that hermeneutic theory guides my analysis of the texts. The use of hermeneutic theory also offers criteria for understanding rigour and validity for the research, which is worth reflecting on before moving forward. While replicability is a concern for many quantitative research methods, hermeneutic research is significantly more concerned with validity in practice. This means that rigour and validity of hermeneutic research are inherently related to the research's reception in

105. Baxter, "Content," 394.

106. Schreier, *Qualitative in Practice*, 22–28.

107. Timmer, "Radical Defenselessness," 114.

108. Krippendorff, *Content Analysis*, 35.

109. Krippendorff, *Content Analysis*, 34–35.

110. Erlingsson and Brysiewicz, "Hands–on Guide," 94; Julien, "Content Analysis," 120.

the practice from which it arises. Expanding on this point, Moules et al. describes rigour in hermeneutic research as "careful attention to the treatment of topics such that the work engenders trustworthiness and believability."[111] In other words, validity will be found in the research's *ability to be enacted in practice*, as well as its ability to *be recognized as believably plausible*, even if one disagrees with the inferences or conclusions that are ultimately developed. Thus, in the development of a coding frame, the research can be understood as valid insomuch as the categories are appropriately representative of core concepts.[112] How the above discussion relates to the validity of *this* project will be discussed in later chapters. The project's coding frame will be developed in chapter 3, the coding process further described in chapter 4 along with the coding outcomes, and my interpretation of the coding discussed in chapter 5.

## Data Gathering

Because of the variety of data types that can be utilized in content analysis, I had to decide on the specific types I would focus on gathering. While my natural inclination would be to conduct interviews, my core assumptions—namely, that people do not know, or know how to articulate, how they interpret Scripture—would mean that any invitation to practitioners or laity to reflect on and describe their practice would obfuscate what truly happens in their interpretive practice. Rather than describe what their practice is, I expect they would instead reflect on what they think they ought to have done and then match their description of interpretation to that expectation, deforming the self-description of their practice. While I do not know other practitioner's interpretive prejudices, I am at least able to be honestly reflexive about my own prejudices, which allows observations I make during the research to be a degree more objective than those of interviewed subjects would allow.

Due to this, I decided to gather publicly available examples of pastors and Christian leaders describing their interpretive practice. To gather data, between June 25th and August 31st, 2021, I data crawled CBOQ church and affiliate websites using Google's search site functionality.[113] Doing so

---

111. Moules et al., *Conducting Hermeneutic*, 172.

112. Schreier, *Qualitative in Practice*, 175.

113. This method of search is done using search commands that direct the search engine to find specific phrases on particular websites. The basic command formula is:

leveraged the search engine to look through websites for keywords, some of which existed in website source codes and others of which were tagged by the search engine's AI. For each website, a preliminary list of pages with possible connection to the topic were found by searching sites for keywords, including: *LGBT, homosexuality, queer, inclusive,* and *affirming.* Each page was then visited and evaluated as to whether the content of the page fit, broadly, within the purview of the project. After this, content of qualifying pages was evaluated based on whether a sufficient description of interpretive practice was given. Sources found to offer sufficient description of interpretive practice were saved and subsequently transcribed and coded.

Due to Canada's cultural climate, which has begun to treat anti-LG-BTQ sentiment with hostility, and evangelicalism's cultural climate which has historically treated pro-LGBTQ sentiment with hostility, collecting sufficient publicly available data was a concern for my research design. Thus, while data gathering from CBOQ sources was prioritized, a small expanded pool of data was used as a supplement, so that meaningful inferences could be drawn from the data pool. This supplemental data includes broadly evangelical Anabaptist (that is, "re-baptizing") sources from the Mennonite Brethren Church in Canada (MBCC), chosen because the denomination had been engaged in similarly public debates regarding homosexuality at the time of data's collection. The collected data includes statements, exegeses, blog posts, transcribed audio or video (e.g., sermons, Bible studies, local church conferences), and other such publicly available material that give a broad sense of the debate. This data also includes sources churches have either adopted or used as resources that are explicitly stated as broadly representative of constituent churches' views.

Furthermore, the contentiousness of this debate means that the project design must be ethically informed to reasonably protect churches and leaders, especially those whose opinions differ from those of their denomination. Thus, the project has been designed in line with *Tri-Council Policy Statement* (TCPS2) standards. While TCPS2 allows for research involving publicly available documents that have no reasonable expectation of privacy—including audio, video, text, performances, interviews, and other such sources—to not require research ethics board approval, there is still an ethical expectation that researchers preserve privacy by redacting identifying information in the data.[114] This is especially true if there is a reasonable

---

site:URL "KEYWORD."

114. TCPS2, 15–16.

chance of negative consequences due to a source's inclusion in a project, which I believe one could make a reasonable argument for in this case. This concern includes the possibility of data linkage, due to the reality of internet-based sources being easily traceable. These concerns will inform the research design, which will be discussed alongside a description of the data gathering and analysis procedure in chapter 4.

## INCITING SITUATION

Before moving forward, it is imperative to more fully consider the context from which this project has arisen from my professional practice. Having begun working in a CBOQ church, I was quickly introduced to the debate about homosexuality as fellow ministers began talking about whether LGBTQ-affirming theology would eventually divide our convention of churches. In multiple meetings and learning sessions, leadership from various churches struggled with what to when and as same-sex couples asked for them to officiate a wedding ceremony (and what the repercussions of doing so might be), the extent to which a shift the denomination's posture could be made that would allow member churches to embrace LGBTQ affirmation, and how to speak with others in the denomination who had fundamentally conflicting convictions.

While sexuality has been a topic some churches have been publicly thinking through over the past two decades, since the legalization of same sex marriage in Ontario, it was not until recently that CBOQ churches began more vigorously to participate in the debate. In 2018, a motion was proposed at the convention's Assembly (annual general meeting) to better resource churches for ministering to LGBTQ peoples.[115] This motion set off a firestorm, galvanizing conversation and causing some who held the LGBTQ affirming position to begin strategizing about moving the convention towards, at the very least, allowing their view and making a variety of practice regarding marriage and sexual ethics permissible rather than just those as traditionally defined and historically confessed by Canadian Baptists.[116]

It was in this context that I began writing my ordination statement in 2018. Under the supervision of a local pastor, I was encouraged to reflect on and write about topics of ongoing debate within our denomination,

115. CBOQ, "Assembly 2017 Summary," 3.

116. CBWC, "Identity Statement," para. 20; CBOQ, *This We Believe*, §8.2.1; CBAC, "General Operating Bylaw," appx. D§8.

particularly the debate about sexuality. It was in the process of writing this document, and then sharing its content with my church, ministerial colleagues, and other churches via the ordination process, I began realizing that in the context of this debate many people—both pastors and laity—were generally unable to describe, let alone critically reflect on, their interpretive process. It was in this realization that the present project began germinating, as I began wondering whether there was a way to help Christians both describe and reflect on their biblical interpretive practice. This project is the sprout of my wonderings.

# 2

---

# Hermeneutics, Revelation, and
# Integrative Theological Method

THREE ELEMENTS MUST BE sufficiently accounted for if the project is to be successful—the elements of theory, theology, and practice. In the following chapter, I establish a context for the project by discussing key ideas and scholarship related to each of these elements, which will create fertile soil for understanding and the development of new theoretical knowledge regarding interpretive practice.[1] For my theory, I will discuss the concurrent development of hermeneutic theory and the cultural epochs of modernism, postmodernism, and metamodernism, setting the stage for a novel analytical construct outlined in chapter 3. Regarding theology, I will discuss doctrines of Scripture, with special emphasis on the work of Peter Jensen and his articulation of Scripture as revelation. Jensen's work will be brought into critical conversation with other scholars, particularly John Webster, to provide a thick description of Scripture as authoritative revelation. Finally, the practice of biblical interpretation as an act of discipleship will be overviewed in relation to the development of theological reflection methods, especially as conceived of and utilized in the field of practical theology. This will lay the groundwork for a re-articulation of the so-called Wesleyan Quadrilateral, which is the construct at the heart of the Transformative Reading Paradigm proposed in chapter 6.

---

1. Moules et al., *Conducting Hermeneutic*, 38–39.

## THEORY: HERMENEUTICS IN RECENT CULTURAL EPOCHS

It has been repeatedly noted by scholars that the twentieth century has seen three distinct foci in hermeneutics that continue to shape the practice of interpretation—author-centered, text-centered, and reader-centered approaches to reading texts (particularly the Bible).[2] It has also been well established that the development of each of these foci have largely been in step with broader cultural movements, specifically those of modernism and postmodernism.[3] In modernism, hermeneutics moved towards author-centeredness where the author and the construction of the authors' world (the world behind the text) was given authority to create meaning. Next came postmodernism and the movement of hermeneutics away from the author towards being reader-centered, which developed as a consequence of what I describe as an intermediate text-centeredness phase. This move placed authority over meaning with the reader, who creates meaning in conversation with the author or text in some sense. Understanding each of these foci, and their relationship with modernism and postmodernism, will set the groundwork for understanding interpretive practice in the now developing epoch of metamodernity.

In the following section, I offer a broad overview of relevant work from scholars considered to be influential for the development of each form of hermeneutical centeredness mentioned above. This is not to provide a thorough engagement with their work but rather a critical summary, setting the stage for discussing the philosophical hermeneutics of Gadamer and the recent development of the theological interpretation of Scripture movement which is, in many ways, a product of the metamodern mood within evangelicalism.

## Author-Centered Hermeneutic and Modernism

Although a complex movement of philosophy and art, it is well established that modernism developed in the context of Romanticism and the Enlightenment, taking on characteristics of each.[4] Romanticism's emphases on the lived experience of individuals and its distrust of rationalism, and

---

2. Tate, *Biblical Interpretation*, 2–5; Brown, *Communication*, 47–48; Vanhoozer, *Meaning*, 25–29.

3. Village, *Bible and Lay People*, 19; Rogers, *Congregational Hermeneutics*, 41–42.

4. Anderson, *Shape*, 15–16.

the Enlightenment focus on personal liberty, form much of the foundation for hermeneutical developments during the late nineteenth and early twentieth centuries.[5] Prior to the nineteenth century, hermeneutics had more to do with methods of interpretation than understanding the process of understanding in interpretation.[6] This changed in response to the above intellectual developments, and particularly in the wake of Friedrich Schleiermacher (1768–1834).

Schleiermacher is widely considered to be the father of both philosophical hermeneutics and the discipline of practical theology.[7] Living in the long shadow of Gutenberg when people were able to read the Bible for themselves for the first time, Schleiermacher began questioning how we understand Scripture. But the question of understanding was larger than simply understanding Scripture; Schleiermacher wondered how we understood anything, and began to apply his hermeneutical insights across disciplines, developing philosophical hermeneutics in the process. In catalyzing the development of philosophical hermeneutics, Schleiermacher broadened the applicability of hermeneutics, expanding it from being specific to understanding Scripture and other ancient texts to understanding *understanding*; moving from special hermeneutics to general hermeneutics.[8] This allowed Schleiermacher to recognize and account for the importance of both author and text in interpretation, and articulate a more developed notion of what is now known as the hermeneutical circle.[9]

According to the hermeneutical circle theory, one treats a text and the text's author as dialogue partners, allowing the grammatical-linguistic investigation of a text to inform a psychological analysis of the author and vice versa.[10] For Schleiermacher, if one can understand the author—through immersion in the author's world, in order to access the author's mind—they will be able to understand a given text and its definitive (original) meaning.[11] Schleiermacher explained that the grammatical and psychological elements

---

5. Bartholomew, *Introduction*, 305.

6. Bartholomew, *Introduction*, 289.

7. Anderson, *Shape*, 24.

8. Thiselton, *New Horizons*, 204; Brown, *Communication*, 48.

9. While not innovated by him, having been previously developed by Freidrich August Wolf and Freidrich Ast, Schleiermacher certainly provided the first comprehensive description of the hermeneutical circle theory, thus popularizing it. Bartholomew, *Introduction*, 307; Thiselton, *New Horizons*, 204.

10. Westphal, *Whose Community?*, 28.

11. Osborne, *Spiral*, 468.

of hermeneutics were equally important because understanding involves both; that "to understand what is said in the context of the language with its possibilities and to understand it as a fact in the thinking of the speaker. . . . [T]hese two hermeneutical tasks are completely equal."[12] However, Schleiermacher did not treat them equally. His romanticism-influenced emphasis on lived experience led him towards psychologism, moving the focus of interpretation away from what the text actually says to the psychologically-informed lived experience of the author, even to the point of arguing that the interpreter's goal is understanding the text better than the author could have by uncovering the author's biases and assumptions.[13]

Thus began the era of author-centered reading. While Schleiermacher's work formed the basis of author-centered reading, it was Wilhelm Dilthey (1833–1911) who championed it. Dilthey asserted Schleiermacher's goal of understanding a text's author in absolute terms—"*We can* understand an author better than he understood himself."[14] One of Dilthey's most important contributions to hermeneutics was his articulation of "lived experience," which he argued provides intelligibility but not understanding.[15] In other words, lived experience becomes an intermediary to understanding, and "understanding is inseparable from interpretation."[16] This insight is important, as Dilthey's application of it to historiography meant an increased recognition of the historically conditioned nature of understanding—that is, both authors and texts are historically conditioned. Moreover, it allowed Dilthey to look back and strengthen his claim of knowing the author better than they knew themselves, thus making knowing the author (as a historical person) and an author's intention in writing a text the ultimate goal of interpretation.[17]

Generally speaking, knowing the author and their intention epitomized modernist hermeneutics, both inside and outside the church. While secular (and theologically liberal) modernists focused on the human authors of Scripture and their historical locatedness, fundamentalists focused on the divine author. Indeed, Schleiermacher's vision of hermeneutics being applicable to many areas of life and study inherently pushed the divine author

12. Schleiermacher, *Handwritten Manuscripts*, 98–99.

13. Schleiermacher, *Hermeneutics and Criticism*, 23, 92.

14. Dilthey, "On Understanding," 232; emphasis added.

15. Makkreel, "Dilthey," 79.

16. Makkreel, "Dilthey," 79.

17. Brown, *Communication*, 49.

to the sidelines of interpretation, because it would not make sense to speak of divine authorship for all texts generally. The tension between these different foci crescendoed in the twentieth century modernist-fundamentalist debates, which in part led to a reappraisal of author-centered readings.

## Text-Centered Hermeneutic and the Interim

Can we ever really know the author of a text, let alone know that author better than they knew themselves? By the mid-twentieth century, with historical reconstruction becoming a core method of biblical scholarship, scholars began answering the above questions by interrogating author-centered readings.[18] Their interrogation was due to a number of reasons, primary to which was the penchant for those who focused on historical reconstruction had for ignoring the text of Scripture, and its meaning, *as written*.[19] Furthermore, author-centered readings gave the impression that the meaning of a text was located fully in the past, which made discerning application difficult if not cumbersome apart from psychologism. Nonetheless, a reappraisal of readings centered on authors, in the sense described above, led to the realization that a text's meaning was not stuck in the past but discernible from the text. This would begin to move hermeneutics away from focusing on the author to derive understanding and towards focusing on the text itself—a move that took decades to develop and set the stage for the reader-centered focus of postmodernism.

Utilizing text-centered developments in biblical studies as point of comparison, scholars highlight the mid-century literary movement of *New Criticism* as a cipher for understanding the text-centered hermeneutical approach for biblical interpretation.[20] Developing between the 1920s and 1940s, *New Criticism* began "focusing on texts as linguistic systems," such that "meaning arises from an interplay of different forces within a text, regardless of what an author might intend."[21] Indeed, in their influential article "The Intentional Fallacy," Wimsatt and Beardsley argued the "design or intention of the author is neither available nor desirable as a standard for judging the success of a work of literary art."[22] In other words, authorial intention

18. Brown, *Communication*, 52.

19. Brown, *Communication*, 52–53.

20. Brown, *Communication*, 53.

21. Thiselton, *New Horizons*, 472. See also Village, *Bible and Lay People*, 21.

22. Wimsatt and Beardsley, "Intentional Fallacy," 468.

should not matter when interpreting a piece of literature. While it may, at first blush, seem a forgettable or self-evident development to contemporary readers, text-centered readings may have been the most radical development in hermeneutics during the past two centuries, with everything coming after it (including postmodernism's reader-centered reading) developing as a consequence of this shift. Indeed, I have described its development as happening in the interim period between modernism and postmodernism, as text-centered reading both recognized the flaws of modernist hermeneutics while giving postmodern readers the tools to criticize those hermeneutics and develop approaches to understanding meaning.

The shift from author to text-centeredness in biblical studies seems to have happened well after the emergence of literary criticism, around the time of postmodernism's emergence and the publication of Roland Barthes' article, "Death of the Author." Barthes, a literary critic who was frustrated that *New Criticism*'s critique of the author led to the "sway" of the author being "consolidated," argued that the notion of the author was an essentially "modern" invention.[23] In fact, Barthes argues, texts are absent of authors; they are "a tissue of signs" that have a variety of meanings depending on how a reader understands those signs—for the author, having long passed, cannot tell the reader what the sign means.[24] In this short essay, appearing near the end of *New Criticism*'s emergence, Barthes takes the *New Criticism* critique of the author to its logical end, removing the author from the equation, leaving only text and reader.

The shift to text-centeredness was monumental, and contributed to the field of biblical studies and biblical hermeneutics by giving exegetes tools to better understand the biblical texts *as texts*.[25] However, as Thiselton notes, these tools—which include textual criticism, narrative theory, redaction criticism, rhetorical criticism, poetics, and others—do not take into account the nature of Scripture as *divine* text.[26] To rephrase Thiselton's point as a question, how does the Christian confession that Scripture is, in some sense, authored by God via the inspiration of the Holy Spirit factored into one's reading of biblical texts? In many ways, this question underlies an important tension this project seeks to address. Barthes gave an answer to the question

---

23. Barthes, "Death," 143.
24. Barthes, "Death," 142–43, 145, 147.
25. Brown *Communication*, 55.
26. Thiselton, *New Horizons*, 471.

of an authorial importance, which ushered in the postmodern epoch: "the birth of the reader must be at the cost of the death of the Author."[27]

## Reader-Centered Hermeneutic and Postmodernism

The reader-centered approach is, in many ways, a natural consequence of the turn away from the author and towards the text. Indeed, left only with the text one is left wondering whether the text is the arbiter of its meaning or whether oneself, as the reader, is. In a post-World War world, when countries and cultures have become increasingly accessible via travel and mass communication, postmodernism's insight that social systems play a role in understanding has facilitated meaning being tied to readers and reading communities in a way that was previously unrecognized. Namely, as Thiselton argued, a reader-centered posture assumes that texts "remain an abstraction until it is interpreted and understood by its reader . . . the reader is not a passive spectator but actively contributes something to the meaning. He or she is more than a passive observer."[28] In other words, as Tate summarizes, "the text means nothing until someone means something by it," and thus a text is meaningless until a reader means something from it.[29] In the reader-centered approach, it is acknowledged that readers bring experiences, presuppositions, and methodologies to the interpretive practice, which the reader uses to create meaning.

Reader-centered hermeneutics developed in many ways, which one would expect for an approach that emphasizes intersubjectivity as a foundation for understanding. One of the most consequential forms for biblical interpretation has been reader-response theory, generally typified by Stanley Fish.[30] Developing as opposition to the *New Criticism*'s focus on textual authority, Fish argues in his book *Is There a Text in This Class?* that when interpreting texts "the reader's response is not *to* the meaning: it *is*

---

27. Barthes, "Death," 148. In the essay, Barthes quips that texts do not have single meanings as though given by an "Author-God," a metaphorical turn of phrase that also strongly implies the death of God as the Bible's author. Barthes, "Death," 146.

28. Thiselton, *Introduction*, 256.

29. Tate, *Biblical Interpretation*, 4.

30. Other scholars, such as Edgar McKnight, applied reader-response criticism to biblical interpretation more explicitly, but they fundamentally build off of Fish's work such that it is largely sufficient, for the purpose of this survey, to engage with the foundation laid by Fish, while recognizing other scholars will have more nuanced views.

the meaning."[31] In other words, the meaning of a text develops as readers read, disentangling references and ambiguities, and ruling out certain meanings—a complex process Fish argues happens every time interpretation happens.[32] When anyone reads and interprets a text, they have a complex matrix of assumptions and biases behind their interpretive practice that informs their understanding and therefore shapes meaning.

An author not often associated positively with reader-centered hermeneutics is E. D. Hirsch. Indeed, Hirsch is seen by many as the polar opposite of Fish—including by Fish himself.[33] While important within some evangelical hermeneutical works in particular, which see Hirsch's defense of authorial intention as a useful tool to protect notions of divine authorial intent with Scripture, I remain unconvinced of the utility of his work for this purpose. Nevertheless, Hirsch's work made significant contributions to the field of hermeneutics. In his most well-known work, *Validity in Practice*, Hirsch argues in defense of authorial intention by making a distinction between meaning and significance. Though he walked a strong distinction back later in his career, Hirsch contended that meaning was what an author meant by using a particular sign sequence, "that which is represented by a text," while significance "names a relationship between that meaning and . . . anything imaginable."[34] Importantly, for authorial intention, Hirsch says that understanding what one has "willed to convey" through the use of particular signs essentially binds the interpretation of a text.[35]

Both Fish and Hirsch have been influential in discussions of hermeneutics, including in the church, during the postmodern epoch. While Fish tends to represent an extreme of reader-oriented hermeneutics, emphasizing the intersubjectivity of meaning making readers undertake in interpretive practice, Hirsch is regularly seen as the opposite extreme, defending authorial intention as an important guardrail for coming to valid interpretations of texts. There is now a final significant figure in hermeneutics that I wish to engage with: Hans-Georg Gadamer.

31. Fish, *Text in Class*, 3.
32. Fish, *Text in Class*, 145.
33. Fish, *Text in Class*, vii.
34. Hirsch, *Validity*, 8.
35. Hirsch, *Validity*, 31.

## Hans-Georg Gadamer

In 1960 Gadamer released his seminal book *Truth and Method*, a dense text that enlivened philosophical hermeneutic discussions by offering what amounts to a multifaceted attack against method in interpretation.[36] Whereas previous scholars attempted to derive methods of interpretation that would consistently and accurately uncover meaning (either via the author or the text), Gadamer's work focused on understanding *understanding itself*, and proposed a descriptive theory of interpretation that explains what is happening when one interprets.[37] In developing his hermeneutic, Gadamer's concern for the basis of understanding, in which he criticized criticism (in other words, Gadamer is *metacritical*) led his project to straddle the line between modernism and postmodernism.[38] Indeed, rather than throw out the insights of past generations, Gadamer integrated those insights while building off of them. Furthermore, Gadamer also made clear, throughout his career, that he believed his philosophical hermeneutic to be ontological, and specifically Platonic—that is, in line with the tradition of Platonism—which matches recent developments within the church. These developments, which are largely an attempt to return to premodern metaphysics as a way to move beyond the modern and postmodern projects, will be described in a following section.[39]

It would be anachronistic to claim Gadamer was metamodern in the 1960s, but his hermeneutic is certainly a precursor to the metamodern mood, and as such continues to shape the contemporary age.[40] Indeed, Gadamer's hermeneutic has been used since the turn of the millennium to make sense of the extremes of modernism and postmodernism's

---

36. Thiselton, *New Horizons*, 313. Briggs describes Gadamer's "hermeneutical moral" as "if you want truth you must sit light to method, and if you specify method then you *will* end up sitting light to truth . . . you cannot have them both together" ("Practical Theology," 211).

37. Gadamer, *Truth and Method*, xxii; Westphal, *Whose Community?*, 69.

38. Thiselton, *New Horizons*, 314–16, 320; Bartholomew, *Introduction*, 310–12.

39. Fortin, "Gadamer on Strauss," 10; Porter and Robinson, *Hermeneutics*, 81.

40. For example, Gadamer was concerned with the objective/subjective divide related to truth, seeing this bifurcation as a false dichotomy that misunderstands the dynamic nature of understanding. Yet, as is assumed via oscillation and will be discussed in the following chapter, it is this very bifurcation that marks the metamodern mood as modernist objectivity and postmodern (inter)subjectivity play defining roles for these respective cultural movements. See Porter and Robinson, *Hermeneutics*, 82–83.

hermeneutical postures on a cultural level.[41] Gadamer moved the discipline of hermeneutics "from a study of method to the adopting of a fundamental attitude."[42] As such, his hermeneutic has a great deal of utility, and is a solid foundation from which emerging metamodern hermeneutic theorists can build from if they are to move towards describing understanding while holding the roles authors, texts, and readers each play in interpretive practice in creative tension.

Building off the work of his teacher, Martin Heidegger, who recognized "the radical historicity of hermeneutics," such that "the question of Being can only be asked within time,"[43] Gadamer focused attention on the locatedness of the reader and how their location shapes interpretation. Because of this, Gadamer's hermeneutic has been labeled "absolute relativism" by some.[44] Yet, the so-called relativism within his work is not a claim about the impossibility of objectivity as one might assume. Gadamer did not view objectivity and subjectivity as diametrically opposed but dialogically connected, recognizing that humans are enculturated beings, which shapes the process of understanding texts. Indeed, pushing back against author-centered hermeneutics, Gadamer argues that seeking to understand a text is to seek to understand "the truth of what the Thou [that is, the voice of the text] says to us."[45]

Importantly, regarding enculturation, the notion of tradition is essential to Gadamer's work. In one sense, Gadamer sees traditions in reference to what Leiviskä described as "the entire process of tradition, a continuum of historical influences."[46] This is best typified in Gadamer's notion of the "historically effected consciousness," which he uses to draw attention to the locatedness of interpreters in situations, and through this the prejudices of

41. By the turn of the twenty-first century, cultural theorists began to articulate new notions of what was happening in culture. For example, Tom Turner called for a post-postmodern turn in 1995 in his book *City as Landscape*, and Alan Kirby articulated *pseudomodernism* in his 2006 article "Postmodernism and Beyond," which he later honed in 2009's *Digimodernism*. In 2005, Stephen Feldman argued for a synthesis of Gadamer with Derrida and Habermas to form what he referred to as metamodernism. While not meaning what cultural theorists would later mean by this phrase, it is evidence for how Gadamer was, even then, being seen as foundational for what was to come in the epoch after postmodernism. Feldman, "Problem of Critique," 296–98.

42. Thiselton, *New Horizons*, 317; Moules et al., *Conducting Hermeneutic*, 40.

43. Bartholomew, *Introduction*, 309.

44. Thiselton, *New Horizons*, 314.

45. Gadamer, *Truth and Method*, xxxii; Westphal, *Whose Community?*, 79.

46. Leiviskä, "Gadamer's Concept," 588.

interpreters (and their communities).[47] Due to our locatedness, our points of view limit our understanding—in other words, understanding is histor-ically-effected—such that one needs to take stock of more than just their individual point of view if they are to be able to evaluate where they are and chart a course towards where they want to go.[48] Yet traditions do not just limit. For Gadamer, traditions create the context from which understand-ing can emerge.[49] It is from within traditions that humans engage the world, and we are naïve to think that we engage the world neutrally or objectively, set free from the individual and shared histories that have shaped and, to some extent, helped define us as beings in *a particular* time.[50]

Gadamer described the process of accounting for one's locatedness as a fusion of horizons; a melting together of past and present so understand-ing can emerge.[51] As Moules et al. explains, while Gadamer first applied the fusion of horizons to the interpretation of history, he also went on to apply it to texts, arguing that "to fully engage the meaning of the text, the reader brings his or her own horizon into play."[52] Indeed, for Gadamer, it is a posi-tive (even if inevitable) thing "that one reads and understands the otherness of a text *better* by having an angle of commitment of one's own, but only provided that one can hold that angle as a possibility open to change."[53] By bringing themselves into dialogue with others, reflexively engaging with at least partial awareness of their historical locatedness, interpreters can enter into a process where each time they interpret their understanding is revised, which in turn shapes their present horizon, tradition, and future interpretive practice.[54]

Underpinning all the above notions in Gadamer's hermeneutic, and truly the notion that ties them together, is Gadamer's concept of play. While somewhat underdeveloped, Gadamer's concept of play is what allows his hermeneutic vision to move beyond the subjectivity of postmodernism and towards holding the objective and subjective in creative tension. Indeed, for Gadamer play is not to be understood in a subjective sense (in terms of

47. Gadamer, *Truth and Method*, 301, 312.

48. Gadamer, *Truth and Method*, 312; Moules et al., *Conducting Hermeneutic*, 38.

49. Gadamer, *Truth and Method*, 305–6.

50. Leiviskä, "Gadamer's Concept," 582.

51. Gadamer, *Truth and Method*, 317; Moules et al., *Conducting Hermeneutic*, 47.

52. Moules et al., *Conducting Hermeneutic*, 48.

53. Moules et al., *Conducting Hermeneutic*, 48.

54. Gadamer, *Truth and Method*, 280, 315–17.

one playing a game) but as a description of what is occurring in the process of understanding; what Vilhauer describes as "spontaneous back and forth movement (*Bewegung*) that continually renews itself."[55] Thus, Gadamer argues, "the players are not the subjects of play; instead play merely reaches presentation (*Dastellung*) through the players."[56] Play is therefore something interpreters participate in continually, and by doing so open themselves to (renewed) understanding emerging from the oscillation between horizons and experiences.[57] As Moules et al. describe, "To be caught up in the play of possible meanings demands more than merely forming a subjective opinion, but letting the artwork [text] stand amidst the cross currents of its presence in the world so that the self is being reinterpreted in the light of the work even while the work is interpreted."[58] For Gadamer, the back-and-forth movement of play is what happens in the melting of horizons and the continual revision of understanding through interpretation.[59]

## Biblical Interpretation and the Metamodern Mood

Gadamer's conception of play is a concept that finds congruence with metamodernism—namely, that play is an oscillation between poles for the purpose of renewed understanding. As noted in the introduction, this congruence has been so far ignored within metamodern scholarship, yet it is one that can (positively) constructively inform the metamodern development such that the oscillation of metamodernism can be properly conceptualized in terms of the development of understanding. As such, Gadamer's thought truly bolsters metamodernism.

Related more directly to biblical interpretation, in the twilight of the postmodern epoch there have been recent movements towards more intentionally integrating author, text, and reader when interpreting, such that meaning's locus is found in their tension-filled interplay.[60] However, before continuing in this survey, it is important to briefly note that while my suggestion is that each of the above eras had particular hermeneutical

---

55. Vilhauer, *Gadamer's Ethics of Play*, 39.

56. Gadamer, *Truth and Method*, 107.

57. Gadamer, *Truth and Method*, 103.

58. Moules et al., *Conducting Hermeneutic*, 43.

59. For further discussion regarding Gadamer's concept of play and biblical interpretation, see Judd, *Playing with Scripture*.

60. Merwe, "Reading," 3; Brown, *Communication*, 60.

foci, I am not suggesting their focus was monolithic in dominance. Indeed, part of the hermeneutical complexity of postmodernism, especially in the church, is that both reader and author-centered approaches were operative during the postmodern epoch, even as reader-response criticism grew in popularity. Thus, in the very development of postmodernism are the seeds of a metamodernist approach to understanding the relationship between author, text, and reader that can now help clarify some of the complexities in contemporary interpretive practice.

Some of the more constructive proposals in recent evangelical scholarship have sought to re-evaluate author-centered (and, to some degree, text-centered) readings, but with an emphasis on the divine author rather than the human authors. Jeannine Brown's proposal for understanding hermeneutics as communication is one such development. In her book, *Scripture as Communication*, Brown argues for an interpretive posture that foregrounds authorial intention by viewing Scripture according to its fundamental purpose, which is to communicate. That is, the human authors willed to communicate something to their audience in their contexts when writing the texts of Scripture, and God also willed to communicate something to humanity through these inspired texts. By partnering with enculturated humans, via the inspiration of the Holy Spirit, God ensures that what he wanted to communicate *was* communicated through the writings of the human authors.[61]

The above raises the question about whether one can know—or at least to what extent one can know—what God willed to communicate in Scripture. On this point, scholars such as Rhyne Putman and Kevin Vanhoozer offer significant critiques of postmodern hermeneutical insights. Building off the philosophical presupposition of realism, that reality is independent of the mind (that is, there is a real world, in a sense, outside of our minds), both Putman and Vanhoozer argue for *hermeneutical* realism. In their view, hermeneutical realism "is the position that believes meaning to be prior to and independent of the process of interpretation."[62] Vanhoozer describes this concept by discussing its opposites, naïve hermeneutical realism and hermeneutical non-realism, concluding that both lead to making interpretation unnecessary.[63] In their view, apart from a belief that reality exists outside of the mind, the pillars of the church's theologies of Scripture

61. Brown, *Communication*, 259–64; Putman, *Doctrine Divides*, 44.

62. Vanhoozer, *Meaning*, 48. See also Putman, *Doctrine Divides*, 44.

63. Vanhoozer, *Meaning*, 49.

would cease to exist. Yet, this is not a foregone conclusion, and indeed the perspective mistakes what meaning is with what *understanding meaning* is. In other words, while interpretation is concerned with understanding what an author means, hermeneutical realism asserts that the author does mean something and that this meaning is the only meaning of significance.

Put into Gadamerian terms, this perspective is a paradox, because readers can only ever understand meaning from the confines of their horizon and not from the horizon of the other (whether author or text). The fusion of horizons Gadamer postulates significantly damages the hermeneutical realist perspective, even as this perspective rightly attempts to make sense of the place of divine authorship for understanding Scripture. Even still, hermeneutical realism reminds us, at least in a limited sense, that when interpreting Scripture the fusion of horizons is not two horizons melting together but three—the horizons of readers, human author/text, and divine author/inspired text. In essence, this means there are two horizonal-fusion points that, similar to our view of the sky, could be termed local and celestial horizons. Much like the actual earth–sky and astronomical horizons, the perspective of readers can only ever see one horizon ("earth–sky") and can only seek to understand the other ("celestial") without ever being able to see or know it fully (John 20:29; 1 Cor 13:12; 1 Pet 1:8).

Interestingly, Putman draws a line from the hermeneutical realism position to premodern hermeneutics, arguing that both premodern and modern interpreters understood that "texts have meaning independent of their interpreters."[64] This marks another growing hermeneutical trend during the metamodern epoch that has earlier been noted, a return to the premodern. Indeed, this has been marked by a return to metaphysical concerns, even though theorists are often cautious to clarify that any return is more a revival of interest in metaphysics than anything else.[65] For example, Zachary Stein names the revival of metaphysics from premodern thought as a critical element of metamodernity, though he is careful to clarify his proposal is not to return to premodern metaphysics as such but an articulation of metaphysics that is certainly informed by modern and postmodern critiques.[66]

---

64. Putman, *Doctrine Divides*, 45.

65. Stein, "Love in a Time Between Worlds," 188. D. C. Schindler ("Premodern Forebear," para. 8.) has also argued that premodern conceptions may be an ally to metamodernism's ongoing development.

66. Stein, "Love in a Time Between Worlds," 188.

Within evangelicalism, this return to the premodern is perhaps best exemplified in the development of the theological interpretation of Scripture movement. Typified by scholars such as Fowl, Volf, and Carter, the theological interpretation of Scripture argues that one's interpretation of Scripture is informed by what one supposes Scripture is.[67] In other words, biblical interpretation is profoundly informed by theological assumptions about the Bible, and that holding proper assumptions (that is, orthodox theology regarding Scripture) is a necessity for rightly interpreting the Bible. David Steinmetz even goes so far as to argue that the precritical (that is, premodern) hermeneutical viewpoint of the early church is actually a midway point between the extremes of modern and postmodern hermeneutical postures.[68] Thus, the theological interpretation of Scripture movement is, in at least some sense, metamodern in flavour, being developed in the wake of postmodernism but not naïvely returning to modernism.

It is argued by some in the movement that the early church's allegorical approach to exegesis should be readopted, particularly in light of modernism and postmodernism. Carter is a recent proponent of this perspective who rightly recognizes that speaking of a single biblical author, even of many books of Scripture, is incoherent because their authors are either unknown or the book has been heavily edited.[69] As Carter notes, "Arbitrating among the obscure intentions of an unknown number of authors and editors is hopeless."[70] Indeed, it has been in attempting to arbitrate them that the various hermeneutic postures of the past centuries were developed. By bringing focus back to the church's past interpretive practice, Carter argues for seeing a *sensus plenior* or deeper meaning, which is not read into Scripture by readers but exists due to the intent of both the divine and human authors of the biblical texts, leaving room for recognizing layers of meaning in a given passage.[71]

One potential downside of this movement, however, is that some in the movement seem to describe their project as being a return to *premodernism* because, in their view, the modern and postmodern projects have been a disaster. As Carter puts it, believers must "regard modernity in general, and the Enlightenment in particular, as a wrong turn in biblical

---

67. Webster, *Domain*, 30.

68. Steinmetz, "Pre-critical Exegesis," 36–38. See also Carter, *Great Tradition*, 5.

69. Carter, *Great Tradition*, 40.

70. Carter, *Great Tradition*, 44.

71. Carter, *Great Tradition*, xiv.

interpretation."[72] Yet this seems, to me, to somewhat ignore modernism and postmodernism in favour of a sort of "golden age" of precritical, pre-Enlightenment thinking. If taken up, it is not clear to me that the insights of modernism and postmodernism would not simply be reasserted, especially if, as I suspect, postmodernists view any move towards "precritical" understanding as an attempt to preserve power by those who have lost it culturally. Instead, I think it more productive to answer Steinmetz's call to "a hermeneutical theory adequate to the nature of the text which it is interpreting,"[73] that is not simply a return to the premodern but a complex integration of the best of modern, postmodern, *and* premodern thought, which a metamodern approach to biblical interpretation (and, indeed, theological reflection) aims to accomplish.

In my estimation, one of the more important aspects of the theological interpretation movement has been a renewed emphasis on the metaphysics undergirding the church's doctrines and interpretive practice throughout history. Carter, Boersma, and others describe their perspective as "Christian Platonism," by which they do not mean a Christianity where Plato has been shoehorned and forced to overtake Hebraic thought.[74] Christian Platonism is, instead, an assertion that Platonism's core metaphysics find their fullest expression and fulfillment in Christian theism, and thus best make sense of reality—insomuch as the philosophy is subservient to Christ.[75] While describing Christian Platonism is outside of the goals of this project, it is mentioned here to draw attention to an underlying agreement between Gadamer, metamodernism, and the theological interpretation movement. Gadamer's hermeneutical posture is one that is self-described as ontological and Platonic, informed by his earlier work on Plato while studying under Heidegger.[76] This opens the door for Gadamer's thought to bridge some of the gaps in interpretive practice I have been describing, particularly in confessional contexts where one's understanding of Scripture's character *is* considered a critical element of interpretation.

72. Carter, *Great Tradition*, 126.

73. Steinmetz, "Pre-critical Exegesis," 38.

74. Tyson, *Reality*, 126; Carter, *Great Tradition*, 61–91.

75. Boersma, *Theologians Wish*, 43; Carter, *Great Tradition*, 79–84.

76. Fuyarchuk, *Gadamer's Path to Plato*, xiii, 1–2.

## Conclusion: Hermeneutic Theory

Further aspects of *Truth and Method*, and other parts of Gadamer's work that have import for the project will be reviewed throughout as needed. Suffice to say, my goal has not been to summarize every aspect of Gadamer or other hermeneutic scholar's work so much as to situate some of their core insights in the timeline of metamodernism's emergence, which will ultimately inform both my use of Gadamer's hermeneutic theory and my understanding of others' understanding in the context of their interpretive practice.

## THEOLOGY: SCRIPTURE AS REVELATION

As described in the first chapter, the theologies of Scripture's authority and inspiration form this project's theological core. Yet, I will not be treating them separately, because these theologies come together in the doctrine of revelation. The following section is an attempt to foreground my own theological prejudices regarding the doctrine of revelation and its implications, in a Gadamerian sense, through dialogue with relevant scholarship, as my understanding—while it may not be agreeable to every reader—will shape the project. My hope in articulating this section is to invite the reader into deeper reflection on this doctrine such that, even if in disagreement, the ends of the project and my overarching argument will still be found to be coherent and useful. In a limited sense, foregrounding a theology of Scripture in order to understand interpretive practice may suggest that this project emerges from the theological interpretation of Scripture movement. While this would not, in my view, be an inappropriate suggestion, it is not my intention. Instead, as I will argue, a Gadamerian approach to hermeneutics necessarily includes foregrounding presuppositions, as possible, making reflection on my prejudices regarding Scripture both proper and necessary because of the role theological assumptions regarding revelation will come to play in understanding differences in interpretive practice later in the project.

In his book *The Revelation of God*, Peter Jensen argues for understanding God's self revelation in light of (or through the lens of) the gospel. Jensen traces contemporary notions of revelation in a way that maps onto the developments of modernism and postmodernism outlined in the previous section. In essence, Jensen argues that in modernism revelation related to texts *as written by authors*, such that it was the author who was to be considered revelatory or inspired over and against the text.[77] In this mode, textual transmission became an important part of understanding what parts of a text are inspired. John Webster argues this is to make the mistake of assuming that texts and their reception history are dominant over "the self-presentation of the triune God, of which the text is a servant and by which readers are accosted, as by a word of supreme dignity, legitimacy, and effectiveness."[78] Modernism's flaw in conceptualizing revelation was to overemphasize the role and importance of Scripture's human authors to the detriment of the text and divine author.

According to Jensen, postmodernism has led to a redefinition of Scripture's position as revelation as the inspiration of the reader, emphasizing "the experience of divine–human encounter," favouring "a dynamic revelation focusing on God's historical deeds rather than on a static set of words."[79] In other words, it is the reader and their understanding that is inspired rather than the text being read. This development has a significant positive edge in its ability to account for divine saving action in how the church thinks theologically, helpfully emphasizing illumination in the hermeneutical process. Indeed, this insight has been a significant influence on the contemporary field of biblical theology and the development of canonical criticism.[80] However, taken on its own without the recognition that the words used in Scripture have significance because they are Holy Spirit generated and preserve the account of God's self-communication with his creation,[81] what is left is either assessing Scripture as literary documents that must be evaluated in the same manner as any other ancient cultural artifact or with an approach to understanding revelation that prioritizes one's experience of Scripture to understand what the text means.[82] While

77. Jensen, *Revelation*, 213–14.

78. Webster, *Scripture*, 6. Webster goes on to describe how Scripture's inspiration has been either objectified ("the inspired product is given priority over . . . the divine agent") or spiritualized ("shifting center of gravity away from the text towards . . . authors or readers"), both of which can be seen in modernism and postmodernism's understandings of revelation. Ultimately, Webster makes the case that while these are dangers, their cures can also trend towards Docetism because they both tend to treat the divine author of Scripture as inaccessible. Webster, *Scripture*, 33–35.

79. Jensen, *Revelation*, 19.

80. McKnight, *Postmodern Use of the Bible*, 70, 75.

81. Webster, *Scripture*, 29.

82. McKnight, *Postmodern Use of the Bible*, 226. For example, Brian McLaren argued for Christians learning to "enter the text . . . feel the flow of its arguments, get stuck in its points of tension, and struggle with its unfolding plot . . . [so that] *God's revelation can*

readers are certainly illuminated by the Spirit in their reading, the text's generation was also inspired, which postmodern notions of revelation have difficulty accounting for.

As previously noted, renewed attention on the theological interpretation of Scripture has also brought with it a renewed emphasis on the divine author of Scripture. Indeed, theological interpretations are enlivened by the insight that God authored Scripture (1 Cor 2:12–13; 2 Tim 3:16; 2 Pet 2:20–21). As Carter describes, the church's understanding of co-authorship enabled the recognition of both divine and human authorial intent, which fundamentally informed interpretive practice until recently.[83] This understanding presupposes an important point that should not be missed: that God utilizes partnership with humanity to communicate who God is and what God has done in history. The divine-human partnership is revealed in two ways in Scripture. The first is a theme found throughout Scripture of the Lord speaking and the Lord's people writing what is said down. For example, in Jeremiah 36:2 God tells the prophet to "Take a scroll and write on it all the words I have spoken to you." Similar scenes marked by the Lord initiating contact and giving an instruction to write are also described in Exod 17:14; 24:4; 34:27; Isa 8:1; 30:8; Jer 30:2; Hab 2:2; and Rev 1:10–11. Secondly, and critically, the divine-human partnership is shown in the fact that the Bible is written in human language. By utilizing the language of created beings, God (the Creator) binds the church to the Scriptures as texts which definitively communicate truth about reality and history— particularly the *salvation* history that Scripture preserves. The above offers a hint as to why Scripture is regularly found at the center of theological debates, because the church is bound not just to Scripture but to all that Scripture reveals, which means that prejudices regarding Scripture (such as one's conception of the doctrine of revelation) are critically important for all number of theological debates.

Similarly emphasized in recent literature, as well as by Jensen, is the conviction that because Scripture was inspired by God, God will illuminate the minds of readers via the Holy Spirit so that they can understand the Bible's meaning. This pneumatological claim sees the Holy Spirit's activity in both Scripture and the human person as being a bridge for understanding between the horizons of the text and reader. Indeed, Jesus promises that "the Holy Spirit . . . will teach you all everything . . ." (John 14:26) and

---

happen to us." McLaren, *New Kind of Christianity*, 91; emphasis added.

83. Carter, *Great Tradition*, xvi.

"When the Spirit of truth comes, he will guide you into all the truth . . ."
(John 16:13). As Christians read the Bible, the Holy Spirit transforms them
by the renewal of their mind in Christ Jesus and helps them to further understand the Bible's message and precepts.

Many early church theologians explicitly argue that the Holy Spirit's
supernatural help is required for rightly understanding Scripture.[84] This
assertion presupposes that application is a necessary part of the act of interpretation—that is, "interpretation" is not complete without embodied
understanding. Indeed, the illumination of Scripture by the Spirit is related
primarily to application.[85] When Scripture is interpreted, the Holy Spirit
illuminates understanding enough that the interpreter can know how they
might live, in response to God's self-disclosure, as citizens of God's Kingdom. Yet Jensen reminds us this is itself not a separate revelatory act on
God's part but built into the very nature of Scripture as inspired text. As
Jensen comments, "While the knowledge of God may be offered in propositions, it is entirely personal."[86] And it is this personal knowledge—that
is, knowledge of the Triune God—that the Holy Spirit offers, particularly
through Scripture.

Jensen's theology of revelation builds its foundations on the knowledge of God, grounded in the message of the gospel which makes such
knowledge attainable. Doing this helps Jensen connect the revelation
of Christ to biblical revelation, arguing that Scripture is an extension of
Christ's revelation and that the core of the Bible's revelation is a procla-
mation about a person: that Jesus of Nazareth is the Christ and Lord.[87]
Indeed, Scripture can be considered inspired and authoritative because
of the knowledge it shares, which is a knowledge of God through Christ.
Jensen argues that the gospel's covenantal nature, which calls people to
repentance and obedience according to the covenant's promises, suggests
the nature of biblical authority is covenantal, making the ability to "trust
and obey words, sentences, and paragraphs" of the biblical text critical for
faithful living as disciples of Jesus.[88]

The above has important implications for the understanding of revelation I am putting forward. First, if Scripture has a covenantal character,

84. Graves, *Inspiration and Interpretation*, 43; Putman, *Doctrine Divides*, 62.

85. Graves, *Inspiration and Interpretation*, 48.

86. Jensen, *Revelation*, 236.

87. Jensen, *Revelation*, 31, 72.

88. Jensen, *Revelation*, 83.

its function in the Christian community (and the lives of individuals) will serve that character. Scripture certainly has a didactic function, Jensen says, but it also functions to "create and sustain our relationship with the living God."[89] Thus, as God's self-revelation, Scripture must be regarded as more than mere didactic text and instead be treated as the communication from its author, the living God, that it is. This clarifies metamodern biblical interpretive practice, as it reminds believers that while the Bible is useful for teaching, rebuking, correcting, and training (2 Tim 3:16–17), interpretations of Scripture should lead towards knowing the God who speaks, in some sense, through the text to teach, rebuke, correct, and train *us* in righteousness, so that the church might be equipped for every good work.

Secondly, Jensen argues that the covenantal character of Scripture connects obedience to Scripture with obedience to Christ.[90] In his view, when one confesses that Jesus is Lord, their confession reorients them to consider Christ as authoritative in a personal sense. Christians, in particular, live under the rule and reign of Christ the King as citizens of his Kingdom (Eph 2:19; Phil 3:20). Thus, when believers interpret Scripture, they are not simply searching for abstract truths. Interpreting Scripture is, instead, listening for God's invitation to live faithfully as the Lord's people. Indeed, because the authority of Scripture is "the personal authority of the Lord over the people whom he has saved,"[91] when God's Word is opened there is a dual exception: that the hearers would listen to the Word, and that they would put the Word into practice (Matt 7:24–27; Jas 1:22). As Carter comments, "Nothing is more fundamental to the Christian life than reading the text of Scripture and submitting one's life to the One who speaks His Word through the human words of the inspired text."[92]

Jensen repeatedly draws attention to how modernism and postmodernism both led Christians towards devaluing the authority of Scripture, attacking its unity and truthfulness by evaluating Scripture primarily using tools whose epistemological basis did not have a category for supernatural elements. Yet, because Scripture is revelation it must have the character of the one whom it reveals—namely, the Triune God. Because God is a tri-unity, Scripture has a character of unity, and because God cannot lie (which is to say God is fully truthful), Scripture also has a character of

---

89. Jensen, *Revelation*, 82.

90. Jensen, *Revelation*, 150–52.

91. Jensen, *Revelation*, 154.

92. Carter, *Great Tradition*, 32.

truthfulness.[93] To what end? Christians informed by modernism and post-modernism would agree, Scripture leads us towards what Jensen rightly describes as an inescapable question: "Do you believe that God raised Jesus Christ from the dead?"[94] For "If you declare with your mouth, 'Jesus is Lord,' and believe in your heart that God raised him from the dead, you will be saved" (Rom 10:9).

Answering the above question in the affirmative will shape how one reads the Bible, as the text draws readers towards ever deeper covenantal relationship with God through Christ and helps them understand what kind of unity and truthfulness to expect from Scripture. Yet there remains a difference in how that unity and truthfulness are understood, in part because of the approaches interpreters take in focusing on the role of authors and readers in their interpretive process. Yet, no matter one's hermeneutical bent, there is a shared recognition that, rather than a simple unity, Scripture is a unity-in-difference that reflects the unified-difference in the Godhead between Father, Son, and Holy Spirit, while also reflecting the complexity of human beings who God partnered with to produce the text. In other words, as Jensen comments, "if the Bible is to do its job presenting Jesus Christ as Lord in all his fullness, it needs the complex unity that emerges from the coexistence of many parts and many different types of literature."[95] This is a complex unity that is not easy to untangle let alone understand.

Likewise, Scripture's truthfulness is a relational truthfulness, and thus intrinsically tied to faith. In effect this suggests that one is only able to trust Scripture as revelation to the extent that they trust God, and to the extent that Scripture is undermined as untrustworthy one's relationship with God is weakened.[96] Thus, while contradictions or issues may arise that may make one question Scripture's truthfulness, conviction regarding who God is should lead believers towards a deeper study of the text—and a reflexive posture regarding interpretive processes—to gain better understanding and see whether fruitful explanations can be discovered.[97] Indeed, "like the cross, the Scripture is a paradox of God's self-revelation—foolish to the

93. Jensen, *Revelation*, 179.
94. Jensen, *Revelation*, 182.
95. Jensen, *Revelation*, 192.
96. Jensen, *Revelation*, 197.
97. Jensen, *Revelation*, 203.

cultured, but wise beyond all measure to those who are being saved"[98] (1 Cor 1:18–31; 2 Tim 3:15).

While the above may all seem out of place in an academic project, Webster argues (and I would contend with him) this is because post-critical theology tends to proceed from the church's practices rather than God's activity, and is therefore doomed to a broad array of theological issues.[99] Andrew Root makes similar comments regarding the discipline of practical theology, arguing that practical theology has, at times, conflated divine and human actions. Indeed, because, as Root contends, practical theology "studies living human documents first and foremost for the sake of articulating divine encounter, to confess and proclaim how human beings experience and participate in the event of God's becoming among concrete people," the risk of practical theology is focusing on the church's practices (human action) without concern for divine action.[100]

Furthermore, because of Scripture's normative role in the formation of the church, the Bible can be mistaken as the church's book rather than God's, and thereby confuse the church's use of Scripture and God's activity in Scripture. Instead of hearing God's word and putting it into practice, believers may become fixated on improving practice without any sense of what that practice truly ought to be aiming for—which I have argued, for Scripture, is the authoritative articulation of the gospel. A fixation on practice without due consideration of practice's *telos* should not be if the doctrine of revelation is taken seriously, because the church's practices can only be considered such due to God's saving work and our understanding of it as revealed. Certainly, as Webster comments, "Scripture is not the word of the church; the church is the church of the Word."[101]

Thus, building upon Jensen's notion of scriptural authority being covenantal, Webster adds that scriptural authority is not "another way of talking about the accumulated *gravitas* which has been acquired by Scripture."[102] Instead, Scripture is recognized as authoritative because it is judged, by faith, as a text that corresponds to reality precisely because it is the revelation of the One in whom reality is grounded (John 1:1–4). Importantly, if this is not the case, and Scripture's authority is not grounded in

98. Jensen, *Revelation*, 204.

99. Webster, *Holy Scripture*, 43.

100. Root, *Christopraxis*, 147–48; see also 11, 243.

101. Webster, *Holy Scripture*, 44.

102. Webster, *Holy Scripture*, 53.

God via revelation, Scripture can only be considered an artefact of tradition and its authority becomes a matter of capricious power games—a critique that, in my estimation as a practitioner, is becoming increasingly popular in the secular West.[103] Thus, *by faith* is an important clause in the above statement, as it clarifies the nature of biblical authority as being related to ones experience of Christ's lordship. For as Jeff Pool comments, "the Christian Scriptures, whatever intrinsic or objective authority they possess as primary attestations to the history of God's self-disclosure in and to creation, derive their subjective trustworthiness or authority for the Christian from the human's experience of divine love through Christ."[104] By recognizing Scripture as revelation, it can be recognized that Scripture truly communicates something understandable about who God is and what God has done and is doing in the world: God's salvation, and our sanctification, enacted by and through His Word.[105]

## Conclusion: Scripture as Revelation

Grounding the project in doctrines of Scripture, with particular reference to the work of Peter Jensen, I have laid bare my prejudice for understanding the Bible as inspired and authoritative revelation. Indeed, my recognition of the Bible as the revelatory Word of God informs much of my theological vision, and will shape the reappraisal of the process of theological reflection utilizing the Wesleyan Quadrilateral that is to come. Suffice to say, this foundational confession also centers the project as a work of practical theology, insomuch as it ensures the project's concern is with equipping the church to interpret Scripture so that she can hear God's Word and put it into practice.

## PRACTICE: INTERPRETATION AS DISCIPLESHIP AND THEOLOGICAL REFLECTION

Grasping the importance of revelation, a fuller understanding of the nature of the practice this study is investigating can begin to emerge. As an act of discipleship, biblical interpretation should shape people into Christlikeness.

103. Webster, *Holy Scripture*, 53.

104. Pool, "Christ, Conscience, Canon, Community," 420.

105. McFarlane, *Evangelical Theology*, 79.

Or to put this in more doctrinal language, biblical interpretation is an important means of sanctification in the Christian life.

In his book *Sanctifying Interpretation*, Chris Green argues that Scripture is designed by God to shape the hearts and minds of interpreters as they read it.[106] Writing from a Pentecostal perspective, Green begins his study from a conviction tied to the concern of revelation above, namely that when the Bible is read the core questions asked of it should be "Who has given us the Scriptures?" and "Who is he making us to be?"[107] By posing these questions, Green helpfully focuses on God as the author of Scripture—both in terms of production and intent, for if God's intention for Scripture is that through reading it we would be drawn towards Christ, this intent should be held as more important than all other possible intentions ascribable to the human authors.[108] And in this way, we gain a limited clarity regarding the third (celestial) horizon in the fusion of horizons, which will necessarily shape the goals of biblical interpretation. These questions also clarify what interpretation's *telos* is as a practice, which is to wrestle with the text, seeking to bring it to bear in the Church's life in a way faithful to the intent of the divine author; a practice that sanctifies the interpreter and the interpreting community of faith.[109] Thus, Green argues that biblical interpretation invites Christians into a particular vocation—joining Christ in "bringing to bear God's holiness for the good of all creation"[110]—which only happens if and as the Holy Spirit sets God's people apart. Scripture does not just reveal God's past work, Green says, but is, by grace and faith, the instrument by which God works at transforming Christians.[111]

Vanhoozer ends his important volume on hermeneutics by critiquing postmodern hermeneutics, concluding on a similar note to Green that interpretation has a transformational end in mind: the shaping of readers into the image of Christ.[112] Unlike Green, whose insights begin by reflecting on human vocation (by which Green means that which humans were created

---

106. Green, *Sanctifying Interpretation*, 1.

107. Green, *Sanctifying Interpretation*, 5.

108. By this I am not suggesting that the human authorial intent is meaningless, but that it serves the greater intent of the divine author for what the text means and how it should be used.

109. Green, *Sanctifying Interpretation*, 49.

110. Green, *Sanctifying Interpretation*, 125.

111. Green, *Sanctifying Interpretation*, 127.

112. Vanhoozer, *Meaning*, 440.

for) rather than divine revelation,[113] Vanhoozer begins with Christ, arguing for Jesus as the definitive interpreter of Scripture because he is God's ultimate self-communication, the Word made flesh. Building from this, Vanhoozer sees incarnation as central to Christian notions of interpretation, even concluding that "the end of interpretation . . . is embodiment."[114] Just as Jesus, the divine *Logos*, became flesh, those made in Christ's image must enflesh his message and teachings. As such, interpreters become witnesses and bearers of the Word—witnesses because as one interprets Scripture they witness it's message, and bearers in that the message of the Word demands a response.[115]

All of the above makes clear that like the doctrine of revelation, the practice of interpretation is concerned not just with information gathered but information understood and heeded. Indeed, the revelation of God demands a response of obedience and faith. Thus, biblical interpretation can be understood as a practice that shapes believers into increasingly faithful and obedient followers of Christ—in a phrase, it is an act of discipleship. Yet there remains a question about how we go about this practice. Central to it is being self-reflective enough to articulate one's interpretive approach. To this end, evangelical and practical theologians have sought to articulate paradigms or methods to describe how the process of biblical interpretation functions in practice. In essence, what they have described are methods of theological reflection which integrate situational experiences and theological sources (especially, but not exclusively, Scripture). Because the integration of theological sources is an element of the *play* of interpretation, clarifying the process of theological reflection is critical for properly describing and discerning interpretive practice.

Before moving forward, it requires being noted that there is nuance in the relevant literature as to whether or not the use of the phrase *methods*, as above, suggests a methodological approach whereby one must follow a ruleset to arrive at theological conclusions. Some, such as Putman, seem to conceive of theological method procedurally.[116] However, others such as Thorsen and McFarlane take a more paradigmatic approach that understands theological reflection methods to be flexible, recognizing most people do not typically employ procedural methods when thinking—let

---

113. Green, *Sanctifying Interpretation*, 1.

114. Vanhoozer, *Meaning*, 440.

115. Vanhoozer, *Meaning*, 439.

116. Putman, *Method*, 1–4.

alone when thinking theologically.[117] Collins points out that a similar distinction between procedure and paradigm exists in practical theological literature, drawing attention to Whitehead and Whitehead's distinction between "models" of reflection that describe the composite parts of theological reflection pictorially and "methods" as a description of "the dynamic or movement of the reflection."[118] Similar in each of these distinctions, however, is the understanding that theological method develops an orientation or *habitus* to thinking in a particular way about God. Throughout this project, I will use the phrase *method* in relation to theological reflection with a paradigmatic approach in view.

## Theological Reflection and Practical Theology

As the preceding discussion implies, conversations regarding theological reflection have dominated practical theological scholarship in recent years. There are few concepts in practical theology that are as central to the discipline as theological reflection. Indeed, practical theology is regularly described or defined in terms of theological reflection—as I did in the introduction of this project.[119] Because theological reflection is an integral part of practical theological research and a critical element of the practice that I am researching, it is worth further considering what theological reflection is, how practical theologians have thought about it, and how my understanding of it shapes this project.

First published in 1980, James and Evelyn E. Whitehead's book *Method in Ministry* provided an approach to theological reflection designed to equip pastoral leaders for the task. In Whitehead and Whitehead's view, theological reflection is "the process of bringing to bear in the practical decisions of ministry the resources of Christian faith."[120] Though framed in terms of church ministry, this definition helpfully highlights key components of theological reflection that have continued to prove instrumental in how practical theologians understand this practice.

117. Thorsen, *Quadrilateral*, 11; McFarlane, *Evangelical Theology*, 65–67.

118. Collins, *Reordering Reflection*, 16, 148–49. See also Whitehead and Whitehead, *Method in Ministry*, x.

119. As a reminder, I have described practical theology as critically reflexive theological inquiry on the nature and embodiment of Christian practices. See also Ballard and Pritchard, *Practical Theology in Action*, 118; Swinton and Mowat, *Qualitative Research*, 7.

120. Whitehead and Whitehead, *Methods in Ministry*, ix.

First, theological reflection is a process—and more particularly it is a *dialogical* process, an ongoing back and forth between theological sources as well as between reflection and action. Stephen Pattison and James Woodward provide a similar metaphor when they describe practical theology as, "a place where religious belief, tradition, and practice meets contemporary experiences, questions, and actions and *conducts a dialogue* that is mutually enriching, intellectually critical, and practically transforming."[121] As a dialogue, practical theologians understand theological reflection to be about bringing varied sources of theology to bear on the experiences of individuals and communities. What sources are to be brought is debated, though it is generally accepted that Scripture must play a role, even as many do not clarify what this role is or how it operates in practice beyond what, in my view, often amounts to proof-texting. This lack of clarity regarding Scripture's use is an ongoing conversation in the field, which this project will make a contribution towards.

Second, Whitehead and Whitehead's definition points to theological reflection being *concerned with helping Christians live faithfully*. Bringing the resources of the Christian faith into conversation with problematic situations that arise leads towards new insight for how to live faithfully in a given situation. Swinton and Mowat echo this description of theological reflection, and therefore practical theology, saying that theological reflection has "a view to ensuring and enabling faithful participation in God's redemptive practices in, to and for the world."[122] Likewise, Cameron et al. argue that theological reflection "lies at the heart of the Christian commitment to live faithfully in the world for the sake of the world that God loves."[123] Similarly, to biblical interpretation, this connects theological reflection with discipleship in a fundamental way critical to the discipline of practical theology.[124]

Finally, the above means that theological reflection is *fundamentally situational* or *contextual*. This is most clearly seen in how Whitehead and Whitehead see the use of their method as being, primarily, in the midst of what they call pastoral challenges, or what Roger Walton describes as "a pastoral issue [that] is encountered and on which the minister or church

---

121. Pattison and Woodward, "Introduction," 7; emphasis added.

122. Swinton and Mowat, *Qualitative Research*, 14.

123. Cameron et al., *Theological Reflection for Human Flourishing*, 2.

124. Graham et al., *Theological Reflection*, 2; Cahalan and Nieman, "Mapping the Field," 67–70.

community must take action."[125] More recently, Dustin Benac has argued these challenges or issues may be better understood as crises, "experience of being brought up short that requires new interpretive horizons."[126] For each of the above, theological reflection occurs within a particular situation that gives shape to the reflection, which necessarily means experience is an important element for reflection in practical theology. One of the consequences of this insight is an active debate regarding the role of experience in theological reflection. Walton observes that many theological reflection models share a conviction that reflection begins in experience.[127] Likewise, John Paver asserts that "our theology begins not with a proposition, but with experience," and as such experience is properly the starting point of not only theological reflection but theology itself.[128] However, scholars such as Collins have argued that such assertions have led to an overemphasis on experience, leading to recent reappraisals as to where theological reflection *should* start from. While I agree with Collins that there has been an overemphasis on experience in discussions of theological reflection, this overemphasis includes a fundamental insight that should not be ignored— that theological reflection *is* situational and therefore experiential.

Collins offers a compelling reappraisal of other theological reflection models, arguing for what she terms the Scriptural Cycle, whereby one starts theological reflection with reading Scripture. Collins envisions this as not being simply picking and choosing pericopes at random but starting one's reflection with a deep understanding of and dependence on Scripture, on Scripture's unity as God's story, and on Scripture's purpose. This engagement with the Bible then transforms the reader by the Holy Spirit who illuminates their mind and helps them know how they are to "allow God's story to tell our lives."[129] However, in Collins's framing, one must have sufficient knowledge of the Bible to be able to know the story it tells and thus see oneself as part of that story, which inevitably creates a gap in applicability for the model—that is, it may be effective for clergy but not necessarily for laity. The same is true of many other theological reflection methods, which are often articulated in relation not to congregational life and thought but the training of church leaders via theological education. Indeed, Collins

---

125. Walton, "Using the Bible," 135. See also Walton, "Teaching and Learning," 13.

126. Benac, "Theology for Crisis," 750.

127. Collins, *Reordering Reflection*, 155–58.

128. Paver, *Theological Reflection and Education*, 35.

129. Collins, *Reordering Reflection*, 8.

proposal could be an effective tool for spiritual formation, particularly of ordinands and seminarians, as it would help them place themselves coherently in the biblical story, which—in function—is an important identity forming element of biblical interpretation and theological reflection that pastoral leaders in particular are in need of.

Given the above discussion, even though the primary audiences for this project are academics and pastoral leaders—which is to say informed interpreters—I am also aiming to articulate a theological reflection paradigm which *could* be understood and used by laity, and which describes more than how the biblical story plays a part in interpretive practice. Furthermore, one of the underlying convictions of Collins' project is that many people who use theological reflection methods, in her words, "do not understand the Bible as Scripture."[130] This is a conviction I share, though I have particularized this conviction to not just be about the Bible as Scripture but the Bible *as revelation*.[131]

Interestingly, by formulating a theology of Scripture as revelation and bringing this preunderstanding to bear in the context of theological reflection, Scripture and experience can be held in tension in a more sophisticated way that has otherwise been proposed in other works. This is because, by its very nature, revelation needs to be experienced to be known. Put another way, God's self-disclosure—whether through general or special means—can only truly disclose if there is one to whom the disclosure is made; someone who listens and can therefore respond. Thus, there is an oft hidden connection, doctrinally, between Scripture and experience, which I suspect is a contributing factor to confusion regarding the role of each in theological reflection and practical theological inquiry.

One of the most famous dialogical reflection methods in practical theology is the Pastoral Cycle—so famous that Pete Ward quips, "it has in many ways come to define the whole field."[132] In its simplest form, the Pastoral Cycle is a movement from seeing to judging to acting, iterating reflection on experience cyclically to bring about transformation (or, in connection to its roots in liberation theology, the liberation of the

---

130. Collins, *Reordering Reflection*, 8.

131. This particularization is not a novel one for describing underlying differences in theological reflection. As Walton notes, Avery Dulles has described five ways the Bible is perceived and used based on one's understanding of revelation. Walton, "Using the Bible," 165. See also Dulles, *Models of Revelation*.

132. Ward, *Introducing*, 96.

oppressed).[133] Though popular via many iterations, it is noteworthy that the pastoral cycle tends to be described as dialogically heuristic and often communicated (and diagrammed) as an overarching approach to practical theological research that provides little guidance for discerning how to reflect theologically in terms of the integration of theological sources. For example, Ballard and Prichard describe the cycle as Experience, Reflection, Learning, and Action, while Richard Osmer describes it according to tasks: descriptive-empirical, interpretive, normative, and pragmatic.[134] In both, the role of different theological sources, especially Scripture, can be unclear at times, which has not gone unnoticed.[135]

## Core Difference in Models: Correlative verses Integrative

As I hope is beginning to emerge from this brief review, the practical role of theological sources in theological reflection is an area of confusion and debate that continues to mark discussion in the guild. This debate, especially regarding the question of how theological sources relate, may be due to a fundamental difference in conceptions of theological reflection models—whether a given model is correlative or integrative. While both types of models utilize the metaphor of conversation, how the conversation happens is significantly different.

Grounded in the theory of Paul Tillich, correlative methods were popularized in practical theology by David Tracy, Don Browning, Stephen Pattison, and the development of the Pastoral Cycle discussed above.[136] In correlative models, theological sources are brought into dialogue with an assumption that they are, in some sense, equally authoritative.[137] That is, they enter the conversation on an even footing as they contribute theological insight to a topic. This has long been recognized as an issue to overcome by those who utilize correlational methods. For example,

133. Ward, *Introducing*, 97.

134. Ballard and Pritchard, *Practical Theology in Action*, 77–78; Osmer, *Practical Theology*, 4. See also Cameron, et al., *Theological Reflection for Human Flourishing*, 4–7.

135. Espinoza, Review of *Practical Theology*, 212; Smith, Review of *Practical Theology*, 112.

136. See Tracy, *Blessed Rage*; Browning, *Fundamental*; Pattison, "Straws for Bricks."

137. For a summary overview of correlative methods, see Swinton and Mowat, *Qualitative Research*, 73–94. Collins also offers a discussion of correlative methods, which includes a reflection on various shortcomings. Collins, *Reordering Reflection*, 25–52.

Ballard and Pritchard comment that "the issue to be faced with any cor-relational approach to theological reflection is that it may lack criteria for giving adequate relative weighting to different sources of information in the conversation."[138] Thus, what is one to do regarding their hermeneutical prejudice (which includes theological convictions) and how those preju-dices inform theological reflection?

Integrative methods, on the other hand, enter the dialogue of theo-logical reflection with an assumption that some voices should be privileged over others.[139] In this sense, then, as the sources dialogue the goal is to bring their insights together and unify them, in their difference, while maintaining distinctions between them. In essence, this means that in-tegrative models approach theological reflection with a self-awareness of Gadamerian prejudices—such as, for example, the conviction that Scrip-ture is authoritative revelation—and that these prejudices necessarily shape the reflection process. Not only this, but integrative methods give space for these prejudices, especially theologically informed prejudices, to function in such a way that they can be both privileged and confronted for change (in the Gadamerian sense).

Given the above discussion, my conception of practical theology is in line with the integrative approach. This is *not* to suggest the correlative approach is illegitimate. Rather, I only intend to clarify the character of conversation I expect the project to have and make a contribution towards. I therefore view my work as contributing an integrative paradigm for un-derstanding theological reflection and biblical interpretation. Implications of this, particularly in relation to understanding the discipline of practical theology and its relationship with the other theological disciplines, will be discussed in chapter 6.

---

138. Ballard and Pritchard, *Practical Theology in Action*, 123. Related to this project, Ballard and Pritchard name the issue outright: "How much weight . . . is to be given to what the Bible says about homosexuality and how much to the plethora of confusing in-sights from scientific and cultural studies? To reject all that science and anthropology say on the subject because of the teaching of Leviticus or Romans would be folly; to accept the pronouncements of the latest scientific study would be equally unwise and put theo-logical reflection at the mercy of scientific debate" (*Practical Theology in Action*, 124).

139. While some, such as Paver, describe correlative models in terms of integration, their concern is not the integration of theological sources but the integration of academic learning and ministry praxis. This is a subtle but significant difference in our use of this phrase, requiring careful reading and discernment of relevant literature. See Paver, *Theo-logical Reflection and Education*, 32–35.

Given the importance of theological reflection to practical theology, there have been many more models than so far named which have been developed to help researchers, educators, and practitioners do, teach, and lead theological reflection. Suffice to say, the seeming complexity of reflecting theologically also mystifies it. Indeed, Cameron et al. reflect on this issue, saying:

> It seems well recognized within practical theology that it is the theological reflection 'bit' of the [pastoral] cycle which is often most problematic: students can work attentively with experience, and are keen to suggest renewed action, but the making of genuine and transformative connections with theology can often be rather weak or superficial. . . . Is it enough simply to use one Bible passage for reflection, and so avoid the often-complex scriptural picture? . . . Once again, it is a problem of 'making connection,' of being able to articulate faith in, for, and as practice, while having some sense of continuity with the wider Christian tradition which is beyond any one experience or practice.[140]

In their discussion of their theological reflection method, Whitehead and Whitehead outline a possible reason for the kind of mystification described above: most reflection methods are not portable, performable, nor communal enough to be adoptable, particularly by clergy (and thus, by extension, laity).[141] This seems, to me, to be related to the general ambiguity of theological sources in many of the methods—if sources are mentioned at all.

Given the preceding discussion, what might theological reflection have to do with biblical interpretation? If application (in the sense of faithful living in response to the living God) is the end of interpretation, theological reflection is a necessary element for moving from Scripture to the transformation of a situation. This is not to say that Scripture is imposed on a situation, applied without due reflection, but that Scripture must be a central element of the reflection process, especially for evangelicals and other Christians who confess to the authority of Scripture. Indeed, because of this, I view theological reflection as an integral part of the practice of biblical interpretation. I am thus in agreement with Collins regarding the privileged place of Scripture.

However, the insights of Gadamerian hermeneutics, earlier described, complexify the question of the starting point of interpretation and

---

140. Cameron et al., *Talking about God*, 28.
141. Whitehead and Whitehead, *Methods in Ministry*, 3.

theological refection. Gadamer clarifies the dialogical nature of interpretation, offering a leverage point whereby the exegesis of Scripture and theological reflection could be integrated. Indeed, an integration of the contextual
nature of theological reflection (and interpretation), exegesis, and an already well used theological reflection method may help address important
issues with theological reflection that exist in practical theology—namely,
it can lead to developing clear guidance on the role of Scripture in practical
theological works, help practical theologians better describe the place of
empirical research in relation to theological method, and provide a model
that appropriates understanding from various fields so as to ensure a level
of portability, performability, and communal grounding.[142]

Therefore, in this project, I will appropriate an integrative theological reflection method into an interpretive paradigm that can bring the
resources of Christian faith into particular situations to help those who
are theologically reflecting live more faithfully as disciples of Jesus Christ.
Doing so will require developing the paradigm to be remwith, use-
able in practice, and mindful of the place of community. To these ends, I
believe that adopting a method designed by academics for academics may
not be the most effective course of action. Instead, utilizing and integrating
elements of a method that is already well known, and which uses theological sources many evangelicals would already recognize, seems to me
to be a better course. Indeed, there is one integrative theological reflection
method that is very well known within Protestantism and evangelicalism,
and which I believe can be leveraged to bring clarity to interpretive practice: the so-called Wesleyan Quadrilateral.

## Integrative Theological Method: The "Wesleyan" Quadrilateral

The "Wesleyan" Quadrilateral was first articulated by Albert Outler, who
coined the term *quadrilateral* as a way to describe the theological method
of John Wesley.[143] More recently, Donald Thorsen popularized the Quadrilateral as an evangelical theological method in his text *The Wesleyan Quadrilateral*, increasing attention to the benefits—and potential pitfalls—of this
method.

At its core, the Quadrilateral is derived from John Wesley's conviction
that there are four theological sources, or "specific vehicles of God's gracious

---

142. Graham et al., *Theological Reflection*, 8; Walton, "Teaching and Learning," 135.

143. Bevins, "Pentecostal Appropriation," 232–33.

revelation,"[144] that work together in Christian theological reflection: Scripture, Reason, Tradition, and Experience. Because of Wesley's historical context, the Quadrilateral's core notions are informed by the Enlightenment, making the parts not easily transferable into the contemporary era.[145] Thus, if it is to continue being usable in the metamodern frame, the Quadrilateral as a tool will have to undergo a basic reappraisal. However, my concern is not to offer a reappraisal just to return to using the Quadrilateral exactly as Methodists may have intended, even as I acknowledge the formative impact Wesley's theology has had on my faith and the evangelical tradition. Instead, I aim to use it as a foundation for helping to describe contemporary interpretive practice. Doing so will mean discussing the theological sources at greater length, which will occur in the following chapter.

For the purposes of the present survey, I will highlight major works that have wrestled with the Quadrilateral at length, of which there are surprisingly few. However, before doing so it is critical to note that while Wesley certainly did utilize the aforementioned theological sources, the integration of all these sources was not particularly ground-breaking nor did Wesley explicitly articulate their integration. Indeed, Scripture, Reason, and Tradition, had long been core theological sources within Anglicanism, which was Wesley's denominational home.[146] His unique contribution was that of experience as a theological source, a concern developed out of his enlightenment-informed sensibilities.[147] I will discuss this further in the following chapter.

The development of the Quadrilateral into a more structured articulation was an attempt to answer questions such as how one should draw upon and differentiate the importance of the aforementioned sources, and how one should use the sources to judge the Christian character of claims and actions.[148] These are both interpretive questions, which involve biblical

144. Maddox, *Responsible Grace*, 35.

145. McFarlane, *Evangelical Theology*, 66.

146. McAdoo described Anglicanism in these very terms, commenting that "the spirit of Anglicanism, including as it does the centrality of Scripture and the visibility and continuity of the Church, both confirmed by antiquity, and illuminated by the freedom of reason and liberality of view point." McAdoo, *Anglicanism*, 357. It should be noted that this provides good reason for why Wesley did not describe his theological method, because he fought throughout his life to be understood—and indeed understood himself—as an Anglican revivalist rather than a dissenter. Thorsen, *Quadrilateral*, 58.

147. Gregory, "Long Century," 39.

148. Maddox, *Responsible Grace*, 35.

interpretation proper as well as a concern for discipleship, in so much as one's interpretive conclusions are expressed in specific applications. In this sense, then, the Quadrilateral is an interpretive tool for situations that can guide believers towards faithful practice. The strength of this method is its ability to systemize theological thought in a (seemingly) simple way, making it easier for anyone to think theologically about the world and their life.[149] This is a particular benefit for methods of theological reflection that integrate various sources, because, by their design, these methods are more concerned with describing how one believes rather than prescribing what to believe.[150]

Yet there is continual debate about how Wesley understood his own method, and what sources of theology should be integrated within theological reflection methods. Donald Thorsen's important work *The Wesleyan Quadrilateral* first popularized the Quadrilateral reflection paradigm outside of United Methodist circles in the early 1990s. Building from the historical work of Outler, Thorsen sought to present the Quadrilateral as "a genuinely catholic model of theology that considers the interdependent significance of all historic claimants of religious authority—namely, tradition, reason, and experience—in relation to Scripture."[151] Describing Wesley's theological heritage and sociohistorical context, Thorsen shows how enlightenment empiricism led Wesley towards thinking about theology in an integrative way, bringing various sources of knowledge together, in submission to Scripture, to shape an understanding of one's faith and practice.[152]

Thorsen goes on to describe Wesley's notions of the theological sources of Scripture, tradition, reason, and experience—at least, as Outler described them—before arguing that evangelicals do not generally recognize their sources when reflecting theologically. Indeed, the Protestant call of *sola scriptura* has been misunderstood to negate other theological sources, even though the Reformers allowed other theological sources—particularly tradition—to have an important role in their theologizing.[153] Thus, the Quadrilateral is a useful paradigm for reminding interpreters that other theological sources are being utilized, and need to be considered, when reflecting theologically.

149. Bevins, "Pentecostal Appropriation," 223.

150. McFarlane, *Evangelical Theology*, 65.

151. Thorsen, *Quadrilateral*, 6, 10.

152. Thorsen, *Quadrilateral*, 66.

153. Thorsen, *Quadrilateral*, 150.

Importantly, Thorsen drew attention to the fact that while Outler used the term *quadrilateral* because of a history of the phrase's use in Anglican theology, he was concerned about people misunderstanding what it meant. Outler meant the Quadrilateral to be metaphorical and cautioned against conceiving it as a static four-square figure (like a quadrant graph) because such imagery risks assuming that the quadrants were of equal authority or normativity in theological reflection. Indeed, every major work on the Quadrilateral has had to wrestle with the question of whether the term implies relationality or equality between the sources.[154] Outler has even gone so far as to say "the term 'quadrilateral' does not occur in the Wesley corpus—and more than once, I have regretted having coined it for contemporary use, since it has been so widely misconstrued."[155] Thus, Thorsen points to an issue Outler understood regarding the Quadrilateral but for which he was not able to find a workable solution. It is my aim to propose a possible solution that will allow continued use of the term *quadrilateral* while conceiving of it more dynamically than has otherwise yet been proposed.

Alongside an increased interest driven by Thorsen's work, debates increased about the Quadrilateral and how it should be understood and used in United Methodism and beyond. Arising from conversations related to the Quadrilateral stemming from the United Methodist denomination's founding, the volume *Wesley and the Quadrilateral* sought to answer issues about the Quadrilateral's use in contemporary times by better attuning Methodists to the complexities of Wesley's theological thought and practice. With chapters on each theological source, the editors helpfully complexified the United Methodist debates about the Quadrilateral. However, this complexity did not, in both my *and their* estimations, help lead Methodists or holiness movement inspired groups towards a renewed and nuanced use of this tool. Instead, the complexity seems to have overwhelmed without offering viable solutions for practitioners in how to utilize the Quadrilateral. Indeed, one of the aims of the present project is to propose a possible solution for this issue.

After the publication of *Wesley and the Quadrilateral* in 1997, there have been few significant works, particularly monographs, that have continued the conversation about the Quadrilateral that this volume invited.[156]

---

154. Gunter et al., *Wesley and Quadrilateral*, 10–11; McFarlane, *Evangelical Theology*, 67.

155. Outler, *Wesleyan Heritage*, 35–36.

156. While journal articles have been written on the topic of the Quadrilateral, and

More recently, Graham McFarlane took up this invitation by proposing an expressly evangelical theological model for reflection based on the Quadrilateral. However, McFarlane adds the novel category of "Community" to the sources, the addition of which he argues is what allows the method to be considered evangelical. Thus, he describes what he terms a "quintilateral"[157]—though it is more properly described as a *quincunx,* with Scripture at its center.[158]

McFarlane argues for adding community to Scripture, reason, tradition, and experience for three reasons. First, McFarlane understands the proper context for theology to occur is within the church.[159] Thus, without a community of faith for whom one is serving through their theological reasoning, and to whom the theologian is theologically accountable to, the theological vision that is developed can only be considered impoverished. Second, McFarlane takes seriously evangelicalism's core conviction of evangelism, which clarifies that the church is a witness to the Gospel both within its community and outside of it. In other words, the church has responded to Christ's call to follow and now invites others to follow as well—a dynamic McFarlane thinks should inform an evangelical theological method.[160] Finally, McFarlane clarifies that evangelical theology (like all faithful theology ought to do) is done in the presence of a Triune God—*coram Deo.*[161] This ultimately brings the covenantal nature of revelation into focus, as previously discussed. Our theology, and indeed the practice of biblical interpretation, is meant to transform us into the image of Christ, which occurs when these practices are done *coram Deo,* sitting at the foot of the Lord's throne.

While I agree with the majority of McFarlane's premises, I ultimately do not think community is an appropriate source of theology in the same way the other four sources are. Fundamental to my disagreement is that its inclusion as a theological source blurs the lines between the other sources

---

popular level books such as Stone and Duke's *How to Think Theologically* have articulated it for new audiences, I have had difficulty finding works that have made a noticeable impression—in academia or otherwise—in constructively contributing to conversations regarding the Quadrilateral as a theological method.

157. McFarlane, *Evangelical Theology,* 62.

158. A quincunx is a geometrical pattern where five points are arranged in a cross (⁙).

159. McFarlane, *Evangelical Theology,* 206.

160. McFarlane, *Evangelical Theology,* 209.

161. McFarlane, *Evangelical Theology,* 211, 215.

in an unhelpful way. For example, how does one conceive of communal interpretation in a way that does justice to each of the sources—does the community's development of local tradition trump the tradition of the church catholic? Does the experience of the community *en masse* trump the experience of individuals? And what happens when a community today disagrees with the interpretations of faithful communities past, including those from within a church's denominational tradition—does the present always take precedence? In my estimation, each of these is difficult to answer and answering them positively risks causing the Quadrilateral's sources to be prioritized instinctively ("I feel this is right") rather than confessionally or theologically.

However, I think there is a deeper issue in that communities don't truly interpret as a singular unit. Rather, even when together, the individuals who make up the community interpret and bring their conclusions into the community, often for the purpose of application (doing). This certainly does shape the community, but in a way more subtle and complex than what McFarlane presupposes, and in a way where each individual is able to walk away from the community with separate interpretive conclusions rather than some monolithic notion of "this is the community's interpretation." At best, the community ultimately could agree to an articulation of conclusions, but this does not guarantee that those conclusions were reached the same way by all the community members, or even that the community members actually agree with the conclusions (for example, one could choose to submit to conclusions they disagree with for the sake of the church's unity and mission). Thus, I find it incoherent to talk of a church community having an interpretation when, in reality, it is a community of many interpretations that is held in tension by something greater than their differences—namely, a series of theological prejudices whose capstone is the lordship of Christ.

Even still, McFarlane draws attention to an important aspect of interpretation—that the interpretations of individuals are brought to bear in their community, informing and shaping it, and that this dynamic must be accounted for in evangelical models of theological reflection. Indeed, Stanley Grenz and John Franke recognized this when they drew attention to the fact that because the Bible is made by a communal God for a communal people, it must be read with the community in mind. Even so, they reflect on the relationship between individual and community, saying the "sensitivity to reading within community extends to our individual interpretive efforts as well, as our private readings of the text are seasoned with the awareness that, even as the church scattered, each of us remains a participant in a particular gathered community."[162] In this project, the role of community must therefore be accounted for in how the church thinks theologically when interpreting Scripture, even if this accounting takes place in some ways separate from the Quadrilateral construct. On this basis, I will be able to expand the project's outcome to being more than simply a novel description of the Quadrilateral but a novel description of the interpretive paradigms at play when individuals (and therefore communities of interpreters) open God's word to seek to understand what it says.

## Conclusion: Interpretation as Discipleship and Theological Reflection

Through a complex process of developing understanding, biblical interpretation shapes believers into the image of Christ, making this practice one of discipleship. This practice does not take place in a vacuum—it is a dynamic process of bringing theological sources that aid understandings together via theological reflection to understand a passage, its significance, and how it can be lived out individually and communally. The Wesleyan Quadrilateral has been used for this kind of integrative theological reflection, but it is in need of reappraisal to clarify the relationship between theological sources, and offer a viable theological reflection paradigm for the metamodern mood.

### CONCLUDING SUMMARY

With the emergence of metamodernism, the church has an opportunity to clarify its interpretive practice while also strengthening its discipleship. Approaching the question of how we interpret while recognizing the varied postures towards understanding and meaning making we take, based on the influence of modernism and postmodernism, can help clarify why talking about interpretation has become so difficult, and provide useful tools to facilitate productive conversation about sexuality and other pressing topics. Having overviewed the past century of hermeneutics, the stage has been set to now develop an approach for understanding interpretive practice that

162. Grenz and Franke, *Beyond Foundationalism*, 92.

does just this. Furthermore, by conceiving of the Bible as revelation, corollary theological concepts such as inspiration, authority, and illumination, are describable and can clarify the use of Scripture in integrative theological reflection paradigms.

While complex, the process of theological reflection—how one understands Scripture, tradition, reason, and experience integrate as theological sources—is where biblical interpretation becomes practical, informing (and indeed transforming) situations as readers hear God's voice through his Word and put it into practice. With the Quadrilateral paradigm, there exists a generally well-known tool that can help with theological reflection, but that needs further refinement. In the following chapter I will return to the question of metamodernism to create a novel construct for understanding the metamodern hermeneutical mood and describe a revised Quadrilateral. Bringing these constructs together, I will then be able to describe the project's methodology and can begin to explore and describe the complexities of biblical interpretation in the contemporary evangelical Canadian context.

# 3

## Bifurcating the Quadrilateral
### *Visualizing Metamodern Hermeneutics*

HAVING LAID THE FOUNDATIONS for this project, I will now begin erecting the project's proverbial walls by discussing my methodology, hermeneutic content analysis. As described in the introduction, hermeneutic content analysis is a form of qualitative content analysis, and as such utilizes data coding to develop inference that can be used to draw conclusions. Central to coding, which will be described later in the chapter, is the use of a coding frame—a set of specific items that make up a "code book," which a researcher uses to build themes in datasets that helps answer the research question. In order to discuss my coding frame and code book definitions, and therefore detail the project's methodology, I must first develop two analytical constructs related to the project's theory and practice: the Hermeneutical Pendulum and Quadrilateral Matrix.

### HERMENEUTICAL PENDULUM

Building from the groundwork laid in the previous chapter, the first construct of this project is a metamodern approach to understanding hermeneutic practice. As I have argued, the hermeneutical developments throughout the past century have matched the cultural developments of modernism and postmodernism. These cultural developments have influenced hermeneutics by focusing on the three core hermeneutical loci of meaning and understanding in interpretation: the author, the text, and the reader. In modernism, the practice of biblical interpretation moved towards author-centeredness, where the construction of an author's world ("the world behind the text") was given precedence in generating meaning.[1] The development of postmodernism moved hermeneutics towards being text-centered and then reader-centered, with postmodern readings tending to give the reader(s) authority by making them the adjudicator of a text's meaning while engaged in conversation with the text.[2] The still-emerging movement of metamodernism has been developing as an oscillation between modern and postmodern moods (while also being informed to the premodern) to make better sense of the world.[3] Indeed, as crises in economics, climate, and politics have compounded, the West has approached understanding the world from both the modernist and postmodernist frames while increasingly being committed to neither.[4] This tension of oscillation is not meant to negate either perspective, but utilize them each for understanding, participating in the cultural equivalent of a penguin's walk—wobbling to and fro in order to stumble forward. Put into Gadamerian terms, the metamodern mood is *play-filled*, and its oscillation informs (and reforms) understanding.

While metamodernism's oscillation is conceived of as being between modernism and postmodernism, my contention is that this oscillation is applicable to hermeneutics due to the developments that roughly correspond to the modern and postmodern moods outlined above. Indeed, the oscillative tension observed in metamodernism helps make sense of interpretive practice in the contemporary age, which is increasingly fractured and perhaps best summed up in the popular saying, "Well, that is just your interpretation." This phrase implies that all interpretations are valid, and that the speaker thinks their interpretation correct compared to all others—two sentiments that do not make sense together but are still widely held, implying something going on under the surface to make it *seem* like a reasonable sentiment. Recognizing this can create space for conversation and for understanding how interpretive practice is shaped by metamodern tensions.[5]

In recent hermeneutic literature, there has been acceptance that modernism produced author-centered hermeneutical approaches while

---

1. Osborne, *Spiral*, 468.

2. Tate, *Biblical Interpretation*, 4; Westphal, *Whose Community?*, 61; Grenz, *Primer*, 6.

3. Velmeulen and van den Akker, "Metamodernism," para. 1, 15.

4. Velmeulen and van den Akker, "Metamodernism," para. 15.

5. Merwe, "Reading," 3.

postmodernism produced reader-centered approaches.[6] In the epoch of metamodernity, the hermeneutical approach many take is a multifaceted oscillation between modernism and postmodernism such that at different stages in the interpretive process, the majority of readers make decisions (or intuitions) that align with both approaches, "swinging" between them. In order to capture this idea of oscillation in how one thinks about metamodernism, Velmeulen and van den Akker used the metaphor of a pendulum swinging between an infinite number of poles.[7] Applying this metaphor to hermeneutics and the author-text-reader relationship, I am proposing the concept of the *Hermeneutical Pendulum* (Figure 1). This construct is designed, in part, to describe the meaning-making interplay between reader and author. As one interprets a text, the worlds of author and reader dynamically enter into dialogue—in Gadamerian terms, melting together—and thereby swinging the pendulum. As the conversation unfolds (continuously), understanding and meaning develop.

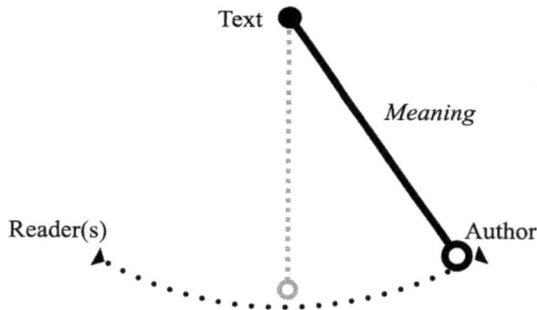

Figure 1: The Hermeneutical Pendulum

The pendulum construct does not seek to describe *how* this oscillation happens. Instead, it describes something that *is* happening. Thus, it is a metaphor for understanding what is occurring during interpretation, helping to clarify how Western culture is attempting to understand understanding in the aftermath of the twentieth century. From there, it is up to a given reader to decide the degree to which author- or reader-centered hermeneutical approaches are appropriate. I will now move on to describing the second

---

6. Brown, *Communication*, 14, 57–78. I would suggest Brown's project is similarly a metamodern project, as she wishes to bring author- and reader-centered approaches into cohesive tension.

7. Velmeulen and van den Akker, "Metamodernism," para. 17.

construct of the project, the Quadrilateral Matrix, before merging the two constructs together to form the research's methodological backbone.

## RETHINKING THE WESLEYAN QUADRILATERAL

As briefly outlined in the previous chapter, Methodist scholars have invited others to use the Wesleyan Quadrilateral while also reappraising it, as doing so might shore up some perceived weaknesses of the reflection method. Initially, Albert Outler's vision for the Quadrilateral was as a metaphor describing the complexity of John Wesley's theological method.[8] Yet, by his own admission, this vision failed to take shape as its users thought about the construction he offered in geometric terms.[9] Outler seems to have believed that the Quadrilateral should have been able to communicate Wesley's theological method in brief while still prioritizing Scripture above all other theological sources.[10] Yet this has not been true of how most have understood the Quadrilateral, at the popular level, since its innovation.

To be sure, issues with the Quadrilateral's reception and use are well documented. In their book *Wesley and the Quadrilateral*, Gunter et al., extend an invitation to renewed conversation about the Quadrilateral, while pointing to multiple important and interrelated issues concerning the Quadrilateral's popular use. Although this initial discussion was limited to Methodist uses, I believe their critique is applicable to the use of the paradigm more generally. Furthermore, the issues they raise provide several points where ongoing theological work is necessary and which this project contributes some answers towards.

First, those who utilize the Quadrilateral tool have tended towards turning it into a formula, whereby if one simply accounts for each "quadrant" of the paradigm they will *de facto* emerge with correct or orthodox theologies.[11] Yet this outcome is not obviously the case. Indeed, this pushes against contemporary notions of hermeneutics, especially that of Gadamer, which strongly critiques such methodological approaches to the development of understanding. It is here where the Quadrilateral's modernist foundations come to light, as this approach to the Quadrilateral is formulaic, expecting that if you plug in the right criteria the right outcomes will

8. Outler, "Quadrilateral," 11.

9. Thorsen, *Quadrilateral*, 6; Outler, "Quadrilateral," 11.

10. Outler, "Quadrilateral," 11.

11. Gunter et al., *Wesley and Quadrilateral*, 38.

occur. Rather than a formula for understanding, the present project aims to use the Quadrilateral as a paradigm for understanding—that is, rather than being formulaic by describing an order of use for theological reflection sources, this project will propose an approach to the Quadrilateral whereby one can "enter" reflection via any quadrant and "leave" from any quadrant.

Secondly, and relatedly, Gunter et al., realized that the formalization of Wesley's theological method as a Quadrilateral undermines usage of the method because people began perceiving the Quadrilateral as *equilateral,* thus regarding each theological source as equally authoritative.[12] On this point it is helpful to visualize how the Quadrilateral has typically been understood. Rather than as a four sides shape with varying length sides, which the name "quadrilateral" would suggests, academic writing has tended to virtualize the Quadrilateral—when it is visualized—as either a sort of flow-chart diagram (Figure 2.a)[13] or as the more popular image of a graph with four equilateral quadrants (Figure 2.b). It is this later visualization that, in my experience, most people think of when thinking about the Quadrilateral. But this has unintended consequences. Ultimately, an equilateral construction can leave the impression that Scripture should be "weighted" with the same authoritativeness as tradition, reason, and experience. In other words, the diagram implies that each quadrant is equally normative in the task of theology. Furthermore, because these diagrams are conceptually static, there is no room for recognizing whether some sources are—or even should be—given more priority over and against the other sources. Thus, the equilateral impression diminishes the capacity of Scripture (and tradition) to norm theological reflection, as they have throughout church history.[14]

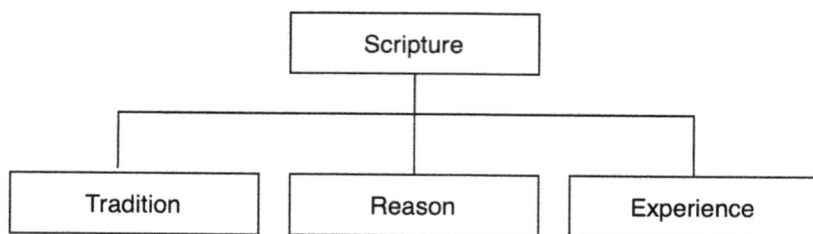

**Figure 2.a: Quadrilateral as Flowchart**

12. Gunter et al., *Wesley and Quadrilateral,* 38, 40–42.

13. McFarlane, *Evangelical Theology,* 67. While he does not produce a drawing in his work, Thorsen's seminal book on the Quadrilateral does have a flowchart diagram on the cover.

14. Gunter et al., *Wesley and Quadrilateral,* 13.

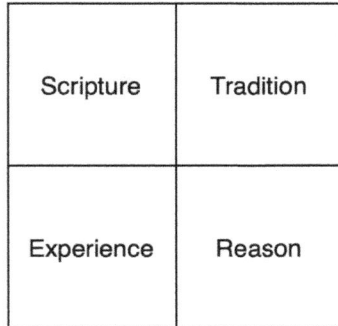

| | |
|---|---|
| Scripture | Tradition |
| Experience | Reason |

**Figure 2.b: Quadrilateral as Graph**

Finally, one of the drawbacks of any diagram, such as the figures above, is that their mode of communication is an image on a page, which limits how one might imagine their use. How to diagram the authority of Scripture is a good case study. In Figure 2.a, Scripture is placed on a different plane than the other sources, such that the diagram logically reads that Scripture is the "top" source. With very little context, it would be easy to assume from this diagram that its writer considered Scripture unique in some sense compared to the others listed. However, the diagram also implies the formulaic understanding of the Quadrilateral, as flowchart diagrams are, by their nature, formulas in some regard (e.g., the social hierarchy of a company, with the CEO at the top). The same cannot be said for Figure 2.b, as it shows no prioritization of sources, no delineation of importance, and no real sense of relationship between the sources other than their simultaneous existence. While more in line with the paradigmatic sense of the Quadrilateral, this diagram also opens the door for competing notions of each source to import understandings in such a way so as to short-circuit one's reflection from the start.

Therefore, rather than being a useful theological reflection method a community could rally around, the popular understanding of the Quadrilateral makes this reflection method problematic as typically utilized. Indeed, rather than being a facilitator for theological unity or ecumenical dialogue, the popular understanding of the Quadrilateral is as likely to facilitate conflict and as it is unity because of its conceptual ambiguity, particularly related to the relative authorities of theological sources.

## Pitfalls of Reappraisals

There have been some reappraisals of the Quadrilateral offered over the past decades, yet in my estimation many are not self-reflective in recognizing the Quadrilateral's theological roots such that they do not recognize how their work might build upon, rather than take away from, previous iterations of the paradigm. This may be due to United Methodists taking ownership of the paradigm, though it is clear in various discourses that few see the Quadrilateral as a purely Methodist construction—it was, after all, a construction derivative of Anglican, and before that Roman Catholic, theological reflection. While the Wesleyan version of it should be considered Methodist, the use of the four theological sources in a way similar to Wesley is not, *de facto*, Wesleyan. Thus, I believe it is appropriate to refer to the Quadrilateral construction as a broadly evangelical construction, and to move forward with its use as such, while still respecting the Methodist roots of the term and its ongoing popularity.

Furthermore, when reappraising the Quadrilateral, many theologians only offer passing mention of the paradigm without engaging its history of use in any meaningful sense. Because of this, evangelical scholars have not tended to treat the Quadrilateral's heritage as our own, even as John Wesley is widely considered one of, if not the, most important Evangelicals of the eighteenth century.[15] By situating this project within a broader conception of evangelicalism, which includes Wesley and the tradition of theological reflection that grew from reflection on his thinking and ministry, I hope to ground a re-articulation of the Quadrilateral in ways that can facilitate the reception of a re-articulated paradigm in theory (within wider cross-denominational conversations about the Quadrilateral) and in practice.

Kevin Lawson provides a positive example of just such an articulation in a paper in the *Christian Education Journal*. Critiquing both the Wesleyan Quadrilateral and John Stackhouse's *Tetralectic* appropriation of the model,[16] Lawson developed a re-articulation that was coherent and

15. Stone and Duke's popular introductory text on theological reflection, *Think Theologically*, is an example of this. Even though they use the same sources of the Quadrilateral, and describe them in a similar fashion (though without any diagraming), they do so with only passing reference. Indeed, they seem to assume the Quadrilateral is correct, saying that using its terms "clarify concerns widely shared by the worldwide community of faith," but offer no forthright reason for using these four sources verses other sources (added or subtracted). Stone and Duke, *Think Theologically*, 47.

16. Stackhouse argues that the theological sources of the Quadrilateral are in "a four way conversation" whereby each source helps us interpret the other sources through

well situated in the wider tradition it emerged from. Many of the concerns Lawson brings up are shared by others, but his proposal goes further than others in two important areas.

First, Lawson accounts for Wesley's thought regarding theological sources. This leads to an interesting reflection on the shortcomings of Stackhouse's proposal related to the places of the Holy Spirit and general revelation in theological reflection. Indeed, it causes Lawson to treat reason less as a source of theology than as the process of understanding that makes theology coherent, especially as it is illuminated by the Holy Spirit. Thus, he adds general revelation in reason's stead as a theological source.[17]

Secondly, he offers a diagrammed approach to theological reflection.[18] This diagraming should not be taken lightly, as many counter proposals to the popular-level understanding of the Quadrilateral do not offer diagrams, and without the simplicity for understanding which diagrams offer it is doubtful whether any new proposal would be capable of overcoming the old. As an adage regarding technology goes, technology is only made obsolete when replaced with something that does the job more simply or effectively. The same is true of diagramed paradigms—replacing a simple paradigm, like the Quadrilateral, with a more complex, less usable form, like Lawson's *tetralectic*, ensures a proposed paradigm will not easily be adopted.

Another possible, yet less effective, example of such a re-articulation is Grenz and Franke, who seem to collapse the Quadrilateral's sources of reason and tradition into a new category, describing their paradigm in terms of Scripture, experience, and *culture*. Yet they do this without giving sufficient reflection on why one should do this. On an important level, this takes for granted the history of theological reflection that articulated the core sources of theology as Scripture, tradition, reason, and to which Wesley added experience. Yet, it is clear that their, and others, reappraisals are for a purpose, even if only sometimes described. In Grenz and Franke's case, while not explicitly described the overarching point of their work points towards to their reasoning. Their move to collapse tradition and reason into the category of culture seems to be related to a postmodern concern for the connection between culture and meaning, which they reflect on by

---

successive conversations on a given topic or situation. Stackhouse, *Making the Best*, 170–78.

17. Lawson, "Theological Reflection," 60–61. Others, such as Morris-Chapman ("Beyond the Quadrilateral," 2, 7), have made a similar argument regarding general revelation (or "nature") in an attempt to describe Wesley's theological epistemology.

18. Lawson, "Theological Reflection," 62.

discussing anthropology and the subjective experience of persons in situations.[19] Collapsing the sources, then, and creating a new category of culture that includes tradition and reason, but also a notion of anthropological development, allows them to propose a theological method they regard as tailored to the postmodern sensibility.

However, I am unsure whether their proposal is effective as a reflection method, in part because it does not truly answer the issues laid out above and creates a new issue of oversimplification. Indeed, if you are willing to utilize "culture" as a category, what stops one from absorbing all tradition and its artefacts (including Scripture) into that category, particularly in light of Christendom? Surely Western culture is so informed by the Christian tradition that their stories are not easily separated. The addition of culture also makes the paradigm's use in practice more difficult by creating a trilateral reflection method that most in the church would find difficult to grasp. In my pastoral experience, the category of culture would cause a general confusion because many are unclear what culture *is*. Furthermore, even if they knew what was meant by "culture," the congregations I have served in have not regularly thought reflexively about culture in a meaningful way. If my cultural exegesis is accurate, and we are in a metamodern mood rather than simply postmodern, Grenz and Franke's method loses some utility because it only accounts for one ("your") culture rather than an endless number of coexisting cultures, complicating reflection to the point of possible absurdity. It is my conviction that a better way forward is offering a reappraisal that reflects on the Quadrilateral's roots and builds on them constructively to chart new, if still familiar, ground rather than dismissing those roots without due consideration.

## DESCRIBING THE QUADRILATERAL: STRUCTURE AND PARTS

Before moving to discussing the Quadrilateral's sources in their particularities, it is worthwhile to consider the overall structure of the Quadrilateral as we approach a reappraisal by asking: why a Quadrilateral? In other words, why utilize only four sources of theology? McFarlane proposes five, adding community, while Grenz and Franke, as discussed, propose three. Others have proposed all manners of constructions, from as many as eight sources

19. Grenz and Franke, *Beyond Foundationalism*, 135–38.

to as few as two.[20] Given the potential of endless options, one must decide where to draw the line and why; whether to complexify, and where to simplify. Because theological reflection is an often-misunderstood topic in the church, even as Christians regularly do think about God's work in their lives, being able to describe theological sources in an understandable way is of understated importance.

For the purposes of the present project, I have chosen to stick closely to Outler's initial construction. I do this for several reasons. First, I believe doing so will make my reappraisal more palatable to the wider Evangelical tradition, including that of Methodism. While my understanding of the sources may be different in places from some, I believe that utilizing the same sources which Outler describes will help make my work applicable and adaptable while still retaining an aura of the initial construction's simplicity—and it should be very easily adaptable to the initial construction, as will be seen shortly. Secondly, due to the popularity of the Quadrilateral, I am unsure whether complexifying the method by adding or contracting sources makes for a more effective method. Rather, the addition of more sources can make the method significantly more confusing and thus unusable in practice. Finally, and importantly, I view my work as emerging from the broad evangelical heritage of Wesley's thought, and reflecting on this foundation I have not been convinced that the addition or subtraction of sources is necessary for improving the paradigm. This includes not adding notations to account for the Holy Spirit's role, as the doctrines of illumination and sanctification, in my mind, appropriately account for the Holy Spirit's work in interpretation and theological reflection.

Thus, having outlined core issues of the Quadrilateral's use in practice, I will now begin reflecting on the four theological sources utilized in this paradigm. Each reflection will discuss Wesley's conception of each theological source and will use these as a jump-off point to describe each in brief. After discussing each, I will propose a re-articulated vision of the Quadrilateral that answers the issues outlined above and, in my estimation, makes the paradigm a more usable theological reflection tool.

---

20. These have been argued by friends and professors at McMaster Divinity College, in both lectures and private conversation.

## Scripture

In every description of the Quadrilateral, one will find Scripture listed first. This is for good reason. In Wesley's theology, and evangelical theology more broadly, the Bible is the foundation of all other theological sources and the criterion by which the information those sources supply are judged.[21] Scripture is the word of God, the inspired revelation of the person of Christ, and as such Scripture bears, in what it communicates, the very authority of the living God. And what does it communicate? The gospel of Jesus Christ, what Thorsen rightly describes as "a trustworthy record of how God provided a way of salvation, especially as revealed through the person and work of Jesus Christ."[22] By all accounts, this is the core of what Wesley believed of the Bible as well, and is congruent with the beliefs of evangelicals today.[23]

As McFarlane describes, Scripture is not just any old book one reflects on; it is the very word of God and the ground from which all theology grows.[24] McFarlane even goes on to make the case for practical theological inquiry, commenting that the most memorable Christian scholars have been those "men and women who engage the Bible *in search of answers to their respective situations.*"[25] Thus, if one wishes to think theologically they must start by thinking biblically, which is not to make a methodological claim but a theological claim that recognizes Scripture's rightful place as the foundation of Christian thought and reflection.

## Tradition

The Christian tradition is, in one sense, the tradition of the Bible's interpretation by the Church, making any notion of tradition tied to Scripture in a dependent way. Tradition is the outcome of the covenantal nature of Scripture; it is where God's promises are actualized within history and handed down for safekeeping from one generation to the next. Indeed, the Bible is received through tradition. To be clear, the tradition of the Bible's

21. Indeed, John Wesley wrote, "I allow no other rule, whether of faith or practice, than the Holy Scriptures." Thorsen, *Quadrilateral*, 76.

22. Thorsen, *Quadrilateral*, 82.

23. Thorsen, *Quadrilateral*, 82; Gunter et al., *Wesley and Quadrilateral*, 47, 50.

24. McFarlane, *Evangelical Theology*, 71.

25. McFarlane, *Evangelical Theology*, 72; emphasis added.

interpretation does not just include facts but necessarily includes the embodiment of understanding—in a phrase, the application of Scripture in real lives—which the church has enacted privately and publicly, individually and corporately, throughout her history. Thus, liturgies and confessions, ethical postures and doctoral pronouncements, and all measure of practices and modes of embodying the faith fall within the scope of what the Christian tradition and sub-traditions truly are.[26]

John Wesley did not formally give tradition *carte blanche* authority in his theological thinking. Instead, Wesley argued that the extent to which a tradition conforms to the Bible is proportional to the extent with which it should be trusted. Whereas Scripture is a "norming norm" for Christians, Wesley believed tradition to be a "normed norm" that can act as a guard rail keeping Christian interpretation, reflection, and practice within the bounds of that which is orthodox.[27] Any traditions that he may have prioritized were, in Wesley's mind, to be prioritized precisely because he believed them more faithful submissions to Scripture (and therefore Christ's Lordship) than other traditions. Thus, in Wesley's estimation, the traditions of Anglicanism and (ante-)Nicene Christianity conformed to the Bible better than other traditions, which made them more authoritative (that is, more trustworthy) than the general historical tradition of the church catholic.[28]

Depending on one's theological presuppositions, they may likewise prioritize certain denominations or theological positions over others: Presbyterian instead of Anglican, Roman Catholic instead of Baptist, Pentecostal instead of Eastern Orthodox, and so on. There is an element of interpreting the development and understanding of Christian tradition that makes it a tricky source to utilize, especially in light of ever-growing fragmentation. Because of this, Wesley's belief that ante-Nicene Christianity is more trustworthy is a good instinct, and one that can be found cross-denominationally in the recitations of creeds and confessions and a respect for the theological insights of the Church Fathers. Indeed, as each generation passes, guarding and confirming what the great cloud of witnesses have said about God, the historic tradition of the church should grow in its trustworthiness compared to the theological innovations of the contemporary age. To what extent trustworthiness should play a role in

26. Stackhouse, *Making the Best*, 171.

27. That is, it helps one remain faithful to God's self-revelation and covenant. Maddox, *Responsible*, 43.

28. Thorsen, *Quadrilateral*, 96, 101; Maddox, *Responsible*, 42.

how the insights of old are translated into the present is up for debate. But what is clear, at least, is the importance of what Stackhouse describes as listening "to the voices of the past, especially those voices whose testimonies have been validated by successive generations of Christians."[29] In other words, if Christians ignore the voices of the communion of the saints, they do so at their own peril—theologically and otherwise.

## Reason

The capacity to reason—to think, comprehend, judge, and imagine—is central to the human experience. Indeed, the Christian faith is a religion of reason, as Christianity is a faith that seeks understanding. This is not to say faith replaces understanding, but that the Christian faith is one that utilizes humanity's rational capacities to understand the reality God has created and that we inhabit as God's image-bearing creation. As a child of the Age of Reason, Wesley believed that truth was knowable through the use of reason and logic and sought to bridge the perceived gap between reason and religion. Wesley even went so far as to speak against enlightenment thinkers who argued against religion while promoting the philosophic foundations of their work, and the enlightenment project in general.[30] For Wesley, theological thought (including one's interpretation of the Bible) must be reasonable—it should make coherent, logical sense—if it is to be considered truthful. Even so, Wesley maintained that reason alone could not produce faith, hope, or love for God.[31] Thus, reason is, like the other sources, not simple to describe. Indeed, describing reason is both to describe the process of thinking and the coherence of this process, both logic and understanding, the *capacity* to both know and do.

It would be difficult to overstate the importance of reason to Wesley's theological method, such that one could consider it the second most important theological source after Scripture. Wesley even commented, "to renounce reason is to renounce religion. . . . [R]eligion and reason go hand in hand, and . . . all irrational religion is false religion."[32] In this, Wesley

---

29. Stackhouse, *Making the Best*, 171.

30. Maddox, *Responsible*, 40; Gregory, "Long Century," 37; MacMillan, "Enlightened," 121.

31. Bevins, "Pentecostal Appropriation," 238–39.

32. Wesley, "To Dr. Rutherford," March 28, 1768, as quoted in Thorsen, *Quadrilateral*, 107.

was arguing for an approach to religion that included structured rational analysis, which was a reaction to an over emotive charismatic expressions of the faith he witnessed that distanced itself from rational analysis and, according to Wesley, made the church unintelligible to the world around it.[33] In the shadow of the enlightenment, this has been a regular issue for the church to address.

Yet, this does not answer how this source functions within the Quadrilateral. To use an architectural metaphor, whereas Scripture is the source that acts as a plumb line, directing the proper place of the other sources, and tradition is the mason-work that has been normed to the plumbline, reason is the framing of the building. It is through reason that life is made intelligible, and through which one comes to know God as God is. Indeed, for Wesley, empirical evidence rightly understood does not point humans away from God but towards God—the God who had made divine providence and the divine nature visible for investigation (Rom 1:20).[34] Thus, Scripture offers categories for thinking about the world theocentrically, and reason is that which allows one to understand what this means. Put another way, reason is a tool for understanding rather than a source of new information (insomuch as insight describes the moment one comes to an understanding of something). As Methodist scholars have noted, without revelation—particularly special revelation—reason is not, in and of itself, able to develop new information about God.[35]

The knowledge of God presupposes elements of both faith and reason, such that without the ability to think logically, rationally, or even imaginatively about the world, no one would be able to claim to have any true knowledge of God.[36] This implies that our reflections should, if they are true to reality, carry elements of rationality, including coherence and logic, and that a lack of these elements suggests a failure to take the source of reason seriously in how we reflect theologically. In different eras of history, how humans have made sense of the world has shifted. A core benefit of reason's inclusion in the Quadrilateral is that it allows for a gracious evaluation of these shifts, seeing them as being reasonable in their contexts, even

33. Boaheng, "Biblical Exegesis," 91.

34. MacMillan, "Enlightened," 125.

35. Gunter et al., *Wesley and Quadrilateral*, 135.

36. Stackhouse makes an argument for imagination being an important element of reason which I find compelling. In short, he argues that it is through the use of imagination that one's reflections "create and critique in hopes of producing the best version of our ideas." Stackhouse, *Making the Best*, 173.

as they can be rightfully critiqued for the purpose of understanding in the contemporary age. Indeed, the coherence of reason as a theological source is not just logic but related to our making sense of personal experiences in light of Scripture—how we understand the ways God's story informs our stories and how we view and interact with the world as the world is.

## Experience

Finally, Wesley's conception of experience as a theological source was as a dialogue partner, whereby one hears the message of the Gospel and then responds to it in how they live. In other words, Wesley's focus was not on experience generally but on one's experience of God. Furthermore, one's response to God includes the Holy Spirit's work in us, such that Wesley considered theology (and theological reflection) experimental and experiential—especially in relation to soteriology. As Thorsen comments, "Although the confirmatory role of experience pertains especially to the assurance of salvation, it also pertains to other truths of Scripture and to doctrines of orthodox Christianity."[37] The truth of Christianity is not just something to be known cognitively but something to be lived, confirmed by the Spirit's work in the believer.

Much of how Wesley approached the experience quadrant's dialogical nature (in relation to the other sources) can be accounted for through his enlightenment sensibilities. Wesley understood experience in terms of knowledge derived via empiricism—that is, the knowledge experience uncovered was observable and measurable or testable—and was, therefore, to be considered 'common sense.' Importantly, if knowledge derived from experience was observable and testable, those observations and results necessarily require interpreting, especially if or when the observations did not seem to make sense in light of what an interpreter previously understood. As such, one's understanding of a given experience is "mediated through [their] pre-existing intellectual concepts."[38] Scripture, as well as the other sources of the Quadrilateral, provide those concepts that allow Christian

37. Thorsen, *Quadrilateral*, 130.

38. Gunter et al., *Wesley and Quadrilateral*, 112–13 See also Gadamer, *Truth and Method*, 315–17. The authors of the Gunter volume go on to reflect on Wesley revising his understanding of spiritual experiences in his life, commenting "in the act of revising Wesley was conceding—at least implicitly—that not even the regenerate can avoid having their experience mediated through their pre-existing expectations and conceptions." Gunter et al., *Wesley and Quadrilateral*, 137.

experience to be mediated—or understood—in a way that draws believers towards Christlikeness and faithful, holy living.[39] Thus, while experience does offer knowledge, it is knowledge subservient to God's revelation in Scripture and Christ, the tradition's witness to this revelation, and the coherence between what one experiences and what the sources of Scripture and tradition promise.

The above way of thinking about experience in theological reflection is significantly different than how many conceptualize it today, with the experience of individuals ("my" experience) being held as sacrosanct in contemporary thought. Yet, if experience is interpreted, those interpretations must be regarded as situational and therefore biased by our prejudices in the Gadamerian sense of preunderstandings.[40] Thus, to be demonstrable in some regard, one's individual experience (or sense of an experience) is not enough to qualify as a theological source. There is a further tension related to how Wesley understood experience, namely that his empiricism is at odds with contemporary notions of constructivism, the idea that reality is socially constructed. If what is true is socially constructed, then truth itself is not just mediated but made via social relationships—an insight completely at odds with Wesley's understanding. His empiricism would have led him towards understanding truth as universally applicable, and thus that the knowledge revealed by experience was objective and universally applicable insomuch as it was testable and repeatable.[41] Yet, in the shadow of postmodernism, this is now seen as naïve because it is recognized that truth, or rather truth understood through application, is contextual, which does not easily allow for testability let alone consistent repeatability or universal applicability. As will be seen, a similar tension exists between modernism and postmodernism related to experience, which I will leverage in my research design.

Within the Quadrilateral, if Scripture can be considered the revelation of God's covenant and tradition the historical fulfillment of this covenant, experience is the present fulfillment of the covenant and reason is that which ties each of the theological sources together. As the covenant's fulfillment, one's experience of God is both individual and communal,

39. Abraham (*Aldersgate*, 5–6) argues that Wesley particularly focused how experience confirmed divine promises in Scripture, showed God's power at work in believers, and promoted one's personal awareness of God's grace, as a basic set of criteria for understanding this experience quadrant.

40. Moules et al., *Conducting Hermeneutic*, 121.

41. Gunter et al., *Wesley and Quadrilateral*, 113.

because God's covenant with humanity is a covenant made by God for both individuals and the community of faith. Thus, as Gunter et al. describe, submitting personal experience to a local body's collective experiences is to acknowledge that "a sister or brother might have a more adequate sense than our own of how to live faithfully as God's people in the world."[42] This may mean taking stock of what others have said or engaging in dialogue as a necessary part of theological reflection—particularly with those in the past, as well as those who disagree with us. This discussion of community is not to say that theological reflection is communal (that is, the community fully shares in the reflection, such that everyone arrives at the same conclusions), but that individuals must theologically reflect in community, building each others' capacity to think about God as they strive towards faithful living in their personal and shared contexts. Indeed, one's personal experience in a situation is the starting point for theological reflection, but within the Quadrilateral paradigm the role of experience necessarily entails the involvement of Christian community.

I think Wesley's impulse to think of experience in a more complex way is a good impulse to emulate. As such, in conceptualizing the Quadrilateral, I would argue for placing experiences in constructive dialogue with other theological sources and with the collective experiences of other Christians. By doing this, one may come to true knowledge of the Christian confession, knowing it not just in mind, but in their heart, soul, and strength as well. Indeed, Wesley believed, and contemporary interpreters would do well to remember, that much of the church's theology was not devised by academics sitting in seminaries but by pastor-theologians seeking to bridge the gap between what Scripture promised and the lives of those God placed in their care.[43]

## THE QUADRILATERAL MATRIX

The preceding descriptions are but introductory reflections on each of the Quadrilateral's sources. However, these brief introductions set the stage for a re-articulation of the Quadrilateral's popular formation and introduces core concepts for this project. As one can surmise from these descriptions, the sources within the Quadrilateral inform each other, and do so in a way that makes the Quadrilateral more complex than it may otherwise seem.

42. Gunter et al., *Wesley and Quadrilateral*, 116.

43. Gunter et al., *Wesley and Quadrilateral*, 125.

Furthermore, how the theological sources interact with one another also makes the misunderstanding of the Quadrilateral as equilateral easier to occur. There is no notion of authoritative hierarchy within the popular understanding of the Quadrilateral, even though descriptions of it tend to describe a theological hierarchy informing how the theological sources should interact. In order to make the Quadrilateral more useful in metamodern practice, I will clarify its complexification and create space for talking more clearly about authority amongst the sources, while ensuring the paradigm's simplicity is maintained for ease of use and adoption.

It is with these in mind that I now offer my reappraisal of Wesley's Quadrilateral, what I am referring to as the *Quadrilateral Matrix*. As described earlier, the Quadrilateral's flow-chart and equilateral graph constructions cause multiple issues with using and applying the method. To overcome these issues, I submit that slightly changing how the quadrants are conceptualized and visualized can help describe their relations to one another. By drawing the Quadrilateral in a way that visually prioritizes sources, one can indicate how they treat each source as authoritative compared to the others, revealing how the theological sources interact in theological reflection and therefore in interpretive practice. Indeed, the visualization need not be static in people's minds but dynamic enough to change depending on the theological prejudices applied to the sources on an individual/contextual basis. In this way, the Quadrilateral might become more akin to a *matrix*, which, in mathematical terms, is a grid that functions using particular "rules" of engagement. For the Quadrilateral, a matrix of theological sources can indicate the "weight" one gives to each source, or how one prioritizes sources, in a way that is both easy to understand and easy to compare.

In Figure 3 below, I offer a diagram of the Quadrilateral Matrix, which includes further description to show the role of situational experiences as incidents that invite—or even require—theological reflection, and which includes biblical interpretation as an important element. This addition will prove important, as it clarifies the nature of experience as generally understood; that is, as Grenz and Franke suggest, "experience does not precede interpretation. Rather, experiences are always filtered by an interpretive framework—a grid—that facilitates their occurrence."[44] Experiences in situations give rise to theological reflection, but it is "cognitive frameworks"

44. Grenz and Franke, *Beyond Foundationalism*, 49.

that make the interpretation of those experiences possible.[45] My suggestion is that the *Quadrilateral Matrix* can, and should, be used as that framework for theological reflection; a tool that can help one bring their Christian faith to bare in the varied situations of their life.

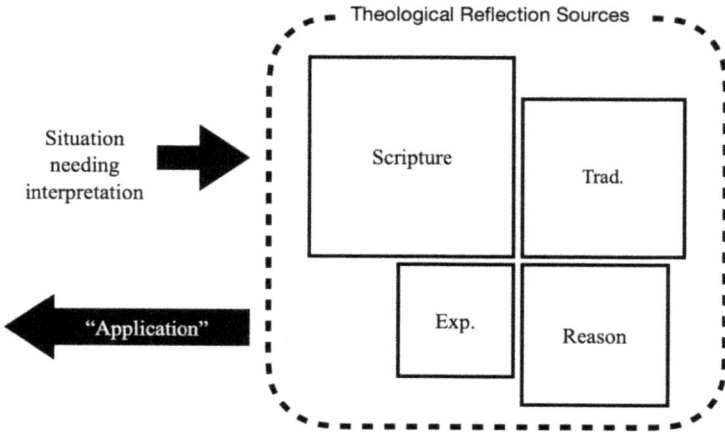

**Figure 3: Quadrilateral Matrix**

Furthermore, it is my conviction, informed by the theological assumptions outlined in the previous chapter, that the configuration I have in offered in Figure 3 should be the normative configuration for evangelicals. This means that the sources of theological reflection are weighted so as to prioritize Scripture, with tradition, reason, and experience having progressively less authority. However, in utilizing the Quadrilateral Matrix descriptively, one must think of it dynamically as a paradigm, allowing it to adapt into many different configurations. Using the Quadrilateral Matrix in such a paradigmatic way allows one to think critically about how the theological sources are utilized and prioritized in interpretation and reflection. Here I am using the phrases *paradigmatic* and *paradigm* in line with its use in the social sciences, which tends to understand paradigms as analytic lenses rather than archetypes or exemplary models. Thus, according to the qualitative use of the phrase, you can "enter" and "exit" a paradigm in varied ways, and for the Quadrilateral Matrix in particular one can imagine countless configurations of the quadrants in order to communicate the relative authoritativeness or weight of each source.

45. Grenz and Franke, *Beyond Foundationalism*, 49.

For example, one could argue that Roman Catholicism priorities the theological source of tradition, whereas Pentecostals prioritize experience, and theological liberalism prioritizes reason. Given these, one could diagram each configuration with the matrix in a coherent way. In *Figure 4* (below), I offer various examples to show this, though these are not to suggest this *is* how each group mentioned above does prioritize theological sources. Instead, it is simply to show how the Quadrilateral Matrix could be utilized and visualize combinations of various possible prioritizations, in order to help the reader imagine the Quadrilateral Matrix's use less as a static method and more the dynamic paradigm it is intended as.

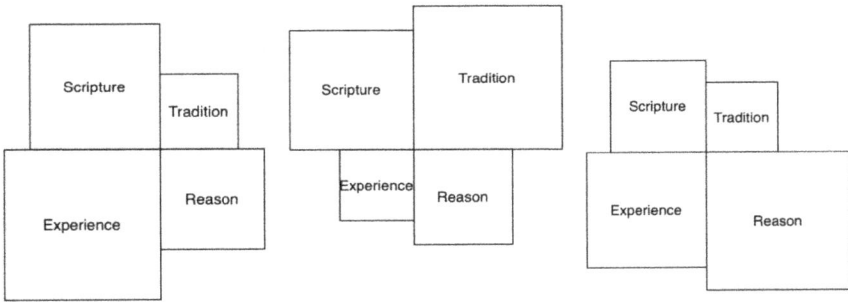

Figure 4: Imaginative Examples Using the Quadrilateral Matrix

I believe this matrix construction of the Quadrilateral makes the paradigm more useful for theological reflection for a number of reasons. First, it overcomes the equilateral issue of other visualizations while maintaining a semblance of the popular notion of the Quadrilateral's use. Because of this, it also maintains a level of simplicity while giving room for complexification in the reflective process. Finally, keeping the same sources as Outler's Quadrilateral ensures a continuity of familiarity across traditions. And, assuming this familiarity, the Quadrilateral Matrix offers a level of pragmatic utility for both self-describing (and reflecting on) one's own prioritization of theological sources, and a framework for discussing these prioritizations. Being fundamentally similar to the popular notion of the Quadrilateral, the basic shift towards imagining the quadrant sizes in terms of a source's prioritization of authority makes the paradigm a dynamic tool for thinking about theological reflection.[46] Furthermore, the summative descriptions I have offered both

---

46. While prioritization of sequence may help reveal a prioritization of authority, it requires an intentional and focused interpretive method, which I do not expect most, if any, of my data sources to describe. Thus, while a prioritization of authority may lead to

clarify what each quadrant is (that is, what I mean when I say "Scripture, tradition, reason, and experience") and how they might be utilized.

## BRINGING THE CONSTRUCTS: HERMENEUTIC CONTENT ANALYSIS

In the first chapter, I outlined in brief the methodology of the project, hermeneutic content analysis. As a reminder, this methodology is used to break texts down into meaning units from which the researcher develops inferences in service to their research question. The process of breaking texts down is called coding, which is performed with the aid of what Krippendorff called analytical constructs. Saldaña describes coding as a researcher's interpretation of data for use in analytical processes (theory building, detecting patterns, and so on).[47] Analytical constructs give structure to this interpretive process by offering the conditions from which stable, meaningful inferences can be made.[48] While Krippendorff's approach was more quantitative than qualitative, coding procedures such as his have become increasingly popular for qualitative research design. Indeed, because qualitative research is, at its core, concerned with developing interpretations of a given data set,[49] coding is a natural method for qualitative data analysis.

When one codes data, there are two main procedures a researcher must decide between using: inductive coding or deductive coding. Inductive coding allows codes and themes to develop as the researcher repeatedly analyzes their dataset. Deductive coding begins with the researcher predetermining a code structure and finding excerpts within their data that meaningfully fit this structure. In the present research, I have chosen to code deductively rather than inductively, as the deductive approach better aligns with my research aims.[50] Namely, deductive coding allows for the use of my analytical constructs to aid in understanding biblical interpretive

a prioritization of sequence, for the purposes of this project the sequence of theological sources interpreters communicate they utilized will not be taken as sufficient ground from which to infer meaningful conclusions regarding their interpretive process.

47. Saldaña, *Coding Manual*, 6.

48. Krippendorff, *Content Analysis*, 30.

49. Schreier, *Qualitative in Practice*, 28.

50. Saldaña (*Coding Manual*, 40) argues that deductive coding is most appropriate for "when your conceptual framework, research questions, and other matters of research design suggest that certain codes, categories, themes, or concepts are most likely to appear in the data you collect."

practice expressed in the texts I will be analyzing. However, this should not be misunderstood to presume that inductive coding will not or cannot take place. These two approaches to coding are dialectical, each feeding into the other, such that inductive coding eventually becomes deductive, and deductive coding must remain open to new knowledge and insight that emerge during data analysis.[51]

While seemingly disparate, the central idea of oscillation, conceptualized via the hermeneutical pendulum introduced at the beginning of this chapter, is not limited just to how one interprets texts. Indeed, conceptualizing "author-centered" and "reader-centered" categories in broad terms allows one to see that the approaches in modernism and postmodernism related to scriptural interpretation are mirrored in the understanding of other theological sources. Thus, if the Quadrilateral's theological sources are bifurcated to account for the varied emphases for understanding the sources in both cultural moods, a coding frame emerges that will allow for mapping varied understandings of theological sources, which will help reveal how the theological reflection sources are being utilized in coming to varied interpretive conclusions.

Coding frames include main code categories that, "symbolically assigns a summative, salient, essence–capturing, and/or evocative attribute for a portion of language based or visual data,"[52] sub-codes that enrich a code entry's understanding, and broad descriptions of the codes to give a sense of what is being looked for in the dataset.[53] In this project, the main code categories are those of the Quadrilateral: Scripture, tradition, reason, and experience. From each, subcategories representing the various "poles" of understanding between modernism and postmodernism can be developed from which inferences can be made regarding interpretive practice.

As already discussed at length, the understanding of Scripture in the modern and postmodern moods has been understood in terms of the poles of author and reader emphases. Thus, these make natural sub-categories to use. Coding these poles will involve discerning the extent to which an interpreter attends to—and though their attending, submits to—the world of the author and/or the world of the reader in their interpretive practice. Understanding the world of the author, and an author's possible intention in writing a text, includes the author's world and words—through historical

---

51. Saldaña, *Coding Manual*, 41.

52. Saldaña, *Coding Manual*, 5.

53. Saldaña, *Coding Manual*, 41–44, 121.

reconstruction, and especially within their literary context. Likewise, prioritizing the world of the reader is, in effect, to disallow the world of the author to confront or challenge the reader, instead imposing the reader's perspective on a text's meaning while dismissing the author. It should be noted that if Western culture is indeed functioning in the metamodern mood, I expect to find both poles active in the coded data (for this, as well as the other sources).

In their approach to tradition, the modern and postmodern impulse has been marked by ecumenicalism on the one hand and a form of sectarianism on the other. Indeed, as Jos de Mul has written, "in contrast to the modernist aspiration for unity, totality, and universalism, postmodernism stands for differentiation, pluralism, and particularism."[54] While in my context as a practitioner many self-described postmodernists would claim ecumenicalism as a distinctly postmodern trait, it is rather modernism whose approach to tradition is truly ecumenical due to its fundamental posture rejecting the romantic notion that tradition is an unquestionable historical given,[55] thus opening tradition up to being questioned, challenged, and changed. For the church, this meant tradition lost its position of *de facto* authority, disallowing it from being used as a norming feature of theological reflection. This being the case, the differences between the traditions could be downplayed in favour of "a central unity underlying the seemingly disjointed flux of all experience,"[56] the search for which was a central concern of the modernist project. Furthermore, the modernist critique of tradition led to what has been called the "dislocation and flattening of history"[57] whereby sources from disparate traditions, whose views may even be at significant odds, are brought together without sufficient recognition of their meaningful differences (including historical and theological contexts). This bringing together was informed by modernism's underlying attitude towards unity, which led to the development of ecumenical movements in and throughout the early and mid-twentieth century. Thus, I have sub-coded the modern notion of tradition as ecumenical.

Given the above sub-code, the opposite of ecumenicalism, sectarianism, could be an appropriate sub-code to utilize for the other pole. However, it is important to note that by sectarian I do not mean schismatic,

---

54. Mul, *Romantic Desire*, 18.

55. Gadamer, *Truth and Method*, 293.

56. Grenz, *Primer*, 83.

57. Grenz, *Primer*, 21.

nor fundamentalist, but rather a view of tradition with a recognition of difference that divides (that is, differentiates and particularizes). Indeed, the postmodern notion of tradition does not grant tradition authority, but does recognize traditions as inevitable aspects of culture, understanding them as socially constructed artifacts, of sorts.[58] This enables a level of self-awareness regarding ways various traditions are meaningfully differ- ent, even if this self-awareness comes at the cost of continually critiquing tradition to ensure ongoing faithfulness—a practice which is not at odds with Christianity generally and Protestantism in particular.

For reason, modernism and postmodernism are differentiated by their emphases on objectivity and subjectivity. In modernism, there was a clear sense of a divide between objective and subjective truth. This sense meant one was open to their viewpoint being significantly altered or falsi- fied and their minds changed by receiving new information. Indeed, the principle of falsification is at the heart of the modernist project and is best seen in the development of the scientific method. It can also be clearly seen in Wesley's empiricism, as previously discussed. Postmodernism, on the other hand, abandoned the notion of a knowable universal truth and devel- oped the notion of intersubjectivity, perhaps expressed most clearly in the idea that reality is socially constructed. For postmodernists, it is incoherent to speak of one truth or monolithic understanding of reality; instead, one can only speak of multiple subjectivities which converge via encounters with others.[59] Grenz argues that the differences between modernism and postmodernism be accounted for via their ultimate concerns, both be- ing expressible via contrasting questions. Talking about postmodernists, Grenz says "at issue for them is not 'Is the proposition or theory correct?' but rather 'What does it do?' or 'What is its outcome?'"[60] Indeed, the point Grenz is making is that postmodernism is concerned with power, and view absolute truth claims as an unjust usurpation of the individual; a power grab that requires deconstructing.[61] In modernism the focus of reason is on objective truth while in postmodernism the focus of reason is on the social construction (intersubjectivity) and deconstruction of one's understanding

58. Grenz, *Primer*, 21.

59. Grenz, *Primer*, 42–43.

60. Grenz, *Primer*, 43.

61. As Grenz summarizes, according to postmodern philosopher Michel Foucault "every interpretation of reality . . . [and] every assertion of knowledge is an assertion of power." Grenz, *Primer*, 6.

of reality. Thus, the categories of falsification and intersubjectivity may be used as sub-codes for reason in my content analysis.

Finally, there are differing notions of experience in modernism and postmodernism. As a reminder, Wesley's conception of the Quadrilateral's category of experience is more focused on one's experience of God than on one's life experiences generally. Thus, it is a theological source insomuch as one's experiences correspond to the promises of God's covenant. When coding for experience, I will not code for the mention of experience generally, but for mention of God's action. Importantly, the emphasis for understanding God's work in history has shifted between transcendence and immanence in the cultural epochs. Theologically, transcendence refers to the idea that God is beyond or outside of human perception and understanding, making one's experience of God a mystery or what William James referred to as mystical or religious experiences.[62] Conversely, immanence is related to God being knowable, perceivable, and present, which focuses on God's presence in the here and now.

Modernism is and was, in many ways, marked by debates regarding the relationship between the transcendent and the natural world (including history), due to the effects of a developing scientific project and the onset of wars of unprecedented violence.[63] While these debates did not necessarily approach transcendence as a positive category, it did treat it as a *meaningful* category.[64] Indeed, modernism's focus on the experience of divine mystery, typified by the work of William James at the turn of the nineteenth century but found throughout modernist literature, allows for the use of

62. James defined these experiences according to criteria of ineffability (it defies description), noetic quality (it reveals truth), transiency (does not last long), and passivity (one is taken over, in some sense, by the experience). James, *Religious Experience*, 370–71.

63. Ratté, "Transcendence," 226; Hughes, *Dickinson to Dylan*, 5, 9–10, 13; Kochlefl, "Modernist Transcendence," 7–8.

64. It should be noted that outside of theology transcendence and immanence do not have God as their subject but a notion of mystery more generally. This is why the category of mystical experience is appropriate, as it describes transcendent experience for those who may not believe in God. I recognize, in making my argument in this section, that I am appropriating the general notions of mystery to discuss particular notions relating to God—whether God's mystery, or God's indwelling. Suffice to say, the Christian tradition has a long history of acknowledging mystery, such that I think it both coherent and reasonable to make these appropriations for the sake of this project, even as I recognize the limitations of doing so—namely, making sense of some source materials that would have scant reference to divine personhood but significant reference to some broadly defined "divine" mystery.

transcendence as a sub-code for the modernism-side of the coding frame. The focus on transcendence is also a corollary to the author-centered hermeneutic focus of modernism, which argued for a "distant or 'hidden' God and a correspondingly removed author."[65] This emphasis could also be expressed through an overemphasis on God as being sovereign over history and as a (distant, cosmic) judge,[66] offering a possible tell for discerning when this perspective is present in the data.

Postmodernism, on the other hand, shifted focus away from transcendence and towards immanence, even going so far as to prioritize the immanent nature of situational experience above most other considerations in theological reflection.[67] Indeed, the focus on immanence, particularly in theology, corresponds with the development of reader-focused postmodern hermeneutical postures. In this epoch, a heaven-bound God "was repositioned as an incarnated Jesus, whose counterpart was a textualized author in literature."[68] Interestingly, this led to an overemphasis on Christ's immanence, including and especially his humanity, and a focus on how Christ is like us and how we can mimic his example and live his teachings.[69] Postmodern theorists such as John Caputo have argued for "relocating transcendence on the plane of immanence,"[70] concluding that "Ethics is all the transcendence there is"—and particularly what might be called an ethic of love.[71] Thus, the postmodern experience of God is filtered through a framework that prioritizes the immanent elements of Christ and his ministry—to the poor, the marginalized, and oppressed in particular—while removing transcendent aspects of said ministry, even while acknowledging the otherness of God.[72]

## Notes about Nuance

As some readers may have intuited up to this point in this discussion of methodology, there is a difficulty in that the bifurcations presented above can

65. Kochlefl, "Modernist Transcendence," 3–4.

66. Kochlefl, "Modernist Transcendence," 4, 7.

67. Grenz and Franke, *Beyond Foundationalism*, 49; Taylor, *Secular Age*, 539–93.

68. Kochlefl, "Modernist Transcendence," 4.

69. Kochlefl, "Modernist Transcendence," 125.

70. Caputo and Scanlon, "Introduction," 10.

71. Caputo, "Temporal Transcendence," 188; Caputo and Scanlon, "Introduction," 7.

72. Kochlefl, "Modernist Transcendence," 4.

be misunderstood to be absolute. In other words, the poles I have presented can be misconstrued as absolute opposites with no sense of complexity or a continuum of positions existing between poles. However, such complexity *does* exist. Like the complexity of metamodernism more generally, whose oscillation is noted to have an infinite number of poles, the poles of my coding frame must be understood as extremes between which a variety of positions may be mappable. To use the pendulum metaphor, a pendulum does not jump from one place to another but swings along a trajectory, and every point along the trajectory is a possible pivot-point for oscillation. However, in order to make meaningful inferences about the project data and help both complexify and simplify understanding of the interpretive process, the poles are, for the purpose of the project, being understood as representative of both the extremes *as well as* those positions that mark a trajectory towards or close to each pole. This necessitates that judgment calls will be made about which interpretive trajectory is operative for each code category. However, this is not to suggest that only the extremes of these trajectories are operative. In fact, there is significant nuance, but dissecting this nuance in greater detail is beyond the scope of this project.

The above bifurcation of poles in the coding frame is also an expression of the discussion regarding sexuality in the contemporary West, as it is generally debated by subsuming degrees of belief under large umbrella terms: affirming versus non-affirming, "side A" versus "side B," progressive versus traditional, liberal versus conservative. Yet, as Lawrence Holben pointed out in his book *What Christians Think about Homosexuality*, each category has a number of possible positions within it.[73] In effect, then, the outcome—of being affirming or non-affirming, for example—tends to dictate the contour of the categories, even when there is surprising diversity from one person to the next on the details leading to their good faith conclusions. Thus, I expect to see a variety of configurations regarding the prioritization of theological sources in the coded dataset.

Finally, there are two aspects of the topic that this bifurcation does not adequately deal with. First, modernism and postmodernism, in a very

73. While not an extensive archive of positions, Holben's insight that there is often more going on under the surface of the larger labels is accurate and helpful. Holben maps various positions out with a nod to its extreme poles; the extreme traditional position being "condemnation" and the extreme progressive position "liberation." Apart from these, four other positions are in between: restoration and friendship on the traditional side, and accommodation and affirmation on the progressive side. Hollinger (*Meaning of Sex*, 143–46) provides an apt summery of each of Holben's position descriptions.

general sense and as already noted in the, can be construed as being generative and deconstructive, respectively. That is, modernism is generally concerned with knowledge generation, while postmodernism is generally concerned with the deconstruction of knowledge via critique.[74] *Generally* is an important word in the above explanation, as neither construction nor deconstruction are the only concern of either perspective. However, the underlying assumptions of each tended towards these concerns, which will aid in coding. Looking for constructive or deconstructive statements within the coding will help me discern which sensibility might be operative in a given piece of data. Furthermore, this generalization helps to clarify the metamodernism oscillation, which is, as previously noted, a movement between modern construction and postmodern deconstruction.

The second aspect is premodernism's influence on contemporary interpretive practice, which has multiple converging elements. At its roots, modernism is informed by the enlightenment and romanticism, such that these premodern movements continue to wield influence in contemporary thought. This is especially true for traditions, such as fundamentalism, that sought to reject modernism in favour of the premodern. As such, one should expect to find elements of the premodern in contemporary culture, as has been previously discussed. Furthermore, related to the practice of biblical interpretation, the emergence of the theological interpretation of Scripture movement, which seeks to return to a form of premodern interpretive practice, makes discerning truly premodern interpretive conceptions difficult, as does the possibility that contemporary notions of premodern thought are unreflectively informed by modernism and postmodernism. Suffice to say, all of this means that the coding frame will have difficulty mapping premodern and fundamentalist concepts if or when they arise in the dataset and will not be able to tell truly premodern instances apart from the more recent reactionary move from modern/postmodern to premodern (which, in the sense of being reconstructive, should be considered a metamodern response, even if judged untenable). Because these (though

---

74. As described by Grenz, postmodern deconstruction is the application of the poststructuralist literary critique that argued the meaning of texts are not inherent to the text but emerge through the act of interpretation. Postmodern philosophers applied this to our understanding of the world. "Just as a text will be read differently by each reader, they [postmodern philosophers] said, so reality will be 'read' differently by each knowing self that encounters it. This means there is no one meaning of the world, no transcendent center to reality as a whole." And if this is the case, there is no basis for assuming any knowledge is objective in the modernist sense. Grenz, *Primer*, 6.

fundamentalism especially) tend to mimic aspects of a given dominant cultural milieu, I will map any instances of these perspectives within the bifurcated coding frame as best as I think they may fit, but will return to this issue of nuance as part of the discussion of inferences in the following chapters.

## CONCLUDING SUMMARY AND CODING FRAME

Having discussed Wesley's Quadrilateral in detail, I have proposed a new way of describing this theological reflection paradigm in what I have termed the Quadrilateral Matrix. Furthermore, building on the insights of the previous chapter, I have articulated a construct called the Hermeneutical Pendulum to describe metamodern interpretive practice. Bringing these two constructs together, I have developed a coding frame with which I will engage in a hermeneutic content analysis of gathered data sources. This coding frame, visualized in Figure 5 (below), corresponds to the project's Code Book in Table 1 (below), which broadly describes what was looked for during the coding procedure. In the following chapter, I will review data sources and offer an analysis of their content using this coding frame, which will give insight into biblical interpretation in the metamodern mood. I will then propose a reading paradigm that will be usable in the church to help Christians understand their biblical interpretive practice.

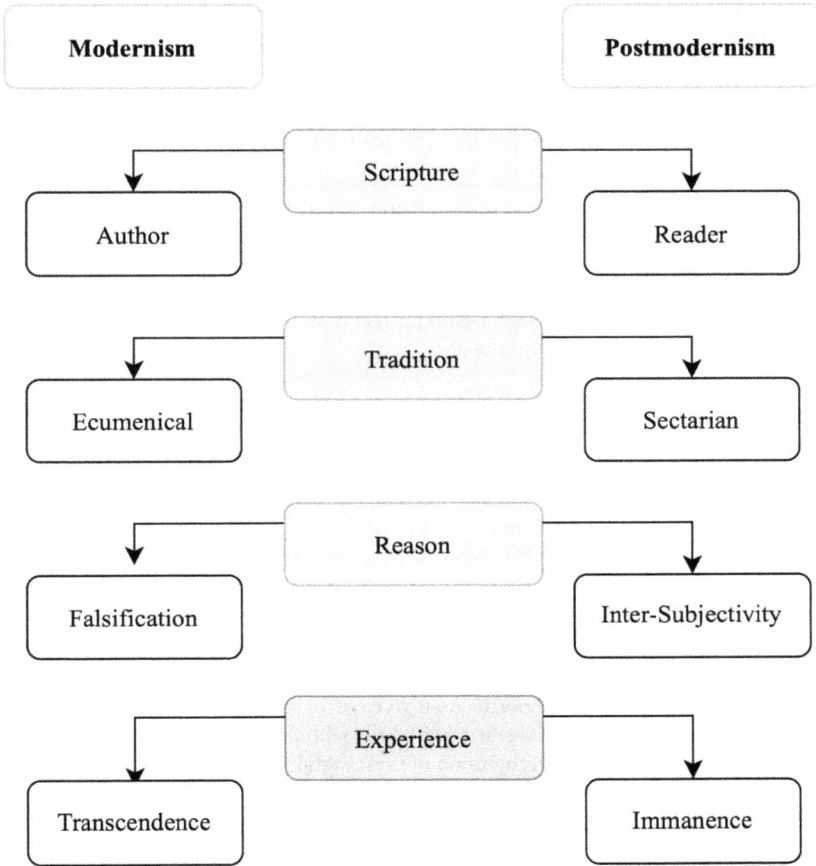

**Figure 5: Project Coding Frame**

**Table 1**: *Project Code Book*

| Category | Sub-Category | Sub-Category Description | Code Example |
|---|---|---|---|
| Scripture | Author | Loci of meaning is placed with the author (includes notions of authorial intent, intertextuality, etc). Goal: Hear the author. | "We're trying to figure out, what is he [Paul] lasering in on? What is he critiquing?" (T15) |
| | Reader | Loci of meaning is placed with the reader (or reading community), whose reception of the text is prioritized. Goal: Distinguish author from reader. | "My sense is that homosexuality is referenced more as an illustration of a point than as the point itself, simply out of Paul's taken for granted assumption that same gender sex is unclean unnatural and completely contrary to God's will. This is not an assumption that I agree with." (T9) |
| Tradition | Ecumenical | Prioritization of unity across denominational traditions, often expressed via the flattening of church history. Historically dislocated. | "Tribalism has been shattered in Christ and we are all on equal footing before God: Jew and Greek, gay and straight, traditional and affirming all alike, all are one in Christ." (T3) |
| | Sectarian | Prioritization given to specific tradition(s), with the recognition of meaningful difference between sects. Historically located. Can be ironic. | "What happens when we see a sister church teaching something that is out of sync with what the majority of Christians throughout history and around the world have interpreted?" (T1) |
| Reason | Falsification | Prioritization of objective-subjective divide; viewpoint changes when offered sufficient evidence. Methodological. Concern: "Is the proposition correct?" | "My first goal, my most important goal is to be faithful to what I understand God to be saying through his word, whether or not I like what I'm reading." (T7) |
| | Intersubjectivity | Prioritization of social construction; multiple subjectivities; lack of falsification; truth is power, deconstruction of truth claims. Concern: "What is a proposition's outcome?" | "[The] LGBTQ issue is not primarily a sexual ethics issue. . . it's a human wellbeing issue." (T13) |

**Table 1**: *Project Code Book*

| Category | Sub-Category | Sub-Category Description | Code Example |
|---|---|---|---|
| Experience *(of God)* | Transcendence | Prioritization given to notions of divine distance; notable emphasis on omnipotence and divine judgment. | "Crossing lines that God has established results in significant harm and dysfunction in this life and exile and death in the life to come." (T5) |
| | Immanence | Prioritization given to notions of divine presence with us; notable emphasis on personal presence of Jesus or leading of the Holy Spirit. | "We can hear [God] speaking through the cries of liberation." (T2) |

# 4

# Analyzing Interpretive Practice

STRUCTURED AROUND THE CODING frame presented in the previous chapter, this chapter will outline my analysis of data gathered from publicly available Canadian evangelical (ana)baptistic sources that exhibit theological reflection on the topic of sexuality. I begin by describing how the data was gathered, stored, and analyzed, before moving on to discussing the prevalence of the coding frame's subcategories within the data. This discussion will then lead into the final chapters of the project, which will describe inferences made within the data, reflect on the implications of this analysis, and propose a reading paradigm to help believers reflect on their practice of biblical interpretation and, therefore, theological reflection.

## OVERVIEW OF THE DATA AND CODING PROCESS

As discussed in chapter 1, the collected data was publicly available at the time of collection. Out of the then-330 churches in the CBOQ, 252 churches with active websites (that I could find) were searched. I utilized search commands to direct the Google search engine to locate specific phrases on church websites, including YouTube autogenerated transcriptions.[1] For

1. Due to the ease of replicability for using these search commands, in keeping with TCPS2's instruction to mitigate the possibility of harm (TCPS2, 21), I have chosen not to replicate the specific command I utilized. This is in order to offer reasonable consideration for protecting the identity of churches whose stated position could warrant discipline or disfellowship in their denominational contexts.

each website, pages associated with the site containing possible connection to the research topic were found, I evaluated the content as to whether sufficient discussion of biblical interpretive practice was given. Sources that seemed, on first glance, to meet my criteria were saved and stored on my personal laptop within a research application used for coding called MAX-QDA. Also searched were non-CBOQ (ana)baptistic church websites that were found through a broad Google search that included denomination names and the same search criteria described above.

The analysis of the data was a two-step process. During both steps, coding involved developing concept codes that were then gathered into "clusters of comparable concepts" within the subcategories of my coding frame.[2] Concept coding is a procedure of drawing out and labeling ideas which are both explicitly and implicitly in a dataset; assigning "a word or short phrase that symbolically represents a suggested meaning . . . beyond the tangible and apparent."[3] To put this another way, concept coding is the development of a metacommentary that seeks to describe an interpretation of the dataset. By looking for repeated words, phrases, and ideas throughout the data and collecting these instances—in one piece of data, and across the collection—I can explicate meaningful inferences that will clarify what is going on when Scripture is interpreted in the metamodern mood.

While it may, on surface, seem that my coding is descriptive, descriptive coding identifies topics in the data but not the content of what is in the data.[4] Because my analysis is *hermeneutic*, which will be further described below, my goal was to summarize my interpretation of the substance of a given excerpt, thus making my method *concept coding*. At the end of the coding process, codes were merged, as appropriate, to create a final group of concept codes that were filtered into the coding frame, summarizing concepts I interpreted as relevant throughout the dataset. It bears repeating that one of the criteria for the project's validity discussed in the introductory chapter was that the research is believably plausible, even if inferences (and conclusions) made are disagreed with.[5] Thus, I considered my coding successful insomuch as the concept codes plausibly represented the elements of the coding frame.

2. Saldaña, *Coding Manual*, 156.

3. Saldaña, *Coding Manual*, 152.

4. Saldaña, *Coding Manual*, 134.

5. Moules et al., *Conducting Hermeneutic*, 172.

An initial coding run was completed during the transcription process, at which time I made a further determination regarding the applicability of the material for the study. Of an initial twenty-three pieces of data collected, seven were disqualified for not sufficiently engaging biblical interpretive practice or theological reflection on the topic of human sexuality.

Thus, in total, sixteen pieces of data were collected for analysis—eight "traditional" and eight "progressive"—including eleven sermons, two Bible studies, one presentation, and two position papers. Of these sixteen, fourteen were from CBOQ sources and two from other contexts. Furthermore, five of the sermons were parts of sermon series: Texts #4, #7, and #9 were part of one series, and Texts #10 and #14 part of another. Texts #1 and #2 were also related as part of a Bible study series. Each of these series had a single speaker throughout, and so each series represents a single distinct voice. I do not view this as a negative for the project, necessarily, as utilizing the same voices over multiple texts may allow for a greater discernment of metamodern interpretive practice across the texts. However, these groups of texts do raise an important issue of sample size. There is debate about the sample size needed in qualitative studies such that no new information is gleaned—that is, when *data saturation* is reached. For most qualitative studies, particularly those engaged in hermeneutic and phenomenological analysis, sample sizes between six and ten tend to produce studies of higher quality. However, for others, such as grounded theory, a sample size no fewer than twelve is argued to be necessary. Because of this uncertainty, I aimed to collect at least six texts (and in the end collected eight) from each of the "traditional" and "affirming" positions, meeting the saturation point of qualitative studies for both. Saturation is still maintained if each series is counted as one datapoint, with six unique speakers for each perspective.[6]

In keeping with TCPS2 best practices for privacy preservation, the data was anonymized in the process of transcription: the names of persons, churches, and communities were all removed, and each text given a random number between one and sixteen using a random number generator. A second coding run was completed on these remaining materials one week after all transcriptions were finished, using a clean (unmarked) transcription. During this second coding run, materials assigned an odd number were coded first followed by those assigned even numbers. The coding from both runs was then compared, and only codes appearing in

6. Bartholomew et al., "Choir or Cacophony," 9; Guest et al., "How Many Interviews?," 78–79.

both coding runs were used for analysis. The above method of working through the content's coding ensures a level of reliability, as it shows that the data was coded in similar ways over a period of time (in other words, the codes are stable), thus implying both reproducibility and reliability.

## Gadamer, Rigor, and the Art of Coding

While my coding method was concept coding, it was informed by Gadamerian hermeneutics such that the core ideas within Gadamer's hermeneutical vision informed my coding decisions. Namely, Gadamer's interrelated notions of language, the fusion of horizons, and prejudice all played an important role in the coding process. Utilizing these concepts, my coding became (and I understood it as being) a practice of interpretation; that is, the codes represented my interpretation of the gathered texts. It bears repeating that while the coding procedure was deductive, the code categories were developed iteratively and reflexively, via personal reflection and through conversation with others about the project. As codes developed, I reflected on the codes, my own interpretive practice, and whether I believed the codes accurately described what was in a given text, which led to ongoing revisions of the concept codes throughout the coding process. This included significantly refining the project code book over the course of the research to clarify, enhance, and sometimes completely redefine the coding frame in order to best describe metamodern interpretive practice. In other words, the codes are not prejudices imposed on the texts but interpretations of the texts informed by the theoretical and theological prejudice outlined in earlier chapters, which were leveraged to gain new insight for how the theological sources of the Quadrilateral are playing a role in contemporary interpretive practice, specifically related to the sexuality debate.

Because the codes are interpretations, the project's capacity to generate new knowledge hinges on the believability of these interpretations, and thus the rigour of the project begins taking shape in the coding process.[7] However, like hermeneutics more generally, the project's rigour is not complete (so to speak) until the point when new knowledge about practice is derived—or put into more common vernacular, until the project's culmination in application. Thus, the believability and trustworthiness of the coding is the ground from which the rigour of the project as a meaningful piece

---

7. Moules et al., *Conducting Hermeneutic*, 172.

of qualitative research finds its roots, and it is in the application of research findings where the project's rigour becomes fully discernible.

As mentioned, utilizing Gadamer's concepts of language, horizons, and prejudice were important to the coding process. For Gadamer, language is the "air that understanding breathes."[8] It is through language that we not only convey concepts but think about concepts such that we can communicate about them at all. This includes communication with ourselves, as humans are constantly in dialogue with themselves, and it is through conversations (with self, and others) that meaning develops.[9] The very notion of dialogue assumes that which is being spoken of is understandable, which is only possible through language.[10] But language is, as human beings are, historically effected—that is, the content of our language is shaped by our historical locatedness (our "horizon" as interpreters). It is meaningful that I am writing this project in English, for example, as this locates me within certain traditions. However, this simply makes the importance of prejudice to understanding clearer. Indeed, language is only understandable if people share certain prejudices such that what we attempt to communicate is communicated.[11] The prejudices of language prepares us for understanding, helping to "accommodate the unknown or unfamiliar . . . by relating it to what is already known or assumed."[12]

Yet again, the confluence of hermeneutic theory and practical theology emerges, as situatedness is an important element for both in developing understanding. In my interpretation of the various gathered texts, a question laying in the background must be whether my prejudices and those of my interlocutors align enough that I am able to understand them (and they, me). While our use of the English language may suggest yes, as does our inhabiting similar church traditions, the development of metamodernism suggests (as my coding frame makes clear) that we may be utilizing different theological dialects, making understanding difficult. In my analysis, the extent to which this complexity makes conversations about biblical interpretation difficult will be clarified.

8. Moules et al., *Conducting Hermeneutic*, 39.

9. Grondin, *Philosophical Hermeneutics*, 39.

10. Gadamer, *Truth and Method*, 415.

11. Gadamer, *Truth and Method*, 280.

12. Malcolm, *Hermeneutics to Exegesis*, 37.

## HERMENEUTIC CONTENT ANALYSIS: OVERVIEWING CATEGORIES AND CODES

The rest of this chapter will proceed in four sections corresponding to the categories of the Quadrilateral, followed by a content analysis of patterns from outside the coding frame and a brief summary of the coding frame findings. Each category section will describe the concept codes that have been clustered into the subcategories of the coding frame, utilizing the voices in the collected texts, to give a thick description of the tensions and differences in contemporary interpretive practice.

To give a sense of the overall dataset, Table 2 (below) shows a visual representation of code instances in the subcategories of the coding frame. While future tables will include the specific numbers of code instances, the visual representation below is important as it helps to communicate the metamodern tension in a qualitative (interpretive) rather than quantitative way. As expected, the majority of texts contained units of meaning that I coded within both modern and postmodern subcategories. Yet, there were a small few that did not contain this oscillation as I had expected. It is critical to note that while the tables that follow may give the impression of the analysis being quantitative in nature, this is not the case. Instead, my qualitative analysis is aided by visualizing the distribution of the codes, which is difficult to do without utilizing quantitative numbering. Indeed, quantitative numbering can be amenable to a significant qualitative analysis, in so much as it helps to visualize code distribution. In fact, because of the nature of the texts (as sermons, studies, and position papers), some code instances that only appear once could reasonably be considered critical to the overall flow of an argument and thus cannot be ignored or dismissed. Thus, these tables should be understood as representative of the underlying codes. Indeed, while the coding frame instances are interesting, such a chart alone does not provide sufficient data to develop meaningful inferences regarding my research question. For this, the concept codes developed from the data are necessary.

**Table 2:** *Coding Frame, Subcategory Code Instances*

| | Scripture | | Tradition | | Reason | | Experience | |
|---|---|---|---|---|---|---|---|---|
| Text (T) | Author | Reader | Ecumenical | Sectarian | Falsification | Inter-subjectivity | Transcend. | Immanence |
| T1 | | | | | | | | |
| T2 | | | | | | | | |
| T3 | | | | | | | | |
| T4 | | | | | | | | |
| T5 | | | | | | | | |
| T6 | | | | | | | | |
| T7 | | | | | | | | |
| T8 | | | | | | | | |
| T9 | | | | | | | | |
| T10 | | | | | | | | |
| T11 | | | | | | | | |
| T12 | | | | | | | | |
| T13 | | | | | | | | |
| T14 | | | | | | | | |
| T15 | | | | | | | | |
| T16 | | | | | | | | |
| **Totals** | 44 | 27 | 21 | 25 | 36 | 36 | 32 | 23 |
| | 71 | | 46 | | 72 | | 55 | |

## Scripture

In each of the following subsections, I will begin with a chart summarizing code instances before describing the concept codes using the language of the texts. Each of the concept codes compiled under the Scripture subcategory (Table 3) involved discerning where attention was given when focusing their discussion of Scripture. Under the subcategory of Author-Centered, the concept codes "God Speaks through the Word," "Obedience," "Intent of the Human Author," and "Authority/Intent of the Divine Author" show deference to the author(s) of Scripture and their (particularly God's) authority mediated through the text. For the subcategory of Reader-Centered, the codes of "Reader Reception," "Authorial Intent is Relative," "(Authority of the) Reading Community," and "Dismissive Laughter" reveal a deference to a reading community over, and sometimes against, the authors of Scripture. A discussion of the Scripture passages used in the texts will appear at the end of this chapter and in chapter 5.

**Table 3**: *Scripture, Concept Code Instances*

| | Author-Centered | | | | Reader-Centered | | |
|---|---|---|---|---|---|---|---|
| | (A) "God Speaks through the Word" | (B) Obedience | (C) Intent of the Human Author | (D) Authority/ Intent of the Divine Author | (A) Reader Reception | (B) Questioning Authorial Intent | (C) Dismissive Laughter |
| T1 | 2 | | 1 | 1 | | | |
| T2 | 3 | | | 1 | | | |
| T3 | | | | | 1 | 2 | 1 |
| T4 | | | | | | | |
| T5 | | | | 2 | | | |
| T6 | | 1 | | 3 | | | |
| T7 | 1 | | | | 2 | 1 | |
| T8 | | | | 2 | | | |
| T9 | | | 1 | | 5 | 1 | |
| T10 | 1 | 2 | | 5 | | | |
| T11 | | | | 1 | 4 | | |
| T12 | 1 | 2 | 1 | 1 | | | |
| T13 | | 1 | | | 4 | | |
| T14 | 1 | | | 2 | | | |
| T15 | | | 4 | | 2 | 1 | 1 |
| T16 | | | 3 | 1 | 1 | 1 | |

## Author-Centered: (A) God Speaks through the Word

"We believe God has spoken and continues to speak to us through his Word." This quote from Text #1 (T1) effectively summarizes many of the units of meaning categorized with this code. In each text, "the Word" was used as a shorthand for the Bible, though some, such as T1, clarified that Jesus is also referred to as the Word of God, offering a complexified understanding of the phrase within Scripture. To my surprise, the phrase "the Word of God" was not used in most texts. However, when it was used, it was connected to hearing this Word and heeding what it says because of who was speaking it. "The Bible and the whole Bible is the Word of God" which believers must submit to and not run away from (T7). And related to sexuality, believers "hear from God" by asking "what does the Bible say about these issues in our society?" (T12). Indeed, Scripture is "God's authoritative word to us," (T2) but this word has a particular purpose: "through it, we come into a relationship with [God]" (T2). This focus on God speaking through the Bible shows a deference to God as author of the text, and points to a theology of revelation operating under the surface—which will be discussed in the following chapters. In these texts, the posture of readers is to be submitted to the text because of who its author is—we "allow the Bible to read [us]" (T2). Importantly, for some texts this includes language, whereby interpreters must allow "definitions as given by God [in the Bible]" (T10) to dictate understanding—especially, for many of these coded texts, God's definition of marriage.

## *Author-Centered: (B) Obedience*

In some texts, hearing God's Word was sometimes referred to in relation to the concept of obedience, which assumes the authority of the speaker over the hearer, and that interpreters can sufficiently understand what God communicates in order to obey. In fact, authority implies obedience. Such an outlook is made explicit in a minority of texts which communicate that saying one must be obedient to Scripture is also to say one must be obedient to God who communicates through Scripture. One way this is stated explicitly in the texts is by drawing attention to one of the so-called Baptist Distinctives, the Lordship of Christ. In one text, the connection between Christ's Lordship and our obedience is made through describing disobedience to Jesus as being "sucked into . . . compromis[ing] God's Word" (T10). This speaker goes on to say that the issue which directs the course of every life, "the determining factor" whether believers will be faithful or not is "who is your God? Is Jesus our Lord?" (T10). If Jesus is our Lord, His Lordship will be expressed through faithfulness in obeying all that Christ taught. Another text made a similar point, saying, "to make a choice against God's word, to disobey God, to go against God, we call that sin" (T12). And in another, Christ commands believers how to live through the Bible (T6). Indeed, as one commentator put it, in the context of the sexuality debate, "we're committed to God's commands . . . what the Bible has to say about sexuality" (T6). In each of these, obedience to Scripture is understood in terms of easily understanding what God means in a given text, and taking this understanding as a universal (for everyone, always). Thus, from the author-centered perspective, to be obedient to Christ means being obedient to Scripture (and vice versa).

## Author-Centered: (C) Intent of the Human Author

Importantly for some texts, focus was drawn towards the intent of the human authors in writing the Bible. This focus most regularly showed up in descriptive language related to passages authored by the Apostle Paul, with a focused concern on what "he" (referring to Paul) was meaning in them. However, sometimes this was made more explicit, such as one text which opined "what is Paul aiming at?" and "We're trying to figure out, what is he [Paul] lasering in on? What is he critiquing?" (T15). A further issue of language appears as well, with one text arguing that written language is only meaningful because of its contextual nature, suggesting that one must understand the context to understand the language. "We must follow the axiom that usage and context establishes meaning. This is the contextual criterion for meaning" (T16). What is important to readers who focus on human authorial meaning is understanding the thought-world of the human author, such that one is able to understand the meaning of a given pericope in its historical context.

## Author-Centered: (D) Authority/Intent of the Divine Author

Much like above, texts that focused on the Bible's divine authorship tend to do so through particular uses of language, especially pronouns, to indicate that God is the Biblical author.[13] As the most prevalent concept code within this portion of the coding frame, many of the instances fall into at least three broader reasonings.

First, some texts indicate God's authorship and authority explicitly. While rare, at least one text imagined God as the one speaking to the

---

13. It should be noted that this does not preclude the fact that some text's view Scripture's authorship in a complex way—that both God and humans authored the Bible in partnership. This, and the previous, concept code is not meant to dismiss this complexity, but rather map how the speakers moved from one to the other in their description of interpretive practice.

church about Scripture's commands, saying, "I've got boundaries, God says, and you need to learn to respect them" (T5). In other words, part of God's intention with Scripture is laying out boundaries within which humans are to live and flourish. Interestingly, while a focus on Paul was consistent through the dataset (because of the importance of key Pauline texts to the debate), less consistent was how speakers referred to the author(s) of Leviticus. It was here one could see a clear demarcation for those focusing on the divine author of the Bible, as author-centered texts repeatedly attributed authorship of Leviticus, and other texts whose authorship is unknown such as Genesis, directly to God. Indeed, for some, the use of the term "abomination" in Levitical texts was not the human authors making a point but God "underscoring and emphasizing [a] particular boundary" (T5).

Likewise, in Genesis, and throughout Scripture, some texts say there is a "God given picture" (T10) or "vision . . . design and template" (T8) related to what marriage is and what human sexuality is for, and it is God's intent that believers live according to this (T10). Some texts posit that God provides clear definitions in Scripture, particularly for marriage. When given, "the definition as given by God" for marriage is founded in Genesis and described as being "a covenant bond . . . defined because of creation" (T10, T8). Again, language is seen to play a vital role in interpretive practice.

Secondly, some texts include explicit discussions of God's authority. For example, one text says "The Christian is bound by the law of God, a higher authority" (T6). Further to this, because the Bible is written by God, it contains all humanity needs to understand who God is and "how we are to called to live" as God's holy people (T2). Indeed, God's authority mediated through Scripture binds our authority in some sense, making it so that "we do not have permission to change what Scripture clearly teaches" (T2). This includes church leaders, God's shepherds, who mediate God's authority, through Scripture, via their interpretive practice. As one text puts it, "Quite simply, Paul's the messenger. I'm the messenger. I'm the shepherd. I'm just telling you what God says, but God's the authority" (T14). This speaker went on to argue that the reality of God's authority, mediated through Scripture and God's shepherds, should lead interpreters to ask a question when they read or hear the Bible, especially if they do not like what they are reading: "What did God say here?" (T14). The implication here is that one should care about what God says, even when delivered through sermons or Bible studies, because God is the authority of what God means in a given Scripture passage.

Finally, some texts include intertextual discussions, arguing that Scripture's meaning can only be ascertained by comparing what one passage says with what other passages say, "allowing the biblical narrative to define the terms" (T16). Thus, "we cannot understand who Jesus is . . . unless we know what God has spoke [*sic*] through the Old Testament" (T1). Though perhaps not obvious, the only way I am able to conceive of this functioning in a meaningful way is if the interpreter believes that God is, at least in some sense, the author of the biblical text such that it has an inherent supernatural unity. Because all of Scripture is God-breathed, the individual books that make up the Bible "form a unified whole" (T1). More pointedly regarding explicit intertextual discussions, one text, explaining Genesis 19, argued that "to be Biblical and understand the reason for God's punishment on Sodom," interpreters must take passages such as Ezekiel 14:49–50 and Isaiah 3 into account (T11). Likewise, another text drew attention to Jesus' intertextual discussion in Matthew 19 in which he refers to Genesis 2 in relation to divorce (T10).

## Reader-Centered: (A) Reader Reception

Within some texts, the reader or reading community was given priority by focusing on their reception of Scripture via the interrogation of reader assumptions. While these readers generally understood what Scripture meant on the author's terms, the authors were not taken to be the arbiters of understanding the texts. In other words, Scripture meant what the readers interpreted it to mean, according to both their assumptions regarding and reactions to the text and their understanding of a biblical author's intended meaning. This reaction seems to have happened at two distinct stages of interpretation: during exegesis, and during theological integration (leading to application).

For some texts, reader reception was a critical part of exegesis, such that specific hermeneutical prejudices informing the interpreter's exegetical practice were recognized. For example, by using qualified language to draw hearers into questioning whether what they think Scripture means what it seems to mean, some interpreters drew attention towards contemporary notions and attitudes and allowed those to direct their exegesis. For example, one text, describing the Pauline context, makes a series of assertions followed by asking "Could Paul have been utilizing [a particular background context]? . . . We can't know for certain, *but let's say that's the case*" (T3, emphasis added). Another text argued that Paul was only concerned with adultery, debauchery, and exploitive sex acts which, they assert, were the context of homosexuality in the ancient world. "*If* this is the context," the speaker says, "this is very relevant hermeneutically for the church today" (T13, emphasis added). Other texts pointed to the history of translation, and how words translated "homosexuality" in particular have a checkered translation history, as the basis for revisiting the treatment given to the "clobber" texts especially. Thus, some texts argue that because lesbianism is not mentioned in the Old Testament "this should raise some red flags when trying to suggest this passage [referring to Leviticus 18 and 20] is about homosexuality" (T11, T7, T15) and thus should open interpreters to develop better translations that is informed by ongoing historical research (T16).

In other texts, reader reception occurred on the level of theological integration, whereby the reader rejected the implications of their exegesis. For example, one text reflected theologically on their understanding of a particular Bible passage by saying "the inclusion of homosexuality in the list [found in 1 Timothy 1] may do more to betray Paul's preconceptions than it does [reveal] God's heart and will" (T9). To be sure, T9 argues explicitly that Paul assumes that homosexual sex was "unclean, unnatural, and completely contrary to God's will" and that "this is not an assumption that I agree with." This sentiment is shared by others as well. Discussing Romans 1, one speaker commented, "there are many of us today, especially people in my generation and younger, for whom that kind of language [in the passage] sounds not only foreign but backward and maybe even repulsive" (T3). And yet another text describes the same passage as "insulting and degrading" if it leads to one concluding that Paul was condemning "people who are trying to follow Jesus within loving, monogamous, caring relationships" (T15).

## Reader-Centered: (B) Questioning Authorial Intent

In some texts, authorial intent is openly questioned, though *not* nefariously. Instead, the interpreters understand their questioning of authorial intent in terms of questioning the applicability of passages written by human authors. Thus, there is a discernible struggle in some texts between what a passage says, what it means, and the extent to which an interpreter thinks what it means is applicable in contemporary culture. Some "questioning" even takes the form of assertion, whereby a speaker will say we can certainly know what would have been on Paul's mind, for example, and that this knowledge should inform our interpretations (T15). In other words, the texts are asking if a given cultural context informing pericopes of Scripture "remain relevant to the church's faithful witness today in the 21st century" (T3). Indeed, it is argued, categories of behavior in the Bible should not be taken "at face value" because the human authors "wrote just like any God-fearing present-day preacher, out of limited knowledge and understanding gained through [their] own human walk with God" (T9). Just as it is possible that "revelations of God's heart" are found in Scripture, is it not equally as possible that there are "deep revelations of [the human authors'] own unexamined prejudices" (T9) in their writings? Note that this approach differentiates between human and divine authorship, focusing on the human (both author and readers) while removing the divine from immediate attention.

## Reader-Centered: (C) Dismissive Laughter

While only appearing in two texts, this phenomenon was noteworthy due to the instances being fundamentally the same—the speaker pointing out an element of a passage as a joke and using the ensuing laughter to dismiss the author's intended meaning. Both instances concerned a single clause in Romans 1:30, "they disobey their parents," and infer through the joke that parental disobedience was not a matter of scriptural obedience or sin. While one could infer more than what these speakers intended from these phenomena, I think they reveal a deference to the reading community over and against the authors of Scripture. While negatively stated, I do not think these instances were intended to make light of Scripture. Instead, they utilized a prejudice of the community—thinking disobedience to parents is not a sin, or if it is sin that it is too prevalent for anyone to do anything about it—to make light of a passage's overarching message.

## RECOGNIZING CODE COMPLEXITY

As I hope the reader has begun to see, and will continue to see, in the code descriptions, many of the codes for the subcategories overlap because of the complex layers of prejudices (especially theological prejudices) that lay in the background of each piece of data. Needless to say, this complexity will inevitably aid in the development of inferences in later chapters regarding all of the subcategories of the coding frame. Furthermore, it is important to note how some of the texts do not fit neatly into modernist or postmodernist categories, particularly those which argue for hearing God through the Word, and which argue, or assume, that God's voice is, in some sense, in the text—and knowable within it. These texts are properly more premodern or fundamentalist in character, even as they represent author-centered approaches to the text. This reveals an already discussed point of tension within the project, which will be further reflected on at the end of the chapter.

## Tradition

Each of the concept codes compiled under this subcategory involved discerning the notions of tradition operative in an interpreter's horizon. Again, I begin by summarizing code instances (Table 4) before describing the concept codes. As discussed at the end of the previous chapter, the insight of modernism being ecumenical and postmodernism being sectarian (that is, self-aware of varied traditions and the meaningful differences between them) helped dictate the concept codes for this category. For the subcategory of Ecumenical, the codes of "Prioritization of Unity" and "Flattening of Church History" reveal a modernist-informed critique of tradition. Under the subcategory of Sectarianism, the concept codes of "Recognition of Traditions (positive or negative)," "Recognition of Own Tradition," and "Consistency in Church Teaching" reveal, in part, interpreter's postmodern attitude regarding church tradition(s).

**Table 4**: *Tradition, Concept Code Instances*

| | Ecumenical | | Sectarian | | |
|---|---|---|---|---|---|
| | (A) Prioritization of Unity | (B) Flattening of Church History | (A) Recognition of Traditions (+/-) | (B) Recognition of Own Tradition | (C) Consistency in Church Teaching |
| T1 | | | | 2 | 2 |
| T2 | | | 1 | 2 | |
| T3 | 2 | 1 | 1 | | |
| T4 | | | | | |
| T5 | | | | | |

**Table 4**: *Tradition, Concept Code Instances*

| | Ecumenical | | Sectarian | | |
|---|---|---|---|---|---|
| | (A) Prioritization of Unity | (B) Flattening of Church History | (A) Recognition of Traditions (+/-) | (B) Recognition of Own Tradition | (C) Consistency in Church Teaching |
| T6 | | | | | |
| T7 | | | | | |
| T8 | | | 1 | | |
| T9 | | 2 | 2 | | |
| T10 | | | | | |
| T11 | | 1 | 1 | | |
| T12 | 1 | | 2 | 2 | 1 |
| T13 | 2 | 2 | 3 | 1 | 1 |
| T14 | | | | | |
| T15 | 3 | | 1 | | |
| T16 | 4 | 3 | 1 | | 1 |

## Ecumenical: (A) Prioritization of Unity

Units of meaning coded with this code prioritized the concept of unity in some way, arguing that differences between traditions were less important than certain universally applicable truths. As one text aptly summarizes, "we have one thing in common, that we've been given new life in Christ," and this one common thing supersedes meaningful divisions between believers (T12). Some texts argue this point by describing unity in terms of our "being embraced by the love of God," which "shatters" all tribalism (T3). Indeed, because "God loves sinners, all of us, and has offered all of us redemption in Christ Jesus," the church must now be unified in difference (T13), particularly regarding the differences of interpretations about human sexuality. "Our unity is deeper than uniformity" (T15), and therefore we should be able to engage in "constructive dialogue with Christians who seek to innovate the traditional definition of marriage" (T16). It is clear, for these texts, that unity is prioritized as a central value—both theologically and practically—such that the extent to which believers are unified corresponds to the extent to which they are faithful to the Gospel that unifies.

## Ecumenical: (B) Flattening of Church History

As described in the previous chapter, the "flattening of church history" is the act of bringing disparate traditions together without sufficient respect for their differences, including for how their theological and historical contexts are treated. Importantly, these texts brought disparate traditions together without acknowledging their diversity in the sense of their differences, only pointing towards diversity as a way to reject and move beyond a given tradition. In a number of texts, as has already been seen in the previous paragraph, a value of unity can cause some to remove complexity from church history to focus on larger themes that may or may not accurately reflect the tradition as a whole, such as "justice, compassion, deliverance, mercy, dignity, the sacred worth of every person, and love of neighbor" (T13). While I think this list would be initially agreeable to everyone, the question is whether what is being referred to in this list is understood similarly by different traditions, and the answer to this question is not clear. Indeed, some texts argue that misinterpretations regarding sexuality are keeping people from God (T9), which some texts describe as unjust, but this would not be an overall agreeable conclusion between all the sources of the study.

Likewise, another text argues that the early church was marked by a pattern of "dialogue and respectful debate" that "stabilized us in the past, curbing extremes, maintaining unity" (T16). Yet, the history of the church is also one of sharp disagreement, sometimes leading early church leaders to harsh public denouncements.[14] Thus, in its flattening, elements of the tradition are lost in service to higher values such as unity (T13, T16), justice (T9), and love (T11).

## Sectarian: (A) Recognition of Traditions (Positive or Negative)

The most frequent concept code in the sectarian subcategory, these coded segments showed recognition for interpretation within church traditions other than their own through both positive and negative comments. While

14. The Apostle John is said to have run from a city while exclaiming, about the Ebionite heretic Cerinthus, "Let us fly, lest even the bath-house fall down, because Cerinthus, the enemy of the truth, is within." Likewise, John's disciple Polycarp is said to have declared Marcion "the first-born of Satan." Irenaeus, *Against Heresies*, 3.3.4 (*ANF* 1:416). And Jesus was known to be harsh as well, calling Pharisees a "brood of vipers" and "evil" (Matt 12:34) as but one example among many in the Gospel narratives.

the coding of positive comments about other traditions is self-explanatory, negative comments were included in this concept code because such references revealed a sectarian element. That is, negative evaluations of other traditions imply a recognition of their existence and belief that they are meaningfully different from one's own.

In many of these texts, the above evaluations are expressed by bringing attention to the church's "heritage" of interpretation (T3), as one text put it. In some texts, this included a recognition of the complex nature of tradition in the Bible itself and its notion of "tradition of the elders" (T9). Such references often reflected—positively—on the Pharisees, and the way their interpretive history shaped the church through the ministry of Jesus (T8, T9). In others, this code is expressed by drawing attention to particular eras of church history such as the Reformation (T13) or to the witness of the Christian tradition over millennia. Finally, some texts refer to the history of the church by discussing the history of Bible translation and how mistranslation has negatively informed interpretive practice (T11, T15, T16). Interestingly, each of these codes did not approach tradition as an authoritative voice but as an informative source, especially with regards to contemporary theological integration. Thus, the texts held that interpreters can learn from different eras of church history, but they are also free to critique those eras in order to discern how to faithfully follow Christ today (T13).

## Sectarian: (B) Recognition of Own Tradition

Interestingly, there is little recognition of the Baptist or Anabaptist traditions from the authors of the gathered texts regarding their denominational beliefs about human sexuality. What recognition is made is either in reference to the CBOQ's ongoing debates regarding sexuality and discerning how to vote on motions during CBOQ Assemblies (T1), reciting past Assembly decisions (T2, T12), or in reference to Baptist history unrelated to the topic. One speaker, for example, argued that because Baptists have been persecuted for beliefs about baptism, which diverged significantly from Protestant and Roman Catholic traditions when the movement first emerged, they should understand traditions can change (T13).

However, this lack of reflectivity on their own tradition is not a surprise. CBOQ churches have a history, similar to other baptistic denominations, that has prioritized local church autonomy, but this has more recently been expressed with a disregard for the potential that the tradition (what

Baptists have done in the past) could positively inform what Baptists want to do in the present. Thus, as one text discerned the various aspects of the recent debates at Assembly, they left having heard this message from sister churches: "local autonomy and the freedom of interpretation are more authoritative than the historical interpretation of Scripture" (T2). This being the case, is it any wonder why churches would not look with humility to their history (recent, and long past) for guidance in dealing with this, and other, topics?

## Sectarian: (C) Consistency in Church Teaching

The vast majority of texts do not make reference to any notion of consistency in the church's teaching regarding sexuality, and the ones that do are separable by their positive and negative appraisal of the tradition. However, these appraisals are in some way incidental to what they mean; that is, the interpreters are treating the tradition as a tradition. When evaluating tradition positively, texts drew attention to the history of the church as being something to be both celebrated and guarded, and be treated as normative. "What happens when we see a sister church teaching something that is out of sync with what the majority of Christians throughout history and around the world have interpreted?" (T1). The answer, for this text, is accountability and discipline. Another text makes a similar point, arguing that those who are LGBTQ affirming believe themselves to be more accurate in their biblical interpretive practice than "four thousand years of biblical testimony and Christian thought," including believers around the world who have held to a particular (traditional) view "for the past several thousand years, and still hold today" (T12). When evaluated negatively, some texts point out that the church's consistent, traditional, teaching on sexuality "has blocked us from loving our neighbors properly" (T13) and describe the tradition as the "rejection of homosexuality" caused by the interpretation of "standard biblical proof texts" (T16). These texts treat the tradition as tradition, but recognize it as revisable; that is, that Christianity is, fundamentally, a human tradition that we continue to shape. Even still, these examples recognize a consistency to the church's teaching that at least needs to be accounted for.

Interestingly, this code is another example where a strong element of premodernism or fundamentalism can be discerned, as some texts discuss tradition as though it was authoritative in some sense. Yet, it is authoritative, it would seem, only in so much as the interpreter agrees with the tradition, pointing towards a selective understanding of tradition that, as was discussed in the Scripture category, is more complicated than what can neatly fit within the coding frame.

## Reason

The concept codes of this subcategory (Table 5) discerned the differentiation of emphases between objectivity and subjectivity in the gathered texts. Under the subcategory of Falsification, the concept codes of "Proposition Conforms to Objective Reality," "Objective Truth," and "Openness to Being Wrong/Corrected" reveal emphasis on the objective-subjective divide that marks modernist thought. Under the subcategory of Intersubjectivity, concept codes of "Concern for Outcome of Proposition," "Subjectivity/ Subjective Truth," and "Multiplicity of Views" help discern a postmodern emphasis on the social construction of reality via multiple subjectivities.

**Table 5**: *Reason, Concept Code Instances*

| | Falsification | | | Intersubjectivity | | |
|---|---|---|---|---|---|---|
| | (A) Objective Truth | (B) Openness to Being Wrong/ Corrected | (C) Proposition Conforms to Objective Reality | (A) Subjectivity / Subjective Truth | (B) Multiplicity of Views | (C) Concern for Outcome of Truth Claims |
| T1 | 3 | | 1 | | | 1 |
| T2 | | | | 1 | 1 | |
| T3 | | | | | | 1 |
| T4 | | | | | | 1 |
| T5 | | | 1 | | | |
| T6 | 3 | | | | | |
| T7 | 1 | | 1 | | | 2 |
| T8 | 2 | | 2 | | | |
| T9 | | | | | | 1 |
| T10 | 2 | | | 1 | | |
| T11 | | 2 | | | | 1 |
| T12 | 3 | | | | | 1 |
| T13 | | 6 | | 2 | | 9 |

**Table 5**: *Reason, Concept Code Instances*

| | Falsification | | | Intersubjectivity | | |
|---|---|---|---|---|---|---|
| | (A)<br>Objective<br>Truth | (B)<br>Openness<br>to Being<br>Wrong/<br>Corrected | (C)<br>Proposition<br>Conforms<br>to Objective<br>Reality | (A)<br>Subjectivity<br>/ Subjective<br>Truth | (B)<br>Multiplicity<br>of Views | (C)<br>Concern for<br>Outcome<br>of Truth<br>Claims |
| T14 | 5 | 1 | | | | |
| T15 | | | | 1 | 4 | |
| T16 | | 1 | 2 | | 1 | 8 |

## *Falsification: (A) Objective Truth*

Text segments coded with this concept code focused on truth claims re-garding objectivity and universal applicability throughout history. Thus, texts referring to universality were coded with this concept code, such as "What God has said in the past applies to today, and it will apply tomor-row" (T1), "the same spirit of truth has been guiding the church, affirming the eternal truths of God," (T1) and that no one has "the right" to violate Biblical commands (T14). However, the most often coded segments were those that made explicit reference to objective truth as a meaningful cat-egory for discussions regarding sexuality. This included describing biologi-cal truth as objectively true (T6) and that the Bible is the standard of what "absolute truth" is (T14). One text even says, quite provocatively, that to attack the truth of the Bible is to attack God (T12). At least two texts, both sermons, also include critiques of intersubjectivity on the grounds that two contradictory truth claims cannot both be correct; one must be right, one must be wrong (T6, T10). Some texts also used facts and figures such as found in scientific studies to build their rhetorical arguments, the use of which assumes that there is objective truth that is measurable and testable in a scientific sense (T7, T8).

## *Falsification: (B) Openness to Being Wrong/Corrected*

The core idea of this concept code is that Christians should let the evi-dence lead them—especially "when it leads in directions you least expect" (T11). Yes, we need to let Scripture speak, but "transformative encounters with real people" are also necessary to give new perspectives and, perhaps, cause a change of mind (T11, T13). Indeed, interpreters should not be doctrinaire, one speaker argues, which means being "impervious to contrary data" but be willing to listen and be confronted by life stories that may shake understandings and "shatter . . . old paradigms of reading Scripture" (T13). All of these coded segments argue that Christians must be open to being wrong about their interpretive conclusions, and open to change if the evidence leads there—in a phrase, we must be open to falsification. Indeed, many gathered texts assumed falsification, as they explicitly want listeners to change their minds, though few were reflexive on this.[15]

## *Falsification: (C) Truth Claim Conforms to Objective Reality*

Units of meaning coded with this concept code all involved some sort of description of reality as objective; that there is something true about the universe independent of one's subjectivity. For example, God has designed the world (T8), sinfulness is expressed in all areas of life including the sexual, social, and economic (T16, T1), the Christian sexual ethic is attractive because it conforms to God's boundaries (T5), that God speaks and does so through the Bible (T7), and that "there is a genetic biological reality" regarding sex and gender (T8).

One text notably argued that propositions should conform to reality by reflecting negatively on how the inverse of this code is becoming increasingly true—namely, that the outcome of propositions are becoming more important to Canadian Christians in discerning truth. Discussing the Canadian context, the speaker shared, "it is [now thought] the church must change our point of view. Out of love for our friends and family, we tend to relinquish our theological convictions because we don't want to hurt other people's feelings" (T1). In essence, this text argues that the outcome or application of a theological position is not the most important or guiding consideration for whether it is true. Instead, the text says, believers ought to allow the truth of our theology to shape our lives, which may actually lead to discomfort, and even suffering, when faced with inconvenient or

---

15. One text (T15) explicitly states that their goal was not to change listeners' minds. Yet this was said during a sermon where one interpretation was argued for and another dismissed and disparaged, suggesting that the stated goal was at odds with an inherent quality of falsification that lay unreflectively beneath the surface of their thinking.

unpleasant truths about what discipleship in the way of Jesus actually entails (cf. Mark 10:22).

While similar to the Objective Truth concept code, this code is distinguished by a focus on reality (rather than all truth claims generally) as being objective outside of one's subjective frame. Stated as a linguistic metaphor, while language may be socially constructed, that to which language refers is not—and these coded segments draw attention to what is being referenced.

## Intersubjectivity: (A) Subjectivity/Subjective Truth

Like the "Objective Truth" code above, this concept code was used when the idea of subjectivity was explicitly mentioned or described. For some texts, their recognition of subjectivity was one of mourning, as the texts recognized how the idea that truth is fundamentally contextual now permeates Canadian culture. One text reflects that "everyone has a different understanding of truth. We no longer believe in absolute truth" (T2) while another describes the Canadian context as one where "whatever belief you have, [it] is equally as valid as my belief in my God and nobody's wrong" (T10). Approaching subjectivity more positively, another text repeatedly highlighted how the lived experiences of others can teach us about what the Bible says. Indeed, for this text's speaker, bringing together multiple subjectivities is what "opened [their] mind and heart to a reconsideration" of their interpretive practice (T13). In Gadamerian terms, we might say that this concept code is the prioritization of one's own horizon over the horizon of others (including history), such that one's understanding of what is true must necessarily conform to their understanding of their horizon, which is then used to make sense of every other horizon—either through dismissal or by conforming other horizons to our own (or vice-versa).

## Intersubjectivity: (B) Multiplicity of Views

Within this concept code, I did not code every mention that there is a multiplicity of views, generally or about the LGBTQ debate. Instead, I only coded those instances that viewed this multiplicity in a positive or neutral light, which suggests that multiplicity is necessary for developing robust understanding. In the main text this code is found, while describing their approach to discussing sexuality and marriage the speaker reflects on how the multiplicity of views within their church is a benefit because of how it bears witness to unity (T15). In fact, the stated goal in this text is to help people hold whatever position they have come to "as healthy and fruitful[ly] as possible" (T15). While not found extensively in the dataset, this code does correspond to others (such as the prioritization of unity) such that it will be useful for developing inferences and drawing conclusions in later chapters.

## *Intersubjectivity: (C) Concern for Outcome of Truth Claims*

By far the most used concept code within this portion of the coding frame was a concern for the outcome of truth claims or propositions, which appeared often and repeatedly in a majority of texts. In these coded segments, a proposition is judged to be correct according to its perceived outcome. While never using these terms, these code segments are expressions of the postmodern belief that truth claims are, at their core, power claims, and as such must be judged according to how their power is wielded. The church's sexual ethics teaching are thus judged according to whether they have caused pain or hurt (T3, T13), led Christians into deeper practice of love (T4), led to the church justifying prejudice and hatred (T7, T9), caused marginalization and persecution (T11), caused negative health and behavioral problems (T13), caused the church's witness to be damaged (T16), or caused harm (T16). Thus, as one speaker concluded, the "LGBTQ issue is not primarily a sexual ethics issue, . . . it's a human wellbeing issue" (T13).

This concept code represents a concern much deeper than not wanting to hurt the feelings of family and friends (though it should not be considered less). One text in particular summarized this code, and the attitude behind it for many affirming churches in particular, best by saying, "the affirming view . . .[is] often really in tune with the deep pain the church has caused the LGBTQ community. They might see the traditional view as callous and out of touch and bereft to the embodied love of Christ" (T3). Indeed, "the condemnation and rejection of a homosexual person is . . . sinful . . . based on fear and prejudice and has no place in the church" (T12).

## Experience

In this final subcategory, the concept codes describe experiences of God within the sub-categorical frames of transcendence and immanence (Table 6). Under the subcategory of Transcendence, the concept codes of "Moral

Code/Boundaries," "God's Attributes," and "Divine Judgment and Wrath" reveal an emphasis on God as an actor in history who is distant and distinct from (that is, sovereign over) humanity. Under the subcategory of Immanence, concept codes of "Holy Spirit (Divine Presence and Power)" and "God Speaking Apart from Scripture" help describe the postmodern shift away from transcendence and the prioritization of God's nearness (and especially Christ's humanity). After summarizing these final codes, I will move on to discussing other themes and notable patterns within the data that will provide further context for building inferences in chapter 5.

**Table 6**: *Experience, Concept Code Instances*

| | Transcendence | | | Immanence | |
|---|---|---|---|---|---|
| | (A) Moral Code/ Boundaries | (B) God's Attributes | (C) Divine Judgment and Wrath | (A) Holy Spirit / Divine Presence & Power | (B) God Speaking Apart from Scripture |
| T1 | | 1 | 1 | 1 | |
| T2 | | 1 | 1 | 1 | 3 |
| T3 | | | | 1 | 1 |
| T4 | | | | | 2 |
| T5 | 2 | 1 | 3 | | |
| T6 | 1 | 2 | 3 | | |
| T7 | | | | | |
| T8 | | 2 | | | |
| T9 | | | 1 | | 1 |
| T10 | 1 | | 1 | | |
| T11 | | | | | |
| T12 | | 3 | | 1 | |
| T13 | | | 2 | 2 | |
| T14 | 3 | 1 | 1 | 2 | |
| T15 | | | | 4 | 2 |
| T16 | 1 | | | 2 | |

## Transcendence: (A) Moral Code/Boundaries

In some texts, one's experience of God is tied to being given a moral code or boundaries by which God requires us to live. These boundaries are not just given through declaration; they are built into the world, and thus "transcend" our capacity to understand them (and are universally applicable across time and contexts). Through reference to boundaries (T10), crossing lines that ought not be crossed (T5), and the necessity of abiding by God's moral and natural laws (T6, T14), a picture is painted of a God whose boundaries structure human life. In the words of one text that summarizes the point made in many of the coded segments, "crossing lines that God has established results in significant harm and dysfunction in this life and exile and death in the life to come" (T5).

As mentioned in the previous chapter, both transcendence and immanence are connected to author and reader centeredness such that it can be expected that codes and themes will repeat between them—transcendence with a focus on author, and immanence focusing on reader. This seems true of this code, which corresponds with the "Authority/Intent of the Divine Author" concept code in the Scripture category.

## Transcendence: (B) God's Attributes

When discussing ethical questions, such as sexual ethics and marriage, some texts used the topic to reflect on God's attributes and offered explicit recognition of God's distance in terms of otherness. God is eternal (T1, T2), unchanging (T12), the alpha and omega (T12), "sacred, the source of life . . . the source of truth, justice, righteousness, and beauty. He's a creator. God is sacred" (T6). And because humans are made in the image of this God, the breaking of God-given boundaries is akin to both a denial of God's attributes and "vandalism" against God's image bearers (T6, T8, T14). By abiding by God's moral boundaries, particularly regarding sex, Christians bring glory to God. Indeed, the created or natural order is an important element to this in some texts, drawing attention to God's oneness-in-difference and the oneness-in-difference of men and women bound together in marriage (T8) as a way to draw a line from who God is to the conditions God has made that allow for humanity, as a species, to flourish.

## Transcendence: (C) Divine Judgment and Wrath

Above all other actions, God's act of judgment was most regularly referred to in the texts, which consistently included an explicit concern for both people's current circumstance of being under judgment and the expectation of future judgment, especially in the eschatological age to come. As T5 has already been noted as saying, which effectively summarizes an idea found in multiple texts, "crossing lines that God has established will result in chaos and conflict and social dysfunction in the here and now, and then judgment, exile, and death in the life hereafter" (T5; similarly, T2, T6, T10). Talk of judgment is also used as a way of warning those a speaker sees as at risk of being found condemned on the day of judgment. Indeed, working through one's interpretations regarding homosexuality "is for now, but *also* for that moment when Christ returns, that our lives, when they are held in review, may be seen as pure and blameless and fruitful, having brought glory and praise to God" (T13). The above is especially held true for Christian leaders who teach and will be judged more harshly (Jas 3:1), giving a "weightiness" to the responsibility of Christian leadership in the area of interpretation (T13). These texts appear to share a conviction that Christians will all, one day, experience God's just judgment, and for Christian leaders especially this will include the judgment of teaching—which is, necessarily, the articulation of ones interpretations in verbal form.

## *Immanence: (A) Holy Spirit/Divine Presence and Power*

The most prevalent code in this subcategory, segments coded with this concept code draw attention to the fact of the Holy Spirit's immanent presence, and that through this presence humanity has access to God. Importantly, this access is an immanently mediated access—it is the Spirit's presence being mediated by other humans (individually and communally), by nature (in an almost panentheistic sense), and through text such as Scripture.[16] In these codes there was a pattern of insisting that, like the Apostles did (T1), if we stopped to listen—especially to other perspectives—the Holy Spirit would speak to and lead us into all truth in debates about sexuality (T2, T14, T15, T16). At least one text expanded on this, exhorting hearers to "have ears to hear what the Spirit is saying" with the hope that the hearers

---

16. This final point must be differentiated, as the approach to Scripture within this code is reader centered and thus it is Scripture as text, rather than Scripture as *sacred* text, which is in view. In other words, one's experience of the Holy Spirit is mediated through any text, though particularly the Bible because of the Bible's role in the Christian faith. In some sense, this may be describable in terms of the experience of awe-struck inspiration when we witness a majestic sunset, hear beautiful prose, or consume emotional media (moves, TV, books).

would be led "into a space that is beyond the boxes that we can check and . . . into a life in God's kingdom" (T15).

To be sure, the language of "encounter" (T13) summarizes much, as the texts consistently indicate that interpreters both expected and experienced God's presence in various ways, which shaped their interpretive practice (T2, T3, T12, T13, T14, T15). In other words, their experience of the Holy Spirit was one of cooperation, a sort of co-option of the Scripture-focused doctrine of divine accommodation. Interestingly, this expectation was also tied in some texts to the experiences of the Holy Spirit in the early church, namely Peter's vision in Acts 10 and the Council of Jerusalem in Acts 15. For both, the interpreters saw connections between the present debate and the early debates surrounding gentile inclusion in the church's life, arguing that *perhaps* the church today is in "an Acts 15 moment" (T15) for LGBTQ inclusion (T3, T4). If we are to know whether that *perhaps* is a *certainty*, some texts argue, we must look for the Spirit and the fruit of the Spirit's work in the lives of those around us (T15, T16).

## Immanence: (B) God Speaking Apart from Scripture

Finally, some texts indicate that God speaks to the church through means other than the Bible, which informs their interpretations of Scripture. For example, "we can hear [God] speaking through the cries of liberation" (T2), we are to "discern what the Spirit is saying" (T4; similarly, T15), and we listen for God's voice calling to us and follow His lead (T3, T4, T15). Each of these is to inform how the Bible is understood, complexifying its message and enabling believers to think creatively about how they might live as God's people today. Like the previous, this code surmises cooperation between God and human as the foundation of our experience of God. One text also exhorts that God will speak through other people and their stories, if we would only listen (T2). When God speaks, God's people are to listen, even if that speaking is done apart from the pages of the Bible, and should inform how the Bible is understood when it is read. However, this raises an important question: how can we know that we are hearing the voice of God and listening to the Holy Spirit? The coded texts do not broach this issue, leaving a critical gap between their description of interpretive practice and the actual practice itself.

## Conclusion: Coding Frame

In each of the above sections, concept codes representing units of meaning in the gathered texts have been discussed. Each section reviewed subcategories and the respective concept codes grouped together within them, and which, when taken together, begin to help us understand what is going on in the interpretive process. Using these concept codes, I will begin developing inferences and drawing conclusions regarding biblical interpretive practice that will help clarify the complexity of the sexuality debate, which in turn will offer the resources from which a tool to help the church understand, reflect on, and discuss interpretive practice can be developed.

### CONTENT ANALYSIS OUTSIDE THE CODING FRAME

Besides the coding frame, content analysis also involves finding general themes and patterns that can be useful for developing inferences. As such, I discerned four secondary themes that are worth reviewing, as they will be important for discussing hermeneutic conclusions based on the coding frame and concept coding overviewed in this chapter. These themes are the *Use of the Bible, Scripture as Revelation, Hermeneutic Procedures,* and a problem of *Fundamentalism and the Premodern Impulse.* Below, I will briefly describe and discuss each of these themes.

## Use of the Bible

Alongside the core five or six "clobber passages" used in the sexuality debate, other passages regularly appeared in discussion. Interestingly, not every clobber passage was utilized in every sermon, with some sermons focusing only on a handful of texts (or only one at a time). The table below (Table 7) shows which biblical passages, relevant to the sexuality debate, were referenced throughout the texts. This chart will be further analyzed and complexified in the following chapters, as patterns within it will prove valuable when correlated to the coding frame.

**Table** 7: *Relevant Bible Passages Referenced in Data Set*

| | Gen 1/2 | Gen 19 | Lev | Rom 1 | 1 Cor 6 | 1 Tim 1 | Matt 19 | Other Foci |
|---|---|---|---|---|---|---|---|---|
| T1 | X | X | X | X | X | X | X | 2 Tim 3:16 |
| T2 | X | | | | | | | |
| T3 | | | | X | | | | Acts 10 |
| T4 | | | | | | | | Acts 10 |
| T5 | X | | X | | X | | | OT Focus |
| T6 | X | | X | | | | | Mark 12 |
| T7 | | X | X | | | | | OT Only |
| T8 | X | | | | | | X | |
| T9 | | | | X | X | X | | NT Only |
| T10 | X | | X | X | X | | X | |
| T11 | | X | X | X | X | X | | Ezek 16:49–50 |
| T12 | X | | X | X | X | | | |
| T13 | X | X | X | X | X | X | | |
| T14 | X | | X | X | X | | X | |
| T15 | | X | X | X | X | X | | Acts 10, 15 |
| T16 | | X | X | X | X | X | | Jude |

## Scripture as Revelation

There was a theme in some texts (T1, T2, T5, T12, T14) of explicitly referencing a theology of revelation that was operative as part of the interpreter's theological assumptions. One text even explained the interpretive conclusions of those they disagreed with as having "deep respect for biblical revelation" (T3). While not described in any significant detail, each of the texts that discusses revelation is careful to point out the purpose of revelation, which is, as one text puts it, "to reveal God's word in the flesh; that we might know Him and enter into a relationship with Him that never ends" (T1). Indeed, there is a sense in the texts that the Bible reveals something both of whom God is and who God wills for His people to be (T12, T2, T5, T14). The above corresponds with the theology of revelation I described in chapter 2. Furthermore, the instances of a theology of revelation being

verbalized, at least in a limited sense, corresponds to one particular interpretive conclusion, providing an important pattern that will help reveal
part of what is going on under the surface of the sexuality debate.

## Hermeneutical (and Exegetical) Procedure

In a handful of texts, the authors noted the importance of having a proper
procedure of interpretation. As a text puts it, "you should be able to...give an
adequate explanation of why you hold your beliefs about homosexuality and
what the Bible says about it" (T6), even as any interpretation of Scripture is,
at best, an attempt at seeing "at least dimly" (T13)—referring to 1 Cor 13:12.
To this end, one text (T7) gives a specific procedure one should use when
interpreting Scripture: one must (i) pray for God's guidance, (ii) compare
translations, (iii) read the verse in its literary context, and (iv) read the verse
in its cultural context. However, when the speaker then worked through this
procedure, they spent little time on steps one or two and focused the bulk of
attention on steps three and four. In fact, steps three and four were explicitly combined into one step, with the speaker suggesting that these steps are
so "intertwined" one could not perform one without performing the other
simultaneously. This raises questions about hermeneutical procedures more
generally, and about the implications of these procedures. Furthermore, this
theme is a touchpoint for the discussion of rigour which this chapter began
with—for this project will only be able to be considered trustworthy and
rigorous if its outcome is a plausible description of hermeneutical elements
that faithfully describes interpretive practice in a way that is coherent, use-
able, and understandable in the church.

## Fundamentalism and the Premodern Impulse

In the discussion of the Scripture and Tradition codes, there were various
examples of coded texts which did not fit perfectly into the coding frame,
due to the bifurcation of modernism and postmodernism being an imposition on the texts to describe differences. Yet, fundamentalism (and, by
extension, premodernism) has been an active influence in the CBOQ for
more than a century. Thus, how this movement might be coded in the data
is an important, and surprisingly complicated, question.

    While fundamentalism could almost certainly be classified as pre-
modern (that is, pre-critical) during its early decades, by the time it was

most influential in the CBOQ—during the fundamentalism-modernism debate in the 1920s—it had morphed into a distinct modernism-informed movement, whose various elements continue to inform CBOQ churches today. One of the core distinctive features is found in fundamentalism's penchant for co-opting a cultural mood in order to both critique *and answer the critiques of* that mood.[17] By "co-opting" I do not mean to imply ill-intent. The fundamentalist—as everyone does—swims in cultural waters saturated with ideas, now informed by modernism, postmodernism, and all that came before. Given this, it is an inevitability that cultural moods will be absorbed and utilized as one attempts to make sense of the world. In other words, as Bruce Lawrence argues in relation to the twentieth century, fundamentalism "accepts the instrumental benefits of modernity but not its value reorientations."[18] Indeed, as Gideon Aran further clarifies, modernity ended up nurturing fundamentalism, giving it the structures of thought necessary for the movement's survival and growth.[19] Insomuch as this was the case in the early twentieth century, I expect it to also be the case in the twenty first century.

It was for this reason that 1920s-era fundamentalism has been mistaken as anti-modernism, even though the core of the fundamentalist project was distinctly modern—that is, as stated above, fundamentalists used modernist structures of thought to make a case for the faith. Lawrence further clarifies that this does not mean fundamentalism is modernist, even as "fundamentalists are products of modernity"; instead, it is an "ideology differentiated but not separated from . . . the modernist worldview," ironically indebted to it for coherence.[20] Indeed, fundamentalism is so informed by modernism that many of its convictions are, essentially, modernist in character.[21] Critically, this includes its approach to Scripture, which Ammerman describes as a "systemic, rational approach to finding and organizing the facts of Scripture [that] reflects the nineteenth century scientific world from which the movement emerged."[22] Rather than a movement that is in simple opposition to the modernist project, fundamentalism utilized

17. Hoffmeister, "Fundamentalism and Modernity," 5; Ammerman, "North American," 14–15.

18. Lawrence, *Defenders*, 6.

19. Aran, "Zionist Fundamentalism," 331.

20. Lawrence, *Defenders*, 2–3, 20.

21. Ammerman, "North American," 8.

22. Ammerman, "North American," 9.

the structural tools of modernism in order to both critique modernism (and its underlying structure) as well as develop a self-understanding that made sense in the increasingly "modern" world—a habit which continues to inform elements of fundamentalism today.

Similarly, contemporary fundamentalism is, in some ways, postmodern, in so much as it is sectarian (in the sense of my coding frame). Indeed, postmodernism's approach to tradition gives space for fundamentalism. As Caputo has said, tradition is "a responsibility to read, to interpret, to sift and select responsibly among many competing strands of tradition and interpretations of tradition. If you have a tradition, you have to take *responsibility* for it and its multiplicity."[23] The postmodern 'flavour' of fundamentalism takes responsibility for multiplicity by embracing the inevitability and necessity of tradition, but does so while antagonistically rejecting any tradition that challenges the authority of the fundamentalist tradition itself. In this way, while the postmodernism-informed fundamentalism may seem anti-postmodern, it is in fact utilizing the underlying structures of postmodernism to erect a defense and renewed self-understanding in an attempt to make itself comprehensible in the postmodern frame.

The above discussion raises an important question: if fundamentalism takes on elements of a dominant cultural milieu, what might a metamodern fundamentalism look like? As already discussed, it may take the form of (or co-opt) the theological interpretation of Scripture movement, which has already been noted as self-describing as a return to the premodern. Yet, as noted, such a description is not accurate, as a return to the premodern is not possible. I hypothesize that metamodern fundamentalism could be expressed as a prejudiced oscillation between modern and postmodern sensibilities, whose core prejudice will be the self-protection of the fundamentalist self-understanding as *the* faithful Protestant tradition. Indeed, while robustly describing this phenomenon is outside of my project's aim, I suspect that a form of metamodern fundamentalism is present within the dataset, whereby interpreters are selectively utilizing both modern and postmodern concepts in ways that make it seem as though they are premodern, in an attempt to "return" to a place (the premodern) to which it is not possible to return. Because the concepts are hidden behind an unspoken prejudice, teasing them out from either the truly modernist or postmodernist concepts is not possible in the context of the present project. It is on this point that my project may prove helpful, as the paradigm

---

23. Caputo, *Deconstruction*, 37.

proposed in chapter 6 can help bring awareness to the culturally informed oscillations in interpretive practice and help reveal the extent to which one's interpretive practice is not premodern, modern, or postmodern, but metamodern in character.

## CONCLUDING SUMMARY

Having overviewed the coding frame and themes emerging from the dataset, I can now move towards developing inferences to clarify differences in interpretive practice of individuals and churches in the CBOQ and beyond. This analysis has shown the complexity of interpretive practice in the metamodern mood, as interpreters jump between modern and postmodern notions of Scripture, Tradition, Reason, and Experience in an effort to understand the Bible—and through this, understand the world. As the coding has revealed, the various emphases for the modern and postmodern notions of each of the Quadrilateral's sources are sufficiently different from one another that if a conversation about interpretation was had without reflecting on the deeper cultural assumptions informing their theological thinking, conversation partners would be bound to speak past one another, even entering into prolonged conflict because of it.

While possibly unavoidable, conflict about interpretation does not have to be an exercise in devouring one another. Rather, it can be dialogue, which, as iron sharpens iron, can strengthen faith in and fidelity to Christ. This does not preclude division at some stage, but does suggest a better way forward—having conversations about Scripture that are marked by reflexivity, clear theological thinking, and a passion for Christ and his Gospel, such that God is glorified by these conversations as well as the embodiment of our interpretations once those conversations are over. In the following chapter, I will interpret the content analysis and further describe patterns within the dataset, to both understand the present sexuality debate and help describe a better way forward for discussing one's understanding of interpretive practice

# 5

# Describing Interpretive Practice

In the previous chapter, I utilized hermeneutic content analysis to analyze various gathered texts—sermons, studies, and other sources—that discussed biblical interpretive practice regarding sexuality and marriage. In this chapter, I will build on the results of my coding to further describe differences in interpretive practice that will reveal, in part, why the interpretive debate regarding sexuality is so complex. Furthermore, this chapter will also lay the groundwork for developing a tool to aid in understanding and describing biblical interpretive practice. The chapter will begin by overviewing the coding, with an added layer of complexification by acknowledging each text's interpretive conclusion, before revealing patterns in the dataset and describing critical differences in biblical interpretive practice that have emerged from the hermeneutic content analysis.

## CODING PATTERNS AND INFERENCES

While the coding outcomes, showing the prevalence of the code subcategories, were shared in the last chapter, a critical piece of information was missing: interpretive conclusions. While these conclusions, "traditional" and "affirming," were alluded to or confessed in the texts and my discussion, the point of not making these conclusions clear up-front was to allow the reader to perceive the metamodern oscillation in the texts without the prejudice of knowing these conclusions. I also did not want to give the impression that the texts aligned perfectly. Indeed, as discussed at the end of chapter 3, my categorization of poles is representative of a range of views and, as will be seen shortly, the conclusions of the texts are related to, but do not precisely match, patterns of hermeneutic oscillation in and between categories of modernism and postmodernism.

Below (Table 8) is the chart of subcategory coding instances, with each text now labeled and arranged according to its interpretive conclusions regarding sexuality and marriage. As is apparent based on these coding instances, there is oscillation between poles of the coding frame. However, not every text contained these oscillations in every quadrant, and those that did oscillate did not necessarily do so robustly.

**Table 8**: *Coding Frame, Reorganized and Labeled with Interpretive Conclusions*

| Text (T) | TR/AFF | Scripture | | Tradition | | Reason | | Experience | |
|---|---|---|---|---|---|---|---|---|---|
| | | Author | Reader | Ecumenical | Sectarian | Falsification | Inter-subjectivity | Transcend. | Immanence |
| T1 | TR | ▬ | | | ▬ | ▬ | ▪ | ▬ | ▪ |
| T2 | TR | ▬ | | | ▬ | | ▬ | ▬ | ▬ |
| T5 | TR | ▪ | | | | ▪ | | ▬ | |
| T6 | TR | ▬ | | | | ▬ | | ▬ | |
| T8 | TR | ▪ | | | ▪ | ▬ | | ▬ | |
| T10 | TR | ▬ | | | | | ▬ ▪ | ▬ | |
| T12 | TR | ▬ | | ▪ | ▬ | ▬ | ▪ | ▬ | ▪ |
| T14 | TR | ▬ | | | | ▬ | | ▬ | ▪ |
| T3 | AFF | | ▬ | ▬ | ▪ | | ▪ | | ▬ |
| T4 | AFF | | | | | | ▪ | | ▬ |
| T7 | AFF | ▪ | ▬ | | | ▬ | ▬ | | |
| T9 | AFF | ▪ | ▬ | | ▬ ▬ | | ▪ | ▪ | ▪ |
| T11 | AFF | ▪ | ▬ | ▪ | ▪ | ▬ | ▪ | | |
| T13 | AFF | ▪ | ▬ | ▬ | ▬ | ▬ | ▬ | ▬ | ▬ |
| T15 | AFF | ▬ | ▬ | ▬ | ▪ | | ▬ | | ▬ |
| T16 | AFF | ▬ | ▬ | ▬ | ▬ | ▬ | ▬ | ▪ | ▬ |

Postulating why a lack of oscillation occurred may help explain some patterns within the dataset. First, the nature of the debate as being *about* the poles—either you believe in "this" conclusion or "that" conclusion—may make the framing of the discussion more lopsided, even as the interpreters hold a metamodern tension in their interpretive practice. Secondly, it could be an indication of rhetoric; speakers arguing for the LGBTQ-affirming position argue their point knowing that their hearers may carry certain theological presuppositions that will need to be addressed if their interpretation is to be viable for those hearers, whether modernist or postmodernist. Relatedly, the genres of gathered texts may play a role, as each were public attempts at arguing for a given interpretive conclusion. Indeed, it is plausible that, for some, their church community acted as a prejudice that constrained their description of interpretive practice.

The above is especially worth considering further in reference to the CBOQ, as I suspect any distinct lack of oscillation in the description of interpretive practice may be, as mentioned at the end of the previous chapter, an artifact of the modernism-fundamentalism debates the CBOQ endured in the 1920s. This conflict anecdotally continues to mark the denomination's self-understanding and its reputation in North American evangelical church culture. As many CBOQ churches come from either modernist or fundamentalist roots, those wishing to move beyond one or the other must address them directly. At the same time, those looking to keep a status quo (and/or defend themselves) may not feel the need to address competing views in any substantive way, instead choosing to ignore them insomuch as they do not see competing interpretations as valid. This would make oscillations muted in some churches' self-description of interpretation, essentially masking or obfuscating the metamodern mood's effect on interpretive practice.

Given the above possible explanations, I expected those texts arguing for the affirming position to be coded with more regularity on *both* sides of the coding frame than texts arguing for the traditional perspective. Indeed, this was the case. Of 243 code instances, I evaluated that 133 were modern, and 110 were postmodern. However, when broken down, the modernist codes appeared 84 times in "traditional" texts and 49 times in "affirming" texts, while postmodern codes only appeared in 26 "traditional" texts, with the remaining 84 instances appearing in "affirming" texts. This may, on the surface, suggest that modernism-leaning interpreters are bound to be non-affirming and postmodernism-leaning interpreters are bound to be affirming. However, such a conclusion is an oversimplification that ignores the true complexity in contemporary interpretive practice. Indeed, when broken down to individual concept codes, the coding reveals patterns and blind spots for how each conclusion is communicated, revealing fertile ground for describing important differences between perspectives. In the following subsections I will move through each category of the Quadrilateral to briefly discuss the dominant concept codes for each pole of the coding frame, complexified by the added knowledge of the text's interpretive conclusions. From this, I will then begin inferring differences in interpretive practice that my coding analysis has revealed.

## Scripture

Codes for modernism-informed understandings of Scripture were each used by at least one affirming text but were dominated in use by traditional texts. Of note was the "Authority/Intent of the Divine Author" code, which was found in all eight traditional texts and two affirming texts. The "God Speaks through the Word" code was of secondary note, used in five traditional texts and one affirming. The code "Intent of the Human Author" had an interesting usage, as it was discerned in three affirming texts and two traditional, making it the only "affirming" leaning code on the modernism side of the coding frame. This is interesting because the Divine Author code is utilized in the two traditional texts, but this is only utilized in one of the three affirming texts, which may hint towards a difference in how the interpreters understand, and thus approach, the Bible as Scripture. On the postmodernism pole, "Reader Reception" was found in seven out of eight affirming texts and in no traditional texts. Similarly, the code "Questioning Authorial Intent" was in five of eight affirming texts and no traditional texts.

Given the overview of hermeneutics offered in chapter 2, expressed by the author-centered and reader-centered subcategories, the utilized codes of the Scripture quadrant are not surprising. In fact, they fit with the broad strokes of what has already been noted regarding modern and postmodern interpretive practice, though with an added detail of the concern for the divine author in the modernism-coded texts.

## Tradition

What is clear for both poles of the coding frame is that affirming texts more robustly acknowledged tradition in both the ecumenical (modernism) and sectarian (postmodernism) subcategories. In the ecumenical subcategory, "Flattening of Church History" was coded in five affirming texts and "Prioritization of Unity" coded in four affirming and one traditional texts. Under the sectarian category, the code "Recognition of Tradition (positive and negative)" was used in six affirming texts and three traditional, making it the most used code of the Tradition quadrant.

The Tradition quadrant may best illustrate, in the present data set, how the metamodern mood can lead to unexpected hermeneutical tensions. For example, it is noteworthy that traditional texts approach tradition in a postmodern way. Likewise, affirming texts oscillate more robustly between modernism and postmodernism codes in this quadrant while holding to a distinctly modernist approach to tradition. Interestingly, across the board, traditional texts barely reflect on tradition—including their own. While already discussed above, it is critical to again point out that the lack of reflection on tradition may be due to several denomination-specific factors within the CBOQ. Although, while I would expect other denominations with a stronger sense of tradition—such as Roman Catholic, Reformed, Anglican, or Presbyterian churches—to have a more robust oscillation, it is also possible that modernism's approach to tradition is such that reflection on what has been is not held as a high value in theological integration.

## Reason

In the subcategories of the Reason quadrant, the modernism code of "Objective Truth" was used by six traditional texts and one affirming text. This is the only modernism code dominated by traditional texts, as the other falsification concept codes were found in more affirming texts (six) than traditional (three). Of note, T13 had the highest number of code instances on the modernism pole for the code "Open to Being Wrong/Corrected," showing an important modernist impulse that further reveals the metamodern approach at play in the interpreter's practice. This text repeatedly insisted on the importance of listeners being open to having their minds changed and seemed to have been doing this for a rhetorical purpose, as the author's explicit goal was to change the listener's mind. Thus, by repeating the idea of being open to correction, the listener might take on this posture and then be (gently) corrected by the speaker.

Interestingly, T13 also had the highest number of code instances on the postmodern pole—which is also the highest number of code instances for any single code in the entire coding frame. In this text, "Concern for Outcome of Truth Claims" was used nine times, reinforcing the text's rhetorical approach discussed above. Furthermore, this code was utilized in seven of the eight affirming texts and two traditional texts, representing the significant majority of intersubjectivity concept code instances.

The two principal concept codes for this category—"Objective Truth" and "Concern for Outcome of Truth Claims"—represent a critical inflection point or convergent boundary, as they are opposed to one another in a meaningful sense. As discussed in chapter 3, postmodernists are concerned that truth claims are unjust attempts at domination. Thus, a concern for the outcome of propositions is necessarily a concern about power differentials between individuals and groups. Related to the sexuality debates, this is only heightened as modernism-informed interpreters make claims about ultimate reality that postmodernism-leaning interpreters find oppressive on the level of personal identity (that is, the claims oppress who someone *is*). Thus, the modernist concern for objective truth confronts the postmodern concern for how truth claims affect people, creating a significant place of conflict. In my estimation, insomuch as this difference in approach to Reason is left undeclared, conversation regarding sexuality (and other topics) will become increasingly difficult, if not eventually impossible, as the metamodern era continues developing. This point will be further discussed below.

## Experience

Finally, in the Transcendence subcategory, "Divine Judgment and Wrath" is the most utilized code, with instances in six traditional texts and two affirming. However, the code "God's Attributes" is used in seven traditional texts, and "Moral Code/Boundaries" in half of the traditional texts (four) and one affirming text. Unlike these lopsided codings, the Immanence subcategory codes were much less utilized but more balanced between traditional and affirming texts. The code used in the majority of texts was "Holy Spirit/ Divine Presence and Power," which was found in eight texts in total—four traditional and four affirming. The second most used postmodern code in the Immanence category was "God Speaking apart from Scripture," utilized in five texts, four affirming and one traditional.

There is an interesting contrast in how the texts deal with agency in this code category. On the one hand, traditional texts place a great deal of agency with God—it is God who acts, God who creates boundaries, God who judges, etc.—while affirming texts placed more emphasis on co-agency between God and humanity. Yes, God acts, they agree, but these texts also remind us that humans are to act in response, including in the act of biblical interpretation. Thus, God speaks, but are we listening to every avenue by which God speaks? God judges, but do we really know the criteria by which this judgment comes? God gives boundaries, but God can choose to remove boundaries if God wants—and He has done so before, so why suppose it will not happen again? In effect, the codes draw attention to how the texts primarily think about God.

## Initial Reflection on Patterns

Given the above description of the coding and highlighting of dominant codes in each subcategory, I can begin discussing patterns within the dataset that will help make sense of the complexity at hand. Before doing so, it is important to return to and reflect on one final, critical, pattern: if the interpreters are metamodern (which I am presuming they all are; that is, their interpretive practice can be mapped onto some "swing" of my hermeneutical pendulum), some are *not* being metamodern in how they describe their interpretive practice. Indeed, as one can intuit from *Table 8*, at least four texts in total—three traditional (T5, T6, T8) and one affirming (T4) are not metamodern in their descriptions *overall*, and no traditional text is metamodern in their descriptions of Scripture. As discussed in the previous chapter, for traditional texts, this *may* be a sign of a fundamentalist or precritical posture.

However, there appears to be a correlation between the Author-Centered approach to Scripture and Transcendence, such that the two are, in some sense, conceptually connected. And this makes sense, as those who prioritize God's otherness in their experience of God would necessarily prioritize that experience in the context with which they most regularly experience him—through studying the Bible. This may be especially true for fundamentalists, though I suspect it is also true for anyone whose interpretive practice is shaped by the premodern approach to interpretation. Indeed, insomuch as any of the texts are fundamentalist or premodern, they are so only in response to both modernism and postmodernism and via their use of modernist and postmodernist concepts. I suspect this is why some traditional texts seem to dismiss postmodernism, even as many utilize postmodern concepts in their interpretive practice—particularly in their approach to tradition.

As I hope is becoming increasingly clear, the interpretive debate regarding sexuality has multiple fault lines involving critical differences in interpretive practice for each theological source in the Quadrilateral. Indeed, this analysis has revealed fault lines whose implications extend far beyond just one theological debate. In the following section, I will further describe these differences before moving on, in the next chapter, to being more evaluative in approach and describing a reading paradigm that will help believers clarify their biblical interpretive practice.

## UNDERSTANDING THE COMPLEXITIES OF INTERPRETIVE PRACTICE

Having overviewed the coding frame and concept codes in chapter 4 and described patterns within the coding frame in the section above, I can now begin to pull the project's threads together. In the following section, I will begin bringing the coding frame, Gadamer's hermeneutics, and my theological conviction regarding revelation together to describe differences in interpretive practice.

### Scripture: Same Bible, Different Foundations

The coding results, which suggest a difference in approaches to Scripture between modernism and postmodernism, are not surprising. To be sure, the fault line between modernism and postmodernism in terms of author- and reader-centeredness is already well described.[1] On this point, the coding confirms the hermeneutic expectation regarding differences in each cultural milieu's approach to Scripture, respectively.

More interesting than this is the use of Scripture in the texts and how those uses differ. Below is a revised chart of the relevant Scripture passages referenced in the data, with the added information regarding the interpretive conclusions of each text (Table 9, below). In the context of the sexuality debate, much tends to be made of the so-called "clobber passages," with affirming texts, in particular, seeing these texts as the lynchpin of the debate.[2] In other words, many of the affirming texts understood these passages to

---

1. Brown, *Communication*, 47–68.

2. As a reminder, these generally include Lev 18:22; 20:13; Rom 1:18—2:1; 1 Cor 6:9–11; 1 Tim 1:10; as well as Gen 19:1–28; Jude 7; and sometimes Gen 9:20–27 and Judg 19:22–25. Throughout this chapter, unless quoting from these passages, I will refer to them according to book and chapter number and will not be including verse numbers in every mention.

be the guiding passages of the debate, and if one could explain them in an LGBTQ-affirming way, it would open the door to listeners changing their minds (and, thus, their interpretations and practices) related to this topic. Thus, when discussing their interpretive practice, the affirming texts routinely moved through the "clobber" passages, often emphasizing one or both of Leviticus 18 and 20 and Romans 1 (and some to the story of Sodom and Gomorrah in Gen 19).

**Table 9**: *Relevant Bible Passages Referenced in Data Set, Revised*

|          | Gen 1/2 | Gen 19 | Lev | Rom 1 | 1 Cor 6 | 1 Tim 1 | Matt 19 | Other Foci |
|----------|---------|--------|-----|-------|---------|---------|---------|------------|
| T1—TR    | X       | X      | X   | X     | X       | X       | X       | 2 Tim 3:16 |
| T2—TR    | X       |        |     |       |         |         |         |            |
| T5—TR    | X       |        | X   |       | X       |         |         | OT Focus   |
| T6—TR    | X       |        | X   |       |         |         |         | Mark 12    |
| T8—TR    | X       |        |     |       |         |         | X       |            |
| T10—TR   | X       |        | X   | X     | X       |         | X       |            |
| T12—TR   | X       |        | X   | X     | X       |         |         |            |
| T14—TR   | X       |        | X   | X     | X       |         | X       |            |
| T3—AFF   |         |        |     | X     |         |         |         | Acts 10    |
| T4—AFF   |         |        |     |       |         |         |         | Acts 10    |
| T7—AFF   |         | X      | X   |       |         |         |         | OT Only    |
| T9—AFF   |         |        |     | X     | X       | X       |         | NT Only    |
| T11—AFF  |         | X      | X   | X     | X       | X       |         | Ezek 16:49–50 |
| T13—AFF  | X       | X      | X   | X     | X       | X       |         |            |
| T15—AFF  |         | X      | X   | X     | X       | X       |         | Acts 10, 15 |
| T16—AFF  |         | X      | X   | X     | X       | X       |         | Jude       |

There are surprising patterns in the texts' use of Scripture to describe their interpretive practice. First, while a majority (five) of the affirming texts discussed the Sodom and Gomorrah story, only one of those texts utilized Jude as a point of interpretive clarification (as Jude makes direct reference to Gen 19). This is especially notable because Jude's reference connects Sodom's judgment with the city's sexual immorality (Jude 7). Rather than *just* being about inhospitableness, a conclusion some texts seem to have drawn from Ezek 16:49–50, sexual immorality is an important element of the story that deserves further clarification and discussion.[3]

Second, and more surprising, is that while the traditional texts regularly discussed the "clobber" passages, these were *not* the lynchpin of the debate for these texts. Instead, for every traditional text, the most important chapters for the topic of sexuality were Genesis 1–2 (and relatedly, for some, Matt 19:1–12). Critically, only one affirming text discussed Genesis 1–2, and no affirming texts discussed Matthew 19, while every traditional text discussed the first chapters of Genesis, and four discussed Matthew 19. The question is, what lies behind this difference in Scripture usage?

At its core, the issue for the traditional texts seems to be an exegetical prejudice that prioritized the canon for how they understand the topic of marriage. In particular, this prejudice views Jesus' discussion of marriage in Matthew 19 as revealing God's intention for marriage across all of Scripture. Thus, when Jesus references Genesis in the Matthew 19 discourse, the traditional texts take this as an indication of divine intention for understanding the implications of Genesis 1–2 for their theology of marriage, and by extension their theology regarding sexuality. In the words of one traditional text, which is echoed in all eight, "Marriage is defined *because of creation*, not because of culture" (T10, emphasis added). Indeed, one text views this point as so central that they make a brash claim that "Some teachers who say that [sic] homosexuality is correct, but *I don't even have to leave the book of Genesis* to prove you wrong" (T6, emphasis added). More than exegetical prejudice, this also reveals an approach within the traditional texts that understands the debate to be about more than sexuality and marriage—it is about a theological anthropology whose foundation is in the first chapters of Genesis. One text perceived this clearly, commenting, "Evangelical Christians at the dawn of the twenty-first century find themselves living in a period of historical transition as Western cultures become increasingly post-Christian. *It has embarked upon a massive revision of what it means to be a human being*" (T12, emphasis added). And it is those initial passages of Genesis that traditionalists see as the foundation for understanding what it means to be human. Thus, there are different

---

3. Only T11 gave a longer description of this passage of Scripture, while T16 cited it without discussion. Other texts, such as T1, T7, T13, and T15, each reference inhospitableness as an interpretation of the Genesis 19 passage, but do not reference where this interpretation is being derived from. While an argument from silence, I think it most charitable to assume that, at least somewhere in their research, this interpretation was derived from Ezek 16:49–50.

understandings of the scriptural foundations of the debate, and unless each group, traditional or affirming, can clarify their biblical foundations and theological anthropology in an agreeably understandable way, productive (even constructive) conversation will continue to be elusive.

While affirming texts largely ignored Genesis, three utilized another passage to bolster their interpretation which was not used by the traditional texts: Acts 10:9–23. In this passage, Peter receives a vision from God which instructs him that he "should not call anyone impure or unclean" (v. 28), thus opening the door for ministry to the Gentiles. Affirming texts looked to this passage, and a passage with a similar theme in Acts 15, interpreted the present cultural moment as comparable, and either implied or stated outright the belief that, like Peter, God has taught them not to reject those who confess Christ's Lordship. In effect, these Acts passage acts as a canonical prejudice for the affirming texts in much the same way as Matthew 19 acts as a canonical prejudice for traditional texts. Furthermore, the summary of Acts 15 that one text offers could well summarize what many of the affirming texts are ultimately attempting to say: "we got these stories of the people we thought who are out, who are [actually] in because Jesus has accepted them" (T15). This use of Scripture is an expression of the concern for the outcome of truth claims, as exclusion is seen negatively and inclusion is seen positively. Mapped onto the Quadrilateral Matrix, this suggests Scripture would be a strong authority but not the norming norm of theological reflection in the same way as it is for the traditional texts, creating a significant barrier to overcome in how discussion about Scripture occurs between those of the respective interpretive conclusions.

Suffice to say, there is a canonical prejudice informing the exegetical (and therefore interpretive) practice for both traditional and affirming interpreters. However, the extent to which this prejudice is understood as such, and the extent to which it is understood in canonical terms, is unclear. Therefore, clarifying the role of the canon within exegesis, partnered with a recognition of differences in how interpreters treat Scripture as authoritative, could elucidate theological debate and help interlockers better describe how they understand Scripture and how the Bible informs how Christian's are to live in the world.

## Tradition: Prejudices and Language

Based on the coding overviewed in this and the previous chapter, I argue that the traditional texts studied did not give much weight to the Christian tradition. In contrast, the affirming texts did—at least in so much as the meaningfulness of traditions was actively acknowledged. Whether this lack on the part of the traditional texts is for rhetorical purposes or whether Canadian baptistic churches do not have a strong sense of the Christian tradition is cause for further study. However, whatever the case, the lack of reference to the tradition is meaningful because of its implications for both interpretive conclusions.

First, a lack of meaningful reflection on tradition suggests that the interpreters did not think that what has come before is meaningful for understanding where they are or the contours of the issue(s) they are facing. However, Gadamer rightly points out that this is not the case—because our understanding of the world is historically effected by the traditions we are immersed in, traditions and history are sources of knowledge that inform present understanding in both positive and negative ways.[4] Thus, though Canadian Baptist churches may not think about it, and, indeed, may not like it, the larger traditions Baptists emerged from—namely Anglicanism, and before that Roman Catholicism, not to mention the General and Particular Baptist sub-traditions that remain in tension within the denomination—continue to shape their theological imaginations, even as they are left unrecognized.

Second, in a hyper-interconnected world, understanding is influenced by the prejudices of others outside of our traditions whom we allow to speak into our interpretive practice, creating a complex context for understanding to develop. This is heightened for Christians, as different churches speak about theology in different ways that is informed by their tradition's development. While represented in metamodernist literature in the use of the phrase super-hybridity, which describes "the use of a great number of hugely diverse cultural sources to create [artistic] work,"[5] I prefer the term hyperculture. Cultural theorist Byung-Chul Han describes hyperculture as a culture which has "increasingly lost the kind of structure familiar to us from conventional texts or books. . . . The borders or enclosures that convey a semblance of cultural authenticity or genuineness are dissolving. Culture

---

4. Gadamer, *Truth and Method*, 293.
5. Heiser, "Super-Hybridity," 55.

is bursting at the seams, so to speak. It is exploding all ties and joints. It is becoming unbound, un-restricted, un-raveled: a hyperculture."[6] In hypercultural context, meaningful differences are both recognized and dissolved, subsumed and obliterated, and in doing so new understanding develops.

Han notes that in contemporary western cultures individuals express their individualism through consumption, hoarding (like a tourist collecting trinkets) elements of other people's individualism they deem worthy of contributing to the (self)understanding they are constructing. Han refers to this as "hypercultural tourism."[7] As Han describes, "hypercultural tourists" live between the discovery and construction of an infinite number of Heres, in the shadow of understanding whose ground has shifted and is shifting underneath them.[8] Because of this, they grasp for meaning and purpose wherever they sense it may be found, traversing cultures and traditions (including, and especially, religious traditions), unreflectively syncretizing what they find with what they already think. In doing so, hyperculture promotes tensions between traditions that limits reflexivity and flattens tradition while also (ironically) increasing knowledge of traditions and therefore the differences between traditions—all of which enlivens the metamodern oscillation.

Insomuch as one operates as a hypercultural tourist (of theology), one's consumption or collection of theological idea leads to the subsumption of those ideas without properly thinking through the context of their development. This means that hypercultural consumers (which is to say, metamodernists) are rarely thinking through the implications of the varied theologies they are ingesting, the language of those theologies, and how they coalesce. If Gadamer is correct, and language is the oxygen of understanding, the use of multiple *liturgical* languages gathered as trinkets do not necessarily, nor easily, coalesce, and are thus an impediment to understanding that will only continue to grow as the church continues to unreflectively consume theologies from across traditions. Indeed, because the language of tradition is how theological concepts are communicated, Christianity can only make sense according to the historically effected language it uses to describe God and God's work in the world. Understanding how traditions speak of God is, therefore, tied to an understanding of the traditions themselves, such that

---

6. Han, *Hyperculture*, 22.

7. As Taylor comments, "One of the most obvious manifestations of [expressive individualism] has been the consumer revolution" (*Secular Age*, 474).

8. Han, *Hyperculture*, 61.

a simple ecumenicalism is not possible, let alone constructive, in the midst of complex theological debate unless there is recognition of legitimate and meaningful difference amongst traditions. Apart from the language developed in a given tradition, it would be exceptionally difficult to coherently describe one's faith. This is not to suggest dialogue is not possible across traditions, but rather that an awareness that there are differences is necessary for productive, *reflexive* dialogue to take place.

What might the implications of the above be? To start, it suggests that depending on how the metamodern tension is dealt with, the development of two separate traditions along the traditional and affirming fault lines is possible, across multiple—if not all—denominations. As I have already discussed, the differences in the use of Scripture and the tension in the Reason quadrant of the coding frame suggests that, even now, there are traditions of language developing within the church that, if not brought together in constructive dialogue, will develop into sub-traditions that will increasingly become incomprehensible to one another.

Finally, however, there is perhaps *one* tradition that continues to be shared by both traditionalists and progressives, even if their approach to it is different and largely left unrecognized. This tradition is the tradition of Scripture. Indeed, the traditional texts, in particular, make use of Scripture as a sort of linguistic tradition when commenting that "definitions as given by God [in the Bible]" (T10) should shape our understanding of reality. In essence, what is being unreflectively inferred in this statement is that we should submit to a tradition—even as other traditions derived from it are ignored. Yet other, affirming, texts were reflective on the nature of language when they discussed issues with English translations, essentially arguing that the recent tradition of translation related to homosexuality, especially since the 1950s, should not be trusted (T11, T15).[9]

It should be noted I am not attempting to conflate the Christian tradition and Scripture. Instead, I am making a more subtle argument that the Bible is being treated as though it were a tradition. However, treating Scripture as a tradition in this way is problematic when the ability to speak about tradition more broadly has been lost or ignored. Insomuch as Scripture can, at least in a basic sense, be thought of as a tradition, why consider the tradition of Scripture authoritative? What is the character of this tradition that it should be considered trustworthy? Indeed, some might suggest that it is not

---

9. To clarify, these texts are not saying that the Bible should not be trusted but that translations should be treated with suspicion because of their necessary complexity.

trustworthy and thus de-prioritize both Scripture and tradition altogether in their theological thinking. Nevertheless, if Scripture is trustworthy, is it so because of the Holy Spirit's work in and through this tradition? This returns us to the question of discerning the Holy Spirit, which was raised at the end of the previous chapter's review of the Experience quadrant coding. However, setting this question aside, one could easily make a similar claim for the authority of any Christian tradition, contemporary and historical, by declaring that the Holy Spirit is working in and through it. Such an argument could even bolster the claims of those who focus on God's immanence and which may not give adequate space for transcendence, a tension in the experience quadrant of the Quadrilateral to which I will return shortly. If not for the Holy Spirit, is the biblical tradition—and indeed any tradition—trustworthy for a different reason? Suffice it to say, the language of Scripture is a tradition because we receive Scripture as handed down to us, and it is, as the revelation of and from God, the genesis point of the Great Tradition. But this tradition is not considered authoritative simply because it was handed down—it is authoritative *because of its character of revelation*, bearing witness to God over generations.

All of this, together, is to suggest that the lack of reflection on tradition, both particularly ("my" tradition) and generally ("the" tradition) stops the church from being able to use the considerable resources of the communion of saints to give (gift) us positive prejudices that may be worthy of submission.[10] Indeed, while recognition of tradition does not stop one from being biased by tradition, it does allow for self-awareness about the ways tradition informs thinking and practices—and, through self-awareness, the possibility of being confronted, challenged, and changed. Gadamer was certainly correct when he commented, "it is the tyranny of hidden prejudices that makes us deaf to what speaks to us in tradition."[11] Insomuch as Christian's harbour a hidden prejudice *against prejudices*, a refusal to appropriately reflect on tradition, we make ourselves deaf to the wisdom of the past, and how that wisdom has and continues to shape us—and do so to our detriment.

---

10. Gadamer, *Truth and Method*, 291–92.
11. Gadamer, *Truth and Method*, 282.

## Reason: Competing Penultimate Concerns

The coding frame showed that the guiding, penultimate concerns signifi-cantly differed between the traditional and affirming texts in terms of how metamodern interpreters employ reason. I hesitate to call these concerns "ultimate" because I am choosing to assume that the ultimate concern for each text is faithfulness to Christ. As such, their concerns—for objective truth on the modernism pole and the outcome of truth claims or proposi-tions on the postmodernism pole—are penultimate *but still powerful* in how they shape interpretive practice. Indeed, the way these shape interpretation is related to the role of truth and how modernism and postmodernism deal with truth claims. Pivotally, the varied approaches to truth—falsification for modernism, which assumes objectivity, and postmodern intersubjectiv-ity, which (as the name suggests) prioritizes co-construction of reality via multiple subjectivities—are at odds with each other, such that the differ-ence will naturally lead to conflict.

From the perspective of intersubjectivity, this proves a significant issue, because there seems to be an assumption that interpreters must rely on an objective principle to conform subjectivities in a way that protects persons from outcomes they may feel are negative. For the majority of texts, this principle was the principle of love: that we should do all we can to love oth-ers "without strings, without fears" (T4), embracing rather than excluding, just as Christ has embraced us. Many of the texts confessed a version of this principle, but it was the affirming texts that truly leaned on it as a central pillar of their interpretive practice. Indeed, the use of this principle was even described in explicit hermeneutical terms: "Do we read flesh and blood people through the lens of [Bible] texts that we love more, or do we read [Bible] texts [according] to the lens of people we love?" (T13). The above quote implies that the proper way to interpret Scripture is by conforming Scripture to life experience (or more particularly the life experience of others, as we understand it). Furthermore, it implies that biblical interpret-ers should not want to read the Bible in a way that hurts those they love; therefore, if one's interpretation does hurt another, the interpretation must necessarily be wrong (cf. Matt 7:12). For modernism-informed texts, truth exists regardless of our feelings or experience of it, such that the job of in-terpreters is to know the truth and live in light of the truth, which is plainly at odds with the postmodernism-informed perspective of intersubjectivity. In essence, the use of love as a hermeneutical prejudice is, for the interpret-ers, the implementation of a principial theological ethic that is, alongside the author-reader divide of the Scripture quadrant, a central dividing point between modernism and postmodernism poles of the coding frame.

The above discussion matches what others, such as Sam Reimer, have noted regarding contemporary interpretive practice. Namely, Reimer argues that the content of beliefs are becoming more "about *adherence to* (significant others) and less about *assent to* (doctrinal propositions).[12] In other words, the effects a truth claim or proposition has on the ones we love has become a key measure for adjudicating the proposition's truthfulness. In a way similar to the experience quadrant, which will be discussed shortly, Abby Day described this as an 'anthropocentric' belief orientation, arguing that people have begun articulating their beliefs primarily in reference to other people.[13] Day contrasted this with "theocentricity," which articulates belief primarily in reference to God.[14] Both speak to elements of the coding frame and their implications—intersubjectivity in the Reason quadrant, and transcendence in the experience quadrant—and offers evidence of the patterns the coding has uncovered—and which the coding clarifies by naming the underlying culturally-informed oscillations between modernism and postmodernism that is shaping contemporary interpretive practice and, to some extent, belief more generally.

## Experience: Expectations and Distinctions

For one's experience of God, there is an immediately discernible pattern in the coding that points to something significant, but this significant thing remains hidden from view. Namely, traditional texts focus on God's attributes and judgment significantly more than affirming texts do. This is interesting because of what these two concepts communicate, which is *who God is*. Conversely, the Immanence codes essentially represent what God does, particularly for "me." God sends the Holy Spirit, and God speaks apart from Scripture—each of these focuses on the immanent actions of God.

Who God is and what God does, respectively, are the foci for each pole of this category of the Quadrilateral. Moreover, the importance of naming the above distinction should not be understated, as it helps to more fully reveal a theological issue that has been hiding under the surface of the sexuality debate (and the data being discussed)—that the interpreters seem

12. Reimer, *Caught in the Current*, 50.
13. Day, *Believing in Belonging*, 156–57.
14. Day, *Believing in Belonging*, 157.

to have a different underlying understanding of what revelation is and how it functions.

Indeed, their core difference in foci suggests two crucial ideas for consideration. First, by focusing on who God is as a starting point for understanding what God might be saying, there is an implicit divine–human division, which I will refer to as the creator/creation distinction. This distinction is to say that human beings are not God—which is an objective truth claim—and this fact draws believers towards the Lordship of Christ as they seek to be faithful, because only the God who designed and created the universe understands the conditions by which all things are made new and defines the contours of faithful response to divine grace. The distinction of creator from creation is intimately connected to revelation because God's self-revelation in the Word of God is the framework from which believers understand who God is and all of creation's purpose: that everything "was created through him, by him and for him (John 1:1–3; 1 Cor 8:6; Col 1:15–16)."[15]

While the distinction between creator/creation is evident in both modern and postmodern frames, in the postmodern frame it is given a different attention. Rather than who God is, *what God does* (immanently, in one's midst) is considered more critical for one's understanding and experience of God. Like the other subcategory, this is related to the postmodern view of reason, as intersubjectivity's concern for the outcome of truth claims even informs those outcomes caused by God's action in the world. Thus, God can speak beyond Scripture, and such speaking is intelligible to the community of faith apart from Scripture—that is, apart from special revelation. Likewise, the Holy Spirit can act, including in ways that may contradict scriptural revelation, such that the Spirit's present action can be understood to supersede all past action, including revelation of and from the Spirit throughout history. The impulse towards immanence as a foci for understanding God's revealing of God's self, by the Spirit, is one that can bear much fruit for the church. In fact, it may open the door for the church to retrieve a robust doctrine of general revelation that was lost in the throngs of modernism's insistence on scientific falsification, which the metamodern tension is now making more possible. However, to fully retrieve this doctrine, the relationship between general and special revelation needs further clarification in light of the metamodern tension, such that

15. Jensen, *Revelation*, 116.

the foci on who God is and what God does are appropriately understood, and held in tension, in relation to one another.

Astute readers will no doubt also surmise an underlying possible implication of the above discussion, which is the role of ongoing tensions between Classical theism and Relational theism within evangelical circles. Interestingly, this tension is, in large part, a tension between premodernism on the one hand and modernism *alongside* postmodernism on the other, creating a further complex underlying set of theological prejudices needing to be addressed. Indeed, I suspect that a fundamental difference amongst interpreters regarding how they understand God in light of the Classical and Relational traditions exists in the background of the texts in my data set, but further research is required in order to better describe these hermeneutical prejudices and the role they play in contentious theological debates that seem, on the surface, to have nothing to do with the doctrine of God. To be sure, the debates about the doctrine of God are, ultimately, debates about revelation, so it would not be surprising to find that one's conception of God informed other areas of theological thought. Indeed, if my coding frame is accurately describing a tension between transcendence and immanence, it suggests that the doctrine of God is playing a role in the interpretive debate regarding sexuality, albeit obfuscated from view.

## CONCLUDING SUMMARY

If metamodernism is an accurate description of the contemporary cultural mood, as I have argued and expressed throughout the project, for the church to learn how to think and speak coherently across hermeneutical differences it must learn to think reflexively about all that it believes—explicitly and implicitly—that causes believers to theologically reflect in the ways they do. This will involve reflecting on understandings of Scripture, Tradition, Reason, and Experience, and being able to name the complexity of how theological sources are integrated in the process of interpretation. But this will also involve reflecting on the prejudgments people make before ever opening the biblical text. Only then will Christians be able to reason together about Scripture and perhaps speak across differences rather than past them. In the following chapter, I will seek to describe a framework for thinking theologically that will enable the church to do just this work.

# 6

## Discerning Interpretive Practice

Two of the texts gathered and analyzed in this study shared notable comments on the lack of reflection in how the church talks about interpretation. One text confirms an assumption of this project shared at the outset, that "A lot of times . . . we don't give our biblical reasoning. . . . [W]e tell what we believe without explaining the why" (T6). Another laments, "For all the arguing, there is little reflection" (T16). My goal in this final chapter is to reflect on and use the theoretical and theological perspectives developed in earlier chapters in order to reinvigorate the practice of biblical interpretation by clarifying a particular way in which this practice can be done (namely, the way in which I think it should be done). This is meant to illustrate how the research undertaken in this study can lead to greater clarity in how one describes and prescribes biblical interpretive practices. First, I will articulate an approach to understanding interpretive practice, what I have referred to as the Transformative Reading Paradigm, that will help Christians reflect on and articulate their biblical reasoning and enable interpreters to speak about their reasoning as they seek to faithfully heed the Word of God. Second, I will offer evaluative comments related to the analysis in the previous chapters to further describe and prescribe a metamodern approach to interpretation that will help reveal blind spots and produce common ground for mutual understanding across sharp disagreement.

## DESCRIBING DISCERNMENTS

In this chapter, I present what I have called the Transformative Reading Paradigm. With this title, I am suggesting that biblical interpretation should lead interpreters towards being increasingly made into the image of Christ—that is, being transformed into greater Christlikeness. More than this, however, interpretation should transform the situations in which interpreters need God to speak and act in. Stated differently, understanding (in situations) should be transfigured by the grace of God and power of the Holy Spirit, particularly when one encounters God through His Word. Whether recognized or not, when one reads Scripture, they bring questions, longings, hopes, and those situations they need God to move in. Because of this, it is my conviction that interpretive practice should be, in an important sense, an act of situational listening: waiting on the Lord to speak to where we are (present situation) so that God can lead us beyond that "place" and into a better one (a transformed situation).

Before my reading paradigm is presented as a whole, the subsequent subsections will overview various parts of the paradigm. Doing so may read as though I am describing a methodology of interpretation. However, this is not my intention. Instead, my intention is twofold: to describe what is happening when one interprets Scripture and to present a paradigm for integrative theological reflection at the center of this description. In this way, the Transformative Reading Paradigm can be considered a hermeneutic paradigm, describing an approach to understanding that, as Porter and Robinson summarize, is a description of "how we already live and think, . . . a description of what happens over and above our doing or wanting."[1]

## Interpreting Situations and Acknowledging Hermeneutical Prejudice

As discussed throughout the project, the interpretive task takes place in the context of situations. It is out of situations that we begin to interpret, and our interpretation leads us back to the situations—albeit, the situation, or rather our understanding in the midst of it, will have been renewed and/or transformed in the process. This configuration for understanding, an iteration of the practice-theory-practice paradigm, suggests something critical we must pay attention to. That is, there are what Oliver O'Donovan refers to as discernments in the interpretive task: "There is the interpretive

1. Porter and Robinson, *Hermeneutics*, 80.

task of discerning what the text means, on the one hand; and there is the conscientious task of discerning ourselves and our position as agents in relation to the text, on the other."[2] While he reverses the order of approach in contrast to Gadamer, these two discernments are indeed important elements of the interpretive task. But as will be discussed, O'Donovan fails to recognize another crucial discernment central to the interpretive task. While O'Donovan argues that one discernment is "of the text," whereby one discerns Scripture, and another discernment "out of the text,"[3] whereby one discerns themselves, a third discernment of response *to the text* is also required in order to bring the interpretive task to completion.

## *The First Discernment: Discerning Ourselves*

As we have learned from Gadamer, every interpreter comes to the interpretive task with a complex set of prejudices or prejudgments that informs their understanding. In an individualistic culture, one may be tempted to mistake this first discernment as being just about discerning something like identity, an attempt to answer the question "Who am I?" However, it is instead to make explicit the complex and ever-changing assumptions we bring to our interpretations, which is to answer the question (using a Gadamerian concept), "What makes up my horizon?" Discerning ourselves involves foregrounding our prejudices by acknowledging their existence so that understanding can develop, iteratively and reflexively, over time.

We might then ask; how do we do this? However, this is to risk falling into the trap of methodological thinking. Rather than being something we do, as in a process that can be planned, it is something we do unconsciously as a matter of response. In fact, because understanding occurs when something addresses us,[4] our prejudices can only be foregrounded after we have been addressed or, more likely, confronted—either by a situation, or, in the case of biblical interpretation, by God through Scripture. As Gadamer says, "the prejudices and fore-meanings that occupy the interpreter's consciousness are not at his free disposal."[5] It is thus not possible to proceduralize the foregrounding of prejudice, even as many might assume it both possible and necessary. Rather, preunderstandings are brought to the fore by being

2. O'Donovan, *Crisis*, 58.

3. O'Donovan, *Crisis*, 58.

4. Gadamer, *Truth and Method*, 310.

5. Gadamer, *Truth and Method*, 306.

confronted, and only after such confrontation can they be named—if only ever tentatively because our horizon is constantly being formed.[6]

This is not to suggest that we should not reflect on our prejudices. Rather, the first discernment in interpretation is a reminder to be reflexive; to reflect on the matrix of concerns being brought to a text and, as Moules et al. summarizes, "to remain open to the possible surprise of stumbling over our own prejudices or having someone else stumble on them and point them out to us."[7] The above openness is actually an openness to knowing *that we do not know*; that our understanding is limited and thus our prejudices are tentative. As Lacoste commented, "We can learn only to the extent that we can let the unanticipated put our expectations and our prejudices in question. . . . Preunderstanding without honest admission of non-understanding will hardly invite more than the most meager discoveries."[8] In other words, honest reflexivity is a necessary element of interpretive practice. And without ongoing, honest, self-critical reflexivity, the kind of discernment necessary for truly understanding the contours of one's own interpretive practice—let alone that of another—is difficult if not impossible.

However, there is an issue in that we do not know which of our prejudices help or hurt interpretive practice. Or as Gadamer puts it, we "cannot separate in advance the productive prejudices that enable understanding from the prejudices that hinder it and lead to misunderstanding."[9] This can only happen through a confrontation with history—that is, "encountering the past and understanding the tradition from which we come,"[10] which will help reveal our prejudices. It is worth quoting Gadamer at length to expand on this point:

> Every encounter with tradition that takes place within historical consciousness involves the experience of a tension between the text and the present. The hermeneutic task consists in not covering up this tension by attempting a naive assimilation of the two but in consciously bringing it out. This is why it is part of the hermeneutic approach to project a historical horizon that is different from the horizon of the present. Historical consciousness is aware of its own otherness and hence foregrounds the horizon of the past from its own. On the other hand, it is itself . . . only

6. Gadamer, *Truth and Method*, 317.

7. Moules et al., *Conducting Hermeneutic*, 44.

8. Lacoste, "More Haste," 272.

9. Gadamer, *Truth and Method*, 306.

10. Gadamer, *Truth and Method*, 317.

something superimposed upon continuing tradition, and hence it immediately recombines with what it has foregrounded itself from in order to become one with itself again in the unity of the historical horizon it thus acquires.[11]

Here Gadamer argues that it is through the difficult and deliberate work of reflecting on the tradition(s) that we emerge from that we become aware of the horizon of history/tradition. And it is through the tension between that horizon (of the past) and the horizon of the present, melting together, that understanding emerges. But as historically effected beings, if we were to reflect on our present horizon with no regard for the horizon of history, we would not develop an informed self-understanding. Moreover, our capacity for self-understanding would thus be stunted, not able to appropriately apprehend the present horizon and therefore unable to accurately discern situations as they arise nor the scope of transformation the Gospel effectuates.

Through interpretation, one's present situation is brought into conversation with the text being interpreted—a fusion of horizons occurs—which becomes an element of the prejudices brought into interpretive practice. Hermeneutical prejudices are foregrounded by being confronted, and when brought to the fore they can be acknowledged for the dual purpose of being able to acknowledge the text on the text's terms and being open to having those prejudices changed. Then, as they are refined or replaced, the prejudices inform interpretation by becoming a new aspect of ongoing preunderstanding. Westphal writes, "This is the hermeneutical circle in which presuppositions and interpretations mutually determine one another."[12] Yet, this is to discuss the end of the interpretive process and thus get ahead of ourselves in this description.

At this juncture, it is important to note that this first discernment could be characterized as postmodern in character, as it invites critical self-awareness regarding one's context and assumptions. While the postmodern tendency is to then use this self-awareness for deconstructive aims, essentially using the knowing self as a tool to critique perceived power differentials, Gadamer sees it in a more neutral light—that our prejudices may distract us from understanding, which is worthy of critique, but they may also be the very basis by which understanding develops. To make my point more explicitly, while deconstruction may be an outcome, it should not be an immediate outcome, or even necessarily a goal, of this step of

11. Gadamer, *Truth and Method*, 317.
12. Westphal, *Whose Community?*, 13.

discernment. Instead, the metamodern mood would hold that self-aware-ness is just that—an awareness of the self in a context—which should be utilized to aid understanding. Nevertheless, this self-awareness is only pos-sible through wrestling with tradition, which is done through reflexively naming our context in all of its complexity.

I suspect this is part of what is occurring in the affirming texts I have analyzed in the previous chapters; that their more robust approach to tradition led to a deeper self-awareness, as these texts oscillated between modernism and postmodernism poles ("swinging" on the hermeneutic pendulum, as it were). Then, when partnered with a postmodern concern for the outcome of truth claims, this created a critical prejudice that guided the rest of their interpretive practice. However, it is not clear from the texts whether this self-awareness was an ironic or self-critical self-awareness, the difference being in the depth of engagement with tradition that either offers. As noted in the previous chapters, postmodernism's notion of the authority of tradition is, in effect, that its authority is an honorable token of a bygone era, and thus the postmodernist approach to tradition is ironic (amounting to an appeal to authority that is not, and some would argue should not, be trusted).

Similarly, the traditional texts near complete lack of oscillation in the Tradition quadrant suggests an approach to tradition that inherently avoids confrontation and thus keeps self-awareness at bay. Partnered with the modernist attitude of falsification, the prejudice of the traditional texts became focused on objective truth, creating the conditions by which inter-preters would not have to think through the complexities of their interpre-tive practice. Indeed, the lack of oscillation overall in these texts throughout the quadrants reflects a lack of self-awareness and, on some level, a denial of how the contemporary cultural mood has shaped us and is continuing to shape us as human beings.

The disposition away from tradition I have previously noted will leave churches increasingly open to never being confronted into acknowledging their prejudices, particularly those prejudices that may lead to theological misunderstanding. Instead, these prejudices will hide beneath the surface of our thinking, compounding until they are confronted or until they lead to a spiritual death—for what these prejudices will have led us to misun-derstand is none other than the very self-revelation of the living God. By foregrounding self-awareness through this first discernment, fertile ground is cultivated that is needed for faithful interpretations to develop.

## *The Second Discernment: Discerning Scripture*

The second discernment of biblical interpretation is that of discerning Scripture, which is the practice the Church would describe as exegesis: the explanation of a Bible passage with particular reference to its culture, language, and content. Although briefly discussed in the previous chapter, my project cannot deal with questions of exegesis in significant detail. There are in any case numerous works that discuss biblical exegesis. Yet, there is a recurring theme throughout the project's dataset interacting with and reflecting on exegetical methods. Indeed, although there is some debate in the texts of this study over how exactly Christians ought to approach exegesis and how it ought to be carried out, there is a consensus across all the texts that there is a need for Christians to discern what Scripture says through careful reading. So, although the overall process of theological reflection is reflexive and iterative, the process of carefully exegeting the Bible is nevertheless understood as a distinct step that is in some sense logically prior to and significant for theological integration.

Therefore, rather than saving exegesis for the quadrilateral, I submit that discerning Scripture though exegesis ought to be understood as a separate component of interpretation that, isolated from the Quadrilateral, can help one think more clearly about what one thinks faithful exegesis entails—both in terms of methods and in terms of underlying prejudices related to the nature of Scripture. This not only brings out a theme that runs through my dataset, but it also has the potential to stimulate conversations that will further clarify the underlying tensions characterizing theological debates, which may in turn promote constructive theological dialogue. In sum, because of the (necessarily central) place of exegesis in the dataset, because of the usefulness of discussing exegesis separately from the integration of Scripture and other sources of theological reflection, and because my analyzed texts do engage in and reflect on exegesis separately from theological integration, the paradigm I propose gives due consideration to exegesis as a discernment of Scripture.

One crucial aspect of exegesis that the project has already touched on but requires further discussion is the place of cultural reconstruction. One of the differences between the traditional and affirming texts was their use of cultural reconstruction—namely, the point at which cultural reconstruction was utilized to inform their respective understandings. Traditional texts that were explicit about their exegesis engaged in a clear exegetical movement from an overall pericope to its individual verses, only discussing cultural context when wordings or concepts in the passage seemed unclear to the interpreter, before moving towards intertextual connections with the canon of Scripture. In these texts, the doctrine of perspicuity is visible in that interpreters approach a passage as though it should be clear and understandable to the average Christian sitting in a twenty-first century "pew." The affirming texts likewise began their exegesis in the overall pericope. However, they moved to developing a robust cultural reconstruction before returning to a verse-by-verse breakdown of the passage informed by the reconstruction.

The differences in their use of cultural reconstruction means that, on the level of exegesis, the relationship between the Bible and context are meaningfully different—for traditional texts, sociohistorical cultural context can aid understanding but is not necessary for understanding, whereas for affirming texts a sociohistorical cultural reconstruction is necessary. I suspect this is why some affirming texts made more regular appeals to scholarship in their descriptions, especially context-related research, as it is a more critical element of their exegetical process.[13] Furthermore, the movement from pericope to cultural context and back to pericope discernible in affirming texts sometimes skips over the possibility of intertextuality or inter-biblical clarification, which may account for why traditional texts engaged in more intertextual discussions than the affirming texts.

There are, I suggest, issues lurking under the surface of each exegetical approach. For traditional interpreters, more emphasis should be placed on cultural context, such that the importance of culture in the development of meaning should be better recognized and made part of their exegetical procedure. Indeed, insomuch as this element is missing from their exegesis, it means that the horizon of the text cannot be sufficiently formed, leaving their interpretation open to the criticism of not being sufficiently critical.[14] For affirming texts, while they do a better job of accounting for context, they do so without discerning the sources of their reconstruction, leaving them open to the criticism of only using contextual reconstruction as a sort of

13. The important work of "scholars," which seems to represent a broad and ill-defined category, is explicitly mentioned in T3, T11, and T15.

14. N. T. Wright makes a similar point in relation to the jump to application many interpreters like to make without giving due consideration to the underlying cultural tensions that may exist in a passage of Scripture. Discussing Galatians in particular, Wright comments, "This is always the challenge for historical study of the Bible: to resist the lure of quick-and-easy 'application' that reflects too closely the thought patterns of an older theology, and to allow the relevance of the text for our own day—and its effects in 'Christian formation'—to emerge more slowly and steadily as we look at its original meaning." Wright, *Galatians*, 31.

interpretive confirmation bias that props up their prejudices. Furthermore, especially for church leaders and informed interpreters, discerning sources is all the more important because most laity do not have the requisite skills to evaluate biblical scholarship—and in the information age, it has become increasingly harder to evaluate between good and poor scholastic sources for even those with evaluative skills. Indeed, the importance of discerning sources is a distinctly metamodern issue, whereby the super-hybridity of the mood has led to the necessity of people to "develop a sensorium to be able to tell the ingredients apart, . . . crowd wisdom from mob mentality, proper journalism from fabricated misinformation or fake news and actual spontaneous developments from manipulated ones,"[15] and, for our purposes, poor scholarship from good scholarship (not to mention poor from good *readings* of said scholarship).

As mentioned at the end of chapter 4, five texts in particular (T3, T7, T13, T15, T16) speak about cultural context at length, and their description of context at their discussion's outset "opens the door," so to speak, for their eventual conclusions. Two of these, T3 and T16, discuss the passage from Romans 1 by describing a cultural context related to the Roman Emperor Caligula. These texts take cues for their cultural reconstruction from ancient biographers who describe Caligula as a sex-crazed, murderous lunatic. However, as the majority of contemporary Caligula biographers now point out, such descriptions in ancient sources cannot be taken at face value. In fact, "the accounts of Caligula surviving from antiquity pursue the clearly recognizable goal of depicting the emperor as an irrational monster."[16] They do this by "provid[ing] demonstrably false information . . . present[ing] the emperor's actions out of context . . . [and by] offer[ing] assessments of his behavior that often contradict other information contained in their very own accounts."[17] Yet, time and again, these sorts of texts are being taken at face value, without *their* historical contexts being discerned. This example and discussion should not be misinterpreted as an argument against the role of cultural context for interpreting Scripture. Instead, it has been to suggest that discerning sources is an important element of contemporary exegetical practice in the metamodern mood that can, if done well, clarify the Bible's meaning, but when done poorly will accidentally obfuscate its meaning.

15. Heiser, "Super-Hybridity," 65.

16. Winterling, *Caligula*, 4.

17. Winterling, *Caligula*, 4.

Given the above, the discernment of Scripture should not be understood as the discernment of ancient culture *per se* but as the discernment of the text of Scripture and all that the text points towards as meaningful for understanding—which necessarily includes culture, but will also include intertextuality (e.g., an author drawing connections between Testaments). Examples of a marker within a text pointing to information meaningful to its interpretation direct reference to geographic location, people, and events, as well as linguistic markers such as quotations, patterns, and the complex interplay of tense, time, and aspect in Scripture's original languages. Discerning the text of Scripture by discerning markers such as these prioritizes Scripture's claim as revelation, trusting that we have what we need in order to understand the Bible—whether in the Bible itself, through contextual description that clarifies a passage according to linguistic markers within pericopes, or by the Spirit.[18] Furthermore, it is an approach that should naturally foreground the canon as an interpretive key to understanding Scripture, especially for difficult to understand passages.

Yet, this raises an issue regarding how to understand the canon and Scripture as a unified whole. The church receives the Bible as an artefact of tradition, namely in the concept of the canon. Because of this, a crucial principle of canonical theological method may be leveraged to help name a potential starting prejudice that, if agreed upon, would set basic ground rules for contentious conversations about Scripture—particularly those conversations one might consider ethical in nature, involving what W. Ross Hastings describes as "situations that are new, that the Bible does not directly address, and a solution to which cannot be decided in advance."[19] As developed by John C. Peckham, canonical theological method argues all of Scripture is a unified whole, that the best exegetical methods prioritize internal textual indicators, and that each passage's meaning is intrinsically related to the overall meaning of the canon. Peckham further clarifies,

> This approach does not look "behind" the text to a reconstructed precanonical history but focuses on the text's own claims as they appear in the final-form canon. Taking the canon to accurately represent its own history, this approach engages relevant extant historical materials (e.g., other ancient literature, artifacts) while reserving priority for the canonical text. Thus, this canonical approach is interested in historical context to the extent that it is

18. Jensen, *Revelation*, 233.
19. Hastings, *Pastoral Ethics*, 56.

relevant to the canonical context, while avoiding theological conclusions based on decisions between speculative reconstructions
of tradition history.[20]

Indeed, Peckham's canonical method should properly include the message
of the canon itself—that is, the narrative of Scripture, "from creation to
consummation," by which God and the gospel is revealed.[21] In this sense,
the canonical method may be considered a thematic approach, whereby, as
Cameron et al. reflect, the "overall coherence to the Bible as the site of God's
self-revelation" is leveraged to help interpret specific passages of Scripture.[22]

While Peckham (as well as Hastings and others) argues for the pri-
macy of a historical-grammatical exegetical method, I am not convinced
only one exegetical method such as this is necessary. Rather, while the
historical-grammatical method may be an useful starting point for exegesis, I would suggest that some texts will require looking "behind the text
to a reconstructed precanonical history" so that the context of the text's
composition can be understood.[23] In brief, what I am contending for is
that because of the requirement of specialization, which places biblical
interpretation out of reach of the majority of Christians, complex cultural
reconstruction should not be an initial stage of exegetical practice, even if it
may sometimes be required at a later stage of the exegetical process. Indeed,
historico-cultural reconstruction is an exegetical tool that must be used
carefully and critically, lest the reconstruction cause one to ignore what
Peckham describes as "the text's own claims as they appear in the final-
form canon,"[24] and therefore lead to a misunderstanding of what Scripture
says and means.

The above discussion has three implications for the discernment of
Scripture. First, the canonical text becomes the most trustworthy source of
data against which all theological claims must be tested.[25] Secondly, prioritizing internal textual indicators necessarily means the de-prioritization of
external indicators (broadly speaking, "cultural contexts"), which develops
a prejudgment about what faithful exegesis entails. This does not mean ignoring cultural contexts, but rather always using cultural reconstruction in

---

20. Peckham, *Canonical Theology*, 156.

21. Hastings, *Pastoral Ethics*, 56.

22. Cameron et al., *Theological Reflection for Human Flourishing*, 75.

23. Peckham, *Canonical Theology*, 156.

24. Peckham, *Canonical Theology*, 156.

25. Peckham, *Canonical Theology*, 156.

service to the text itself *as it appears* within the canon. Furthermore, it may mean bringing cultural context into the interpretation of a text's meaning later in one's exegetical and interpretive process rather than immediately or up-front. Finally, the canon has a unity-in-diversity that should be expected, as it is the revelation of a triune God of unity-in-diversity. As such, Scripture offers a pluralism of views on numerous topics, but this pluralism helps to discern the boundaries of diversity that is appropriate for continued unity. In other words, "the canon itself provides the limits for accepted diversity . . . there is a place for differences, but not all potential differences are acceptable."[26]

In an important sense, the discernment of Scripture described above could be characterized as a *modern* step of discernment, insomuch as contemporary biblical studies is built on modernist assumptions of objectivity and the ability to know an author's intended meaning in a text. And while some may disagree with my assessment of the discernment of Scripture offered above, I believe this assessment best describes an approach to exegesis that will allow Christians—lay and otherwise—to discern Scripture passages without needing extensive or obscure specialized materials as a necessary starting point for their exegetical practice. Furthermore, based on the discussion so far, although it may give the impression that this assessment will lead to a traditional interpretive conclusion, I do not believe this is necessarily the case. Indeed, if the approach to exegesis I have described—prioritizing Scripture as a means of clarifying Scripture, while cautiously developing cultural reconstruction as a secondary aid—were utilized by those on both sides of the sexuality debate, it would allow for coherent and constructive conversation about this second discernment that is currently not occurring.

After exegesis, one's explanation of the meaning of Scripture becomes part of the preunderstanding they bring into future interpretive practice. But once Scripture is discerned, an interpreter has not finished their hermeneutical work. There is, instead, a third discernment which will lead the interpreter to completing the interpretive task: discerning theological integration.

---

26. Porter, *Interpretation for Preaching*, 32. For a detailed discussion regarding diversity and unity in relation to the canon, see Porter, *Interpretation for Preaching*, 99–119.

## *The Third Discernment: Discerning (Transformative) Theological Integration*

The third discernment is discerning how the message of Scripture changes how one understands oneself, the world, and God—and therefore leads to a transformation in how one lives. As Ward describes, this discernment is in some sense a discernment of the gospel, the combining of an "understanding of God with the embodied and committed lives of individuals."[27] This is a multistep discernment of theological reflection ending in application; allowing God's self-revelation to inform how believers faithfully practice their faith in the varied situations of life.

In this discernment, the Quadrilateral Matrix can be utilized to help Christians understand how they relate the theological sources while also ensuring the lived application of interpretive conclusions at the end of the reflection process is clearly in focus. Indeed, it is in discerning theological integration that the Quadrilateral becomes most helpful, as it clarifies the nature of transformation into Christlikeness according to the authority given to the various theological sources, and invites interpreters to ensure that the transformation implied in their interpretation is truly lived out— particularly within their inciting situation.

It is worth considering here what I mean by the authority of the theological sources because this is a contested concept in the metamodern frame. Before postmodernism's rise, authority was generally understood in terms of its transcendent origin. Even within modernism, where the notion of a transcendent God was being critiqued and replaced with a notion of a transcendent self, authority functioned according to a metaphor of hierarchy that assumed otherness (or, to put it in religious terms, it assumed transcendence). In the postmodern frame, this metaphor breaks down as hierarchy is assumed to be evidence of capricious power games such that the origin of authority could not be found "out there" but only "in here," in what we might call the *intersubjective self*[28] or what Reimer describes as "the move towards internal authority and self-spirituality."[29] In a simplified sense, then, the difference between modern and postmodern notions

---

27. Ward, *Introducing*, 48.

28. Larkin, "Authority for Postmodern Mind," 129. Relatedly, Reimer (*Caught in the Current*, 51) notes Day's observation that "young people's beliefs tend to be co-produced, through participating with family and friends in creating and maintaining beliefs." See also Day, *Believing in Belonging*, 90.

29. Reimer, *Caught in the Current*, 61.

of authority is related to transcendence and immanence, at least in terms of where they find their coherence. In the modern frame, authority comes from outside of oneself, an appeal to power that is *other than* at any given moment. Conversely, in postmodernism, authority is a social construct, an agreed-upon framework of power-sharing, centered on individuals, that functions only so long as the agreement remains intact.

Through the complex integration of theological sources, with their varying degrees of authority decided on—partly—via one's operative prejudices, interpreters can move from exegesis to application and bring interpretation to completion in practice. This integration is done by bringing understandings of Scripture, Tradition, Reason, and Experience together in dialogue. Such is the purpose of the Quadrilateral Matrix, as it allows an interpreter and interpreting community to honestly clarify the degree of authority they give to each of the theological sources, and then wrestle with the implications of this for how they respond to their Discernment of Scripture. Done well, one's theological integration, and therefore their biblical interpretive practice, should lead interpreters towards greater faithfulness as a citizen of God's Kingdom, whereby the gospel, in all its fullness, is brought to bear in and transforms whatever situation the interpreter faces.

## REVELATION, AUTHORITY, AND THE KNOWLEDGE OF GOD

At the outset of the project, I described a guiding prejudice that I hold: that Scripture is revelation. It is worth discussing this prejudice further, as it forms the overall ground for how I approach the three discernments discussed above. As I described in chapter 2, modernism and postmodernism have competing conceptions of revelation—while modernism considers human authors as revelatory rather than Scripture, postmodernism conceived of the reader as the revelatory or inspired agent. I have argued that it is instead Scripture that reveals God and is inspired by God for that purpose. It is my contention that the exact words used in Scripture have significance precisely because of their quality of having been inspired by the Living God. Our knowledge of God, as revealed by God, is then the ground from which I believe Scripture is able to claim authority over all other theological sources. On this point Gadamer is helpful and, again, worth quoting at length:

It is primarily persons that have authority; but the authority of persons is ultimately based not on the subjection and abdication of reason but on the act of acknowledgement and knowledge— the knowledge, namely, that the other is superior to oneself in judgement and insight and that for this reason his judgement takes precedence—i.e., it has priority over one's own. . . . Authority in this sense has nothing to do with blind obedience to commands. Indeed, authority has to do not with obedience but rather with knowledge.[30]

In my view, Scripture is authoritative—it takes precedence—over all other theological sources not because it demands blind obedience but because the knowledge it gives is the knowledge of one whose judgment and insight is definitionally superior to our own, which is a conviction one can only come to by faith. In other words, the Bible's authority is grounded in covenantal relationship with God through Christ—its authority is related to its character as revelation. And only insomuch as an interpreter is a person of the faith can they be expected to regard Scripture as revelation and therefore as authoritative, even as Christians believe that Christ is Lord of all.

The differences between modernism and postmodernism gives rise to areas of concern for both that all interpreters must keep in mind. For modernism, there will be a consistent pull away from Scripture as a revealer of divine relationship, and towards knowing the Bible in the way one would know a textbook—impersonally and only for the information it contains. In other words, modernism's falsification does not lend itself to developing faithful covenant people but hypocrites who know the Bible but who may not know the God the Bible reveals. On the other hand, postmodernism's concern for the subjective operationalization of knowledge, including knowledge of God, problematizes biblical authority. Indeed, as O'Donovan describes, the postmodern posture means "the question of the authority of the biblical text has been refocused from their historical veridically to their moral serviceability," which, O'Donovan argues, has developed into doubt as to whether Scripture is a competent moral guide.[31] This development makes it difficult to even talk about faithfulness, for faithfulness is, at its core, relational knowledge that leads to obedience. Put another way, faithfulness leads to a particular moral life, and it is not a life that pursues happiness as life's *telos*. Indeed, for Christians today, knowledge of

30. Gadamer, *Truth and Method*, 291–92.
31. O'Donovan, *Crisis*, 56–57.

Jesus' Lordship may *not* lead to the kind of moral life that optimizes personal sense of self, liberty, security, or pleasure. Instead, relationship with God may draw someone into situations in which they must choose to do something they would otherwise not want to do, placing them in danger or causing them to suffer. Furthermore, the historical veridically of the story of Christ is important enough that without it the Christian faith falls apart (1 Cor 15:13–19), making the move away from objective truth troublesome if followed to the extreme.

Thus, both perspectives have the potential to lead believers away from deeper relationship with God and, thus, away from discipleship and the transformation which God offers in Christ. However, by being aware of these extremes and the ways one may invariably move towards one or the other situationally, interpretive practice can remain focused on a commitment to faithfully living in obedience to God in accordance with the covenant of grace revealed in the person of Christ and words of Scripture. The above could be said for each of the quadrants of the Quadrilateral, as the goal of metamodern interpretive practice is to hold the poles of the coding frame in tension and make informed, reflective decisions about which interpretive route to take.

It is therefore not enough to be "modern" or "postmodern"; contemporary interpreters must be aware of how both perspectives are operative in their thinking, so that they can come to an informed understanding of how they are reaching their interpretive conclusions, which will equip them to further reflect on, refine, and indeed discuss their interpretive practice coherently with others. For Scripture, metamodern interpreters should take both author and reader centeredness into account, not dismissing one or the other, so that no matter which conclusion one comes to—and no matter which pole of the hermeneutical pendulum one ultimately leans towards—one can describe the road that has been traveled to arrive at their conclusion(s). Likewise, one should not be just ecumenical *or* sectarian in approach to tradition, just objective *or* intersubjective in reasoning, nor just focus on transcendent *or* immanent experiences of God. Rather, it is better to recognize each of these modern and postmodern poles are operative in our thinking at any given time, and by being aware of this we can name how we approach the integration of theological sources and come to a deeper understanding of the competing elements and prejudices from which interpretive disagreements arise. This necessarily means that conflicts will arise in metamodern interpretive practice, but it is within these conflicts—the oscillation between modern and postmodern poles—that true understanding is able to develop. Thus, rather than being an unwanted by-product, complexity that leads to conflict is a necessary element of metamodern interpretive practice, as this is the place from which preunderstandings can be named (and confronted), application formed, and lives transformed by God's revelation in the midst of integrative theological reflection.

## THE TRANSFORMATIVE READING PARADIGM

In the *Transformative Reading Paradigm* (Figure 6, below), the above discernments are brought together into a diagramed description of the process of interpretation. The diagram labels the three discernments, provides some of the possible preunderstandings that interpreters bring to Scripture, includes the Quadrilateral Matrix and my coding categories, and clarifies how one's transformed life situation informs future situations and personal prejudices. Furthermore, one's transformed life situation also shapes the prejudices of the community of faith whom they are interpreting alongside and that community's understanding of other, similar, life situations that may arise in its communal life (and the life of individuals within the community).

One construct explicitly missing from this diagram is the Hermeneutic Pendulum. While I have omitted explicit reference to the Pendulum from the diagram, it is still present conceptually. Indeed, as a tool intended to be usable by the church, the explicit addition of the Pendulum seemed, to me, to risk placing this tool out of the reach of the laity, warranting its exclusion. However, the inclusion of the poles of the coding frame is representative of the pendulum's conceptual inclusion in the diagram, reminding users of the fact that modern and postmodern notions are in constant tension within the metamodern mood throughout the Quadrilateral Matrix, and that the notions of authority given to each theological source are, in many ways, dependent on the extent to which a modern or postmodern impulse is being brought into the paradigm's third discernment. While I suspect the Pendulum may be too confusing for the average lay-interpreter to utilize, church leaders who utilize the paradigm must be aware of the complexity of the metamodern age that the Hermeneutic Pendulum describes, such that they can dissect their own interpretive practice using the Quadrilateral Matrix and become aware of the prejudices they have as metamodern people.

For similar reasons, I have labeled prejudices as "preunderstanding" on the diagram—not because "prejudice" is incorrect but because I have

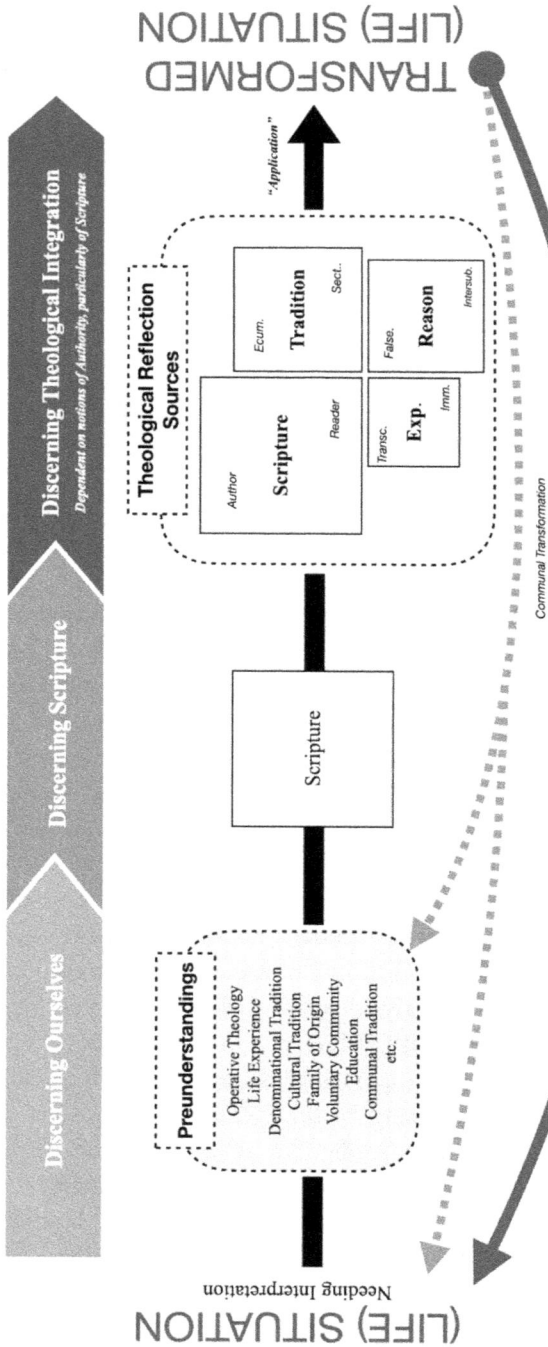

Figure 6: Transformative Reading Paradigm

TRANSFORMED (LIFE) SITUATION

"Application"

Discerning Theological Integration
*Dependent on notions of Authority, particularly of Scripture*

Theological Reflection Sources

Tradition
Ecum.
Sect.

Reason
False.
Intersub.

Scripture
Author
Reader

Exp.
Transc.
Imm.

Communal Transformation

Discerning Scripture

Scripture

Discerning Ourselves

Preunderstandings

Operative Theology
Life Experience
Denominational Tradition
Cultural Tradition
Family of Origin
Voluntary Community
Education
Communal Tradition
etc.

Needing Interpretation

(LIFE) SITUATION

been utilizing it as a technical term whose definition will be unfamiliar in contexts outside of academic discussions about hermeneutics. The phrase "Preunderstanding" does not share the same negative connotation that the phrase "prejudice" has in the contemporary imagination, making it better suited for use in the diagram to describe the Gadamerian concepts at the center of the paradigm's design.

## Using the Paradigm in Practice

There are several ways I can imagine the Transformative Reading Paradigm being utilized, each of which can help reveal how this theological reflection method is rememberable, usable, and appropriately communal, thus meeting the criteria Whitehead and Whitehead outlined for effective theological reflection methods. First, the paradigm could be used by pastors or Bible teachers to better describe their practice of biblical interpretation to their congregations and use it as a discipleship tool for explaining the discernments in interpretation. Having listened to many sermons, studies, and presentations over the course of this project, it is clear—as seen confessed in some of the texts at the beginning of this chapter—that Christian leaders regularly discuss interpretive conclusions without describing the process by which they arrived at those conclusions. By accurately describing their interpretive process, pastoral leaders can disciple their flock in the art of interpretation, helping laity to develop a better understanding of their interpretive processes and thereby equip them for dialogue regarding Scripture, including contentious issues related to biblical interpretation. Furthermore, the paradigm can be broken down to the level of each discernment and contextualized based on the needs of a given audience. Doing this, pastors or church leaders could walk through each element of the paradigm to teach their church how to utilize it, or to walk through it in their own personal study and thus exemplify it in their practice of biblical interpretation which is expressed in how they articulate their interpretations (via sermons, studies, or other outlets). Interpretive clarity from pastors and leaders has the added benefit of helping to name the hermeneutical elements those leaders, and their churches, consider to be important for developing interpretations of Scripture that they consider faithful, further clarifying interpretation. As this project emerged from my own pastoral practice, this use of the paradigm is one that I have utilized in my ministry context to improve my understanding and articulation of interpretation. Namely, it has given me the capacity to better name the elements of theological reflection and describe, for my church community what and why I believe certain interpretations are faithful and others less so.

Second, the paradigm could be used in academic settings such as seminaries to help future pastors and ministry leaders develop a better understanding of interpretation. Namely, the paradigm can help those leaders begin to recognize the place and role of preunderstandings, Scripture, and theological sources for faithful interpretive practice. Furthermore, it can help them clarify the purpose of biblical interpretation, which is transformation in conformity to Christ—and, because of this, help show how integral theological reflection is to interpretation, discipleship, and the church's ongoing mission in the world. The paradigm I am proposing gives a framework for describing interpretive practice that foregrounds key aspects of interpretation, invites its users to articulate their approach to theological reflection, and reminds them that interpretation is only completed once lived. By following along with the paradigm and being humbly honest about their prejudices and notions of authority related to the theological sources, users would be equipped to articulate their interpretive practice to themselves and others, creating a context within which meaningful conversation about the Bible can occur. Indeed, simply by being able to describe each discernment of the paradigm, more clarity can be brought to fraught theological debates that will allow believers to speak about their interpretive process more coherently and, perhaps, develop common ground for mutual understanding and constructive dialogue. Relatedly, the paradigm opens the possibility for articulating the prejudices of one's theological tradition and creates new space for inquiries that can help uncover those prejudices informing current practice so that they can be named, and perhaps challenged or buttressed. As Zoë Bennett and Christopher Rowland argue, creating space for a dialogical encounter with how one's tradition is informing their present understanding "will enable the interpreting subject to see more clearly, and as a result make informed judgements."[32]

As described in chapter 3, the Quadrilateral Matrix is meant to be dynamic rather than static. It thus could be drawn according to *however* an individual or community perceives the sources and their relative weight or authoritativeness. Thus, one could use the paradigm to develop a vision for how the theological sources interact that is different from how it is presented in the above diagram. However, it is important to reiterate that this

32. Bennett and Rowland, *Glass Darkly*, 11.

interplay would be necessarily informed by the notions of authority, requiring interpreters to be honestly explicit in how theological sources function authoritatively in their own theological thinking.

Finally, having developed an understanding of their own interpretive process, leaders—pastoral and academic—could then utilize the paradigm to dialogue across difference. Indeed, partnered with the insights related to the metamodern cultural mood, leaders could facilitate discussion by using the paradigm as a base framework to help others more accurately describe and understand interpretive practice, such that persons with opposing views could speak about their interpretation intelligibly together. However, if there is not a broad understanding of what Scripture is (whether revelation, or otherwise) nor a basic functional shared tradition of theological language, developing a common understanding for how to practice biblical interpretation will be difficult if not impossible to achieve. Nevertheless, talking through the paradigm will at least clarify the reason(s) for the difficulty.

## TRANSFORMATIVE READING AND PRACTICAL THEOLOGY

As described in the introduction of this project, the role of Scripture in practical theology has been a consistent topic of conversation in recent years in the practical theology guild. As noted in the introduction, Mark Cartledge outlined various approaches to the use of the Bible in practical theological work, concluding that "the majority of authors in academic practical theology either use Scripture in a limited manner or not at all."[33] Compounding this, as Collins has mapped, practical theologians have long had disagreements about the starting point of practical theological inquiries, with many simply assuming that practical theology starts in lived experience.[34] And as Ward notes, this assumption "is a political move that puts practical theology on the liberal side of the debates in modern theology."[35] Ward's solution to this issue is to collapse distinctions between liberal and conservative theologies, while Collins argues for a *scriptural cycle* method of theological reflection that starts with Scripture but takes seriously the

33. Cartledge, *Mediation*, 43.
34. Collins, *Reordering Reflection*, 36–38, 57, 97.
35. Ward, *Introducing*, 4.

role of divine agency and the possibility for humans to experience God (particularly through the Holy Spirit).[36]

While Collins' method and my proposed paradigm have much in common—especially in that Collins assumes a particular theology of revelation as a starting point for understanding Scripture and, through its narrative, ourselves[37]—her method fails to adequately account for the fact that interpretation is contextual. That is, when we interpret, we do so coming from a particular situation, carrying a complex set of prejudices, and these prejudices will be further shaped by our discernment of Scripture and discernment of theological integration. Rather than a collapse of liberal and conservative perspectives, as Ward describes, both experience ("life situations") and Scripture are integral to practical theology—and, indeed, interpretation itself. While life situations are the place from which inquiries are seeded, those situations can only be understood (in terms of the gospel) when transformed through discerning Scripture and theological integration. This is what I hope the reading paradigm I have proposed clarifies—that the process of interpretation involves a series of discernments that, following my evangelical convictions, prioritizes Scripture while necessitating experience, as well as theological sources as proposed via the Quadrilateral Matrix, and that this process leads to renewed understanding for faithful practice, which is what practical theological inquiry strives to describe.

The way I have articulated this paradigm also provides a possible way for understanding how Scripture fits into practical theological research, which may lead to more generative conversation about the role of the Bible in the field. In so much as discerning Scripture is related to exegesis, the paradigm's focus on integration rather than correlation can help clarify practical theology's integrative nature. That is, practical theology is a discipline that integrates insights across disciplines. Yet, there is still a generally uneasy relationship between practical theology and the other theological disciplines. While it has been opined this may be because practical theology is enchanted by the social sciences,[38] which I do not think is an unfair criticism, it may also be that the field does not yet provide ways to explicitly describe how exactly one is choosing to integrate other theological disciplines into practical theological inquiries. It is on this point where my paradigm

---

36. Ward, *Introducing*, 5; Collins, *Reordering Reflection*, 150.

37. Collins, *Reordering Reflection*, 150.

38. Cartledge, *Mediation*, 50.

may provide clarity, as it is at the stage of *discerning Scripture* where the other theological disciplines can most clearly be integrated into reflection.[39]

Building from the descriptions of Browning, Ward, Cartledge, and others,[40] there are five core theological disciplines: exegetical theology, biblical theology, systematic or doctrinal theology, historical theology, and practical theology. Of these, practical theology is the only discipline which does not have a clear sense or method for using Scripture in its inquiries. However, it is my contention that practical theology *does not need its own Scriptural method*, instead just requiring its own *posture* towards utilizing the methods of the other disciplines. In saying this, I am proposing that practical theologians begin thinking of their use of Scripture in terms of a posture of integration, utilizing the methods other theological disciplines use for engaging Scripture to inform how we (practical theologians) use Scripture in our inquiries. This also opens the door for naming particular sub-methods within the other disciplines and more fully integrating them into practical theological research—such as the theological interpretation of Scripture, liberationist methods, feminist methods, postcolonial methods, and countless others.

Regarding posture, Cartledge has already proposed a vision for what a practical theological posture towards the use of Scripture might look like: hermeneutical reflexivity, attentiveness to the praxis of individuals and communities, attentiveness to agency in Scripture passages, a holistic practice of interpreting Scripture canonically, and an attentiveness to bringing "contemporary questions and issues emerging from lived reality" to Scripture.[41] It is my contention that my design and description of the Transformative Reading Paradigm matches the vision that Cartledge outlines.

If any of the above postural elements above could be considered critical to the field of practical theology, reflexivity seems to be it. As I have articulated in the introductory chapter, a self-reflective posture—to an entire research inquiry, but also to one's use of the Bible in the context of that inquiry—is critical for good practical theology work, which an integrative posture can help promote. Indeed, an integrative posture towards

39. Briggs hints towards disciplinary integration as a way for practical theologians to think about utilizing Scripture when he suggests, "Arguably a simpler way in to using Scripture in practical theology is through other theologians' readings of biblical texts." Briggs, "Practical Theology," 216.

40. Browning, *Fundamental*, 42–43; Ward, *Introducing*, 119–27; Cartledge, *Mediation*, 32–40.

41. Cartledge, *Mediation*, 45–46.

theological disciplines would necessarily require practical theologians to reflexively name the discipline whose methods they are utilizing when engaging Scripture. For example, my project could be described as utilizing a scriptural method of systematic theology, particularly as advanced by Peter Jensen related to the doctrine of revelation.[42] Practical theologians already reflexively name their social science methodological choices, thus there is precedence for naming methods in this way. Moreover, being open about the integrative nature of the discipline will open the field to further creative engagement with Scripture as the disciplines cross-pollinate, converse, and find coherence in the midst of theological reflection.[43] The vision of theological integration at the center of the Transformative Reading Paradigm thus may bring clarity to the use of Scripture, and open space for understanding practical theological work in a more comprehensive way. As Ward says, these disciplines—including the social sciences—should be understood by practical theologians to be "complementary and helpful . . . there must always be moments in which [each discipline's] insights and approaches are not only helpful but essential."[44] Importantly, this means social scientific methods will continue to serve a critical role in practical theological inquiry, as these methods help to complexify practice as lived. Indeed, these methods can help practical theologians interrogate each of the three discernments, and their relationship with one another, and thereby uncover places where the practices of the church could be more faithfully practiced.

Therefore, in future practical theological work, my paradigm could be used as a tool to structure research projects according to the three discernments described. The Quadrilateral Matrix could offer practical theology projects a potential theological reflection paradigm to organize the theological perspective(s) of their work—one that prioritizes Scripture but still recognizes the roles of other sources of theology and how they are dynamically utilized authoritatively in varied contexts and traditions. Furthermore, as implied above, the paradigm offers researchers specific places within which to locate their research, which may help complexify topics

42. Jensen would be considered my "conversation partner," to use the language of Bennett and Rowland (*Glass Darkly*, 16).

43. To a limited extent, this is evidenced by Zoë Bennett and Christopher Rowland, who worked together across theological disciplines to model a reflexive posture towards the Bible. As they argue, to reflect critically on the Bible in the light of life, and perhaps to even more importantly to reflect critically on life in the light of the Bible, is integral to living a reflective life." Bennett and Rowland, *Glass Darkly*, 4.

44. Ward, *Introducing*, 86.

and uncover hereinto ignored elements of practice—in relation to initial life situations, the relationships between the three discernments, and the expected transformation of situations at the far side of theological integration and biblical interpretive practice.

Finally, I believe this paradigm clarifies the difference between how my work relates to other research projects that investigate biblical interpretation in practical theology. For example, Village and Rogers both produced fruitful research on the interpretive practices of laity and their relationship with the Bible. Yet both focused on the role of prejudices in interpretation; Village seeks to name prejudices that can be triangulated to make predictive inferences, whereas Rogers names positive prejudices that the church can cultivate in Christians to inform faithful interpretive practice. Fit within my Transformative Reading Paradigm, their work is about naming and cultivating prejudices. By comparison, my work has been focused on describing and understanding the process of interpretation, including the role of theological integration. In this way, our research can be seen as fundamentally complementary, revealing different—but equally crucial—elements of biblical interpretation that, taken together, elucidate and improve this practice for the church.

## CONCLUDING SUMMARY

In this chapter I have sought to describe the three discernments of the practice of biblical interpretation. The first discernment, discerning ourselves, involves foregrounding prejudices through an honest openness to being confronted with all that we know and do not know—including what we do not know about ourselves and about our prejudices. This first discernment is an acknowledgment of our horizon so that we, as interpreters, can strive to experience the horizon of the Scripture "on its own terms" (insofar as this is humanly possible). The second discernment is discerning Scripture, or what might otherwise be referred to as exegesis. In this discernment one seeks to view the horizon of the text, and the canonic whole of Scripture, such that a fusion of horizons is able to occur that leads to greater understanding of what Scripture means and how we might live its message out. The final discernment is discerning transformational integration. In this discernment, integrative theological reflection utilizing the theological sources of the Quadrilateral Matrix is utilized in order to understand how the message of Scripture might transform understanding of particular situations according to the gospel. This transformation then becomes part of future preunderstanding, and a prejudice of both the individual and their community, as they face future situations requiring them to think through what it means to live faithfully as disciples of Jesus Christ. The Transformative Reading Paradigm which I have proposed, then, is not transformative because of what it is but because of what is at its center: a declaration from God, and a confession from believers that is the foundation of Christian transformation—that Jesus Christ is Lord of all.

# 7

## Concluding Reflections

SINCE I FIRST BEGAN writing this project in 2021, debates about sexuality and marriage within the CBOQ and throughout the Church worldwide have only intensified. The United Methodist denomination in the United States has seen a major split over the issue. The Christian Reformed Church (CRC) has also gone through a significant and turbulent discernment on this topic, leading to the denomination raising the traditional position on marriage to the status of a "confessional" belief—a seismic event in the life of the denomination, to be sure.[1] And of the many times the Anglican communion has engaged the topic, the 2022 Lambeth Conference in particular was marked by a sharp division between bishops of the Global South and bishops from the West due to differences in their interpretive conclusions regarding homosexuality. Suffice to say, watching these events unfold has sustained my motivation to see this project through to completion. In each of the above situations, participants routinely talked past one another, not realizing (or at least not making explicit) the complex hermeneutical and cultural forces at play in their disagreements. It is my hope that this project and its descriptions and conclusions can help bring some clarity to this theological debate in varied denominational contexts, and perhaps even create the ground for mutual understanding—even if and as conflict and division still come to pass.

---

1. VanderBerg, "Synod 2022 Summary."

185

## SUMMARY OF KEY FINDINGS

My project began with a dual goal: to describe the complexity in the ongoing debates about sexuality, particularly within my denominational context, and to develop a paradigm the church and practical theologians might use to help understand and discuss biblical interpretive practice. Utilizing a renewed form of the Wesleyan Quadrilateral, what I call the Quadrilateral Matrix, and applying the insights of metamodernism to hermeneutic theory, my research showed that interpreters today are moving back and forth between modern and postmodern sensibilities throughout the various stages of interpretation—primarily regarding theological integration. A study of this metamodern oscillation revealed core differences in approaches to understanding and wielding Scripture, Tradition, Reason, and Experience (of God), such that when traditional and affirming interpreters come together they are frequently unable to find very much in common as regards their interpretive practice.

Indeed, the foundations from which interpreters respectively function are significantly different. For Scripture, there are different passages and themes in view. While affirming interpreters pointed to the so-called clobber passages as the most important pericopes for understanding the sexuality debate, traditional texts pointed to Genesis 1–2 as their core texts. This difference in scriptural starting points reveals that the debate is, in some sense, a debate about theological anthropology, particularly for traditional interpreters. Furthermore, each perspective has different starting points in exegesis and utilizes Scripture in different ways, with traditional texts focusing on intertextuality between passages to define faithful response to Scripture, but affirming texts focusing on complex cultural reconstruction and defining faithfulness according to whether an interpretation of the passages causes what they perceive to be harm to others. For Tradition, a lack of meaningful reflection regarding Tradition was recognized for all the texts in the study. However, those who came to an affirming conclusion displayed a comparatively stronger sense of tradition (even if still weak overall), as well as a greater sense of self-awareness. Furthermore, the study discussed how the lack of reflection on tradition left interpreters without a common theological language, impeding the possibility of constructive dialogue across difference—about homosexuality and the church's understanding of sexuality, or any other topic of importance. For Reason, the competing notions of objectivity and intersubjectivity were noted to be in conflict, such that this quadrant has the potential to, by itself, derail attempts at dialogue. Indeed, alongside the author-reader divide in relation to Scripture, different views of human reason were a critical dividing point between the two positions. Finally, for Experience, the texts focused on different elements of God—the modernism-leaning texts on who God is, and the postmodernism-leaning texts on what God is doing. Again, this slight shift in focus is such that when the interpreters talk about their experience of God without clarifying what is in focus, they invariably end up speaking past each other because they are, in fact, discussing different things.

Thus, to help foreground the practice of biblical interpretation and to offer a tool for the church to use to understanding its biblical interpretive practice, I have proposed a Transformative Reading Paradigm. This paradigm, which can be summarized in the three discernments of *ourselves*, *Scripture*, and *transformative integration*, bring postmodern and modern attitudes together to help Christians describe their practice of biblical interpretation in the metamodern mood. What I have proposed will not bring debates, whether regarding homosexuality or other debates or conversations that the paradigm may be used regarding, to a close. However, I do believe this paradigm has the potential to help many denominational traditions understand more clearly what is happening in debates over biblical interpretation and thus dialogue critically and coherently about contested topics such as sexuality. Furthermore, the paradigm may also help bring clarity to debates regarding the role of Scripture in practical theology by creating space for understanding practical theology in ways which highlight its integrative posture towards multiple fields of study, theological and otherwise.

## FUTURE RESEARCH: LIMITATIONS AND OPPORTUNITIES

My findings in this project have uncovered multiple areas where future research can be developed. First, because the project focused on biblical interpretation as an act of discipleship, future research utilizing the Transformative Reading Paradigm could further refine the paradigm. For example, the paradigm could help structure a theological action research project involving a particular Christian community that intentionally reflects on how their practice of biblical interpretation leads them towards faithful living in Christ. Further research could also be done exploring the phenomena of people changing their minds regarding biblical interpretations and their reasons for doing so. Such research would further complexify how hermeneutical prejudices develop and compound over time, and could isolate particular prejudices that more regularly lead to certain interpretive conclusions, for the sexuality debate as well as other contested topics. Such research could also begin to reveal how individual and communal interpretive practices compound over time in complex and interesting ways.

One element of the sexuality debate that my research has revealed is the various fault lines that exist between the two main interpretive conclusions. Of particular interest is the difference in the use of Scripture, which gives rise to further questions regarding the importance of developing a robust theological anthropology. I found it striking that traditional interpreters seemed to hold theological anthropology as the core issue of the debate whereas the affirming interpreters seemed, to me, to think the debate was about sexuality (which I suspect meant they understood it to be about *identity*). Further work investigating the differences in articulation between the positions would help reveal why this element is being left out of the debate, and perhaps help each side develop a more coherent description of theological anthropology from which discussions about sexuality, identity, and other related topics can proceed.

While the research had limitations, each limitation is fertile ground from which future research can be developed. For example, one limitation of the study was that source materials were largely sermons or studies performed by Pastors in local congregations. As such, the type of metamodern oscillation I expected to find was viewable but not in as pronounced a way as I initially expected, especially in comparison to my reflections on the complexity of my own interpretive practice. Relatedly, some degree of self-censorship is likely in the sources given their genres (sermons and recorded studies) and the topic in view. Insomuch as speakers in the data self-censored, my data may not reflect the totality of their interpretive practice but rather what they deemed worth sharing or safe to share. It should be noted that this does not invalidate my research, as observing how leaders model interpretation for their congregation is an important element of communal discipleship for local churches.

Human participant research investigating the above question of pastoral self-censorship could help describe the interpretive process of those public figures who share their interpretive conclusions with others. Such self-censorship does not only shape the communication of conclusions, but also limits information that may lead to other conclusions such that the self-censorship could be an impediment to faithful interpretation, for the hearers (in the short term) and the speaker (in the long term). Indeed, the question has been raised, but to my knowledge not tested, regarding the extent to which preachers, who are the primary authority for how a church community interprets Scripture, might "deliberately ignore certain facets of the Bible, in order to promote a particular understanding and specific ways of behaving."[2] Further research on self-censorship could help substantiate or disavow this assertion, and further complexify the relationship between the practices of biblical interpretation and preaching. Such research could also help describe the relationship between metamodern interpretive practice and fundamentalisms, the latter of which is energized by the interpretation of leaders in the movement.[3]

There was also an important limitation in my capacity to discern the influence of premodern or fundamentalist elements in the collected data. This limitation is also an opportunity for further research into the character of (metamodern) fundamentalism, as well the extent to which premodern ideas continue to be utilized in contemporary thought (that is, in metamodernity), which would further complexify the metamodern oscillation.

My proposed reading paradigm could inform each of the potential research opportunities above, as it can help believers think more carefully about their interpretive practice, give them an understanding—or reveal a lack of understanding—in regard to their (theological) prejudices, and help them to constructively reflect on each of the discernments I have described to equip them for dialogue regarding differences in biblical interpretation. Indeed, each of the above future research opportunities could also complexify the reading paradigm, uncovering areas in need of thicker description, or refining it as an accurate descriptor of biblical interpretive practice.

Further study could also be done on the practice of biblical interpretation in various eras of a church or denominations life, which can help the Church better engage in critical reflection that can inform self-understanding, and therefore decisions being made and issues being addressed. To use my denomination as an example, research could be done on differences in biblical interpretation in the CBOQ during different eras of its history. Made possible via the publication *The Canadian Baptist*, as well as other historical sources, researchers could utilize hermeneutic content analysis or a similar methodology to map the premodern, fundamentalist, modern, and postmodern turns in Canadian Baptist biblical interpretation.

2. Bennett, *Using the Bible*, 15.
3. Lawrence, *Defenders*, 16.

By studying the sermons and studies within historical sources, researchers could help the convention better understand the foundations of many of the theological issues being faced today and clarify the terms of the debate within our local tradition to give Canadian Baptists a greater sense of tradition, which will benefit contemporary theological reflection.

Finally, this work has been descriptive of interpretive practice in the metamodern mood, seeking to elucidate how this practice is currently being carried out. While scholars of metamodernism have, so far, focused on the descriptive task related to this cultural movement's development, Jason Ānanda Josephson Storm's proposal towards reconstructive theory building suggests that constructive theoretical proposals for ways forward—that is, more robust metamodern theory building—is now both required and welcomed in the field. To this end, further work can be done to provide a theoretical vision of metamodern interpretive practice that can leverage description towards the end of theory building, which the hermeneutic phenomenology of Gadamer would aid. Indeed, as has already been noted, Gadamer's work could help metamodern scholarship take the next step towards offering descriptions of the metamodern tension in service to a theoretical prescriptive end, such that researchers can become better equipped to move beyond the vacillative tension between modernism and postmodernism.

## REFLECTING ON PRACTICE

As a practice-led research project, I think it appropriate to share how the writing of this dissertation, and my thinking through the various associated topics, has informed my own interpretive practice, specifically relating to the sexuality debate. First, the dissertation has helped me to realize the complexity in my own theological thinking, and through this the relative complexity of the sexuality debate (as well as other interpretive debates in the church). Bifurcating the Quadrilateral Matrix helped me to understand why, at times, I had difficulty speaking to others about the topic and why I was, at times, finding myself paralyzed by a tension between knowing what was being said but realizing the foundation of our understanding was different in some seemingly ineffable way. This is because, in my own thinking, I was oscillating between modern and postmodern impulses, and doing so without sufficient reflection to become aware that this was happening. Similarly, I was unable to discern which impulses my interlocutors were following and prompting them to place heavy emphasis on some facets of biblical interpretation rather than others. Because of my inability to reflect on this tension appropriately, I was unable to lead and pastor in the ways I needed to at certain times. In pursuing this research, the Lord has given me the language to describe my own interpretive practice, as well as to help others begin to describe theirs, which has equipped me to take a more gracious posture in contentious theological conversations.

Second, the project has reinforced the importance of doctrine as a critical prejudice, cementing—in my mind—the place of proper catechism and theological training in the church. Indeed, the differences the project uncovered between interpretive conclusions in how interpreters seemed to understand the importance of theological anthropology—that is, what it *means* that God created humanity as male and female—as well as an apparent difference in theologies of biblical revelation, crystallized this importance in my mind. Relatedly, the project has shaped my attitude towards Tradition, specifically in a renewed conviction regarding the importance of statements and confessions of faith. Not only are such statements meant to be summaries of a church's core beliefs, they describe what a faith tradition considers the boundaries of faithful interpretation, which is then entrusted to the tradition's catechetical processes. Related to this, part of the CBOQ's issue in having a debate regarding sexuality, as well as any other theological debate, is that the denomination no longer has recognizable and agreed upon boundaries. Thus, individual churches increasingly believe they can do and believe as they please. But without a shared prejudice related to tradition within the denomination, productive conversation can only ever be an uphill battle of misunderstanding and speaking past one another.

Finally, completing this project has also helped me recognize how I prioritize the theological sources of the Wesleyan Quadrilateral. Specifically, it has helped me realize how I prioritize Scripture due to my theological prejudices. Furthermore, while the project gave me a deeper appreciation for Scripture, one of its most surprising gifts has been how it has led me to a genuine respect for interpreters I disagree with, because I am better able to understand their point of view. Furthermore, it has given me a renewed interest in Tradition, and especially in Canadian Baptist history and the history of interpretive practice of the traditions that have shaped me (Roman Catholicism, Anabaptism, Methodism, Anglicanism, and General Baptists). For the CBOQ specifically, my interest is driven by a new conviction that the past saints of our denomination should have a voice in present debates. As I have already discussed, because of this project, CBOQ church's prejudice against their own history—even as shared history is the foundation of Baptist identity and polity—is something I am convicted is both unhealthy and unwise, and must be corrected if the denomination is to have constructive theological debates on any topic, let alone controversial topics, in the future.

In all, my research has helped me become a better practitioner, in that it has helped me understand my own biblical interpretive practice and given me the language to describe that process to others. As I continue in this practice—as a pastor, researcher, and a Christian more generally—I find myself reflecting on Psalm 119 and its beautiful reflections on the word of God. As O'Donovan says, "The prayer of the Psalmist, 'give me life according to your word!' (Ps 119:107) is the prayer of the faithful reader of Scripture who is ready to take the risk of living by it."[4] May we now seek to be faithful interpreters who take the risk of hearing God's Word and putting it into practice; transformed more and more, each day, into the image of Christ as we grow in our knowledge of the Triune God.

4. O'Donovan, *Crisis*, 58.

# Bibliography

Abernethy, Andrew T. *Savouring Scripture: A Six-Step Guide to Studying the Bible*. Downers Grove, IL: IVP Academic, 2022.

Abraham, William J. *Aldersgate and Athens: John Wesley and the Foundations of Christian Belief*. Waco, TX: Baylor University Press, 2010.

Ammerman, Nancy T. "North American Protestant Fundamentalism." In *Fundamentalisms Observed*, edited by Martin E. Marty and R. Scott Appleby, 1–65. Chicago: University of Chicago Press, 1991.

Andersen, Lene Rachel. *Metamodernity: Meaning and Hope in a Complex World*. København: Nordic Bildung, 2019.

Anderson, Ray S. *The Shape of Practical Theology: Empowering Ministry with Theological Praxis*. Downers Grove, IL: InterVarsity, 2001.

Aran, Gideon. "Jewish Zionist Fundamentalism: The Bloc of the Faithful in Israel (Gush Emunim)." In *Fundamentalisms Observed*, edited by Martin E. Marty and R. Scott Appleby, 265–344. Chicago: University of Chicago Press, 1991.

Ballard, Paul. "The Use of Scripture." In *The Wiley-Blackwell Companion to Practical Theology*, edited by Bonnie Miller-McLemore, 163–72. Chichester: Wiley-Blackwell, 2014.

Ballard, Paul, and John Pritchard. *Practical Theology in Action: Christian Thinking in Service of Church and Society*. London: SPCK, 1996.

Bargár, Pavol. "The Modern, the Postmodern, and . . . the Metamodern? Reflections on a Transforming Sensibility from the Perspective of Theological Anthropology." *Transformation* 38 (2021) 3–15.

Barthes, Roland. "The Death of the Author." In *Image, Music, Text*, translated by Stephen Burke, 142–48. London: Fontana, 1977.

Bartholomew, Craig G. *Introducing Biblical Hermeneutics: A Comprehensive Framework for Hearing God in Scripture*. Grand Rapids: Baker Academic, 2015.

Bartholomew, Theodore T., et al. "A Choir or Cacophony? Sample Sizes and Quality of Conveying Participants' Voices in Phenomenological Research." *Methodological Innovations* 14 (2021) 1–14.

Bass, Dorothy C. "Ways of Life Abundant." In *For Life Abundant: Practical Theology, Theological Education, and Christian Ministry*, edited by Dorothy Bass and Craig Dykstra, 21–40. Grand Rapids: Eerdmans, 2008.

Baxter, Jamie. "Content Analysis." In *International Encyclopedia of Human Geography*, edited by Audrey Kobayashi, 2:391–96. Oxford: Elsevier, 2020.

Beaudoin, Tom. "Why Does Practice Matter Theologically?" In *Conundrums in Practical Theology*, edited by Joyce Ann Mercer and Bonnie J. Miller-McLemore, 8–32. Leiden: Brill, 2016.

Bebbington, David W. *Evangelicalism in Modern Britain: A History from the 1730s to the 1980s*. London: Routledge, 1989.

Benac, Dustin D. "Theology for Crisis: Practical Theology and the Practice of Giving an Account." *Practical Theology* 16 (2023) 747–60.

Bennett, Zoë. *Using the Bible in Practical Theology: Historical and Contemporary Perspectives*. Burlington, VT: Ashgate, 2013.

Bennett, Zoë, and Christopher Rowland. *In a Glass Darkly: The Bible, Reflection, and Everyday Life*. London: SCM, 2016.

Bevins, Winfield. "A Pentecostal Appropriation of the Wesleyan Quadrilateral." *Journal of Pentecostal Theology* 14 (2006) 229–46.

Bielo, James S. *Words upon the Word: An Ethnography of Evangelical Group Bible Study*. New York: New York University Press, 2009.

Biggs, Michael, and Daniela Büchler. "Rigor and Practice-Based Research." *Design Issues* 23 (2007) 62–69.

Boaheng, Isaac. "The Wesleyan Quadrilateral and Contemporary Biblical Exegesis." *Journal of Mother-Tongue Biblical Hermeneutics and Theology* 2 (2020) 87–95.

Boersma, Hans. *Five Things Theologians Wish Biblical Scholars Knew*. Downers Grove, IL: IVP Academic, 2021.

Briggs, Richard S. "Biblical Hermeneutics and Practical Theology: Method and Truth in Context." *Anglican Theological Review* 97 (2015) 201–17.

Brown, Jeannine K. *Scripture as Communication: Introducing Biblical Hermeneutics*. 2nd ed. Grand Rapids: Baker Academic, 2021.

Brown, Sally. "Hermeneutical Theory." In *The Wiley-Blackwell Companion to Practical Theology*, edited by Bonnie J. Miller-McLemore, 112–22. Chichester: Wiley-Blackwell, 2014.

Browning, Don S. *A Fundamental Practical Theology: Descriptive and Strategic Proposals*. Minneapolis: Fortress, 1996.

———. *Practical Theology*. San Francisco: Harper & Row, 1983.

Burge, Ryan P. *The Nones: Where They Came From, Who They Are, and Where They Are Going*. Minneapolis: Fortress, 2021.

Byrne, Libby. "Practice-Led Theology: The Studio as a Site for Theology in the Making." *Theology* 120 (2017) 197–207.

Cahalan, Kathleen, and James Nieman. "Mapping the Field of Practical Theology." In *For Life Abundant: Practical Theology, Theological Education, and Christian Ministry*, edited by Dorothy Bass and Craig Dykstra, 62–85. Grand Rapids: Eerdmans, 2008.

Cameron, Helen, et al., eds. *Talking about God in Practice: Theological Action Research and Practical Theology*. London: SCM, 2010.

Cameron, Helen, et al. *Theological Reflection for Human Flourishing: Pastoral Practice and Public Theology*. London: SCM, 2012.

Canadian Baptists of Atlantic Canada. "General Operating Bylaw." https://baptist-atlantic.ca/wp-content/uploads/2021/07/CBAC-General-Operating-Bylaw-Updated-Spring-2021-web.pdf.

# Bibliography

Canadian Baptists of Ontario and Quebec. "CBOQ Assembly 2017 Summary." Etobicoke, ON: Canadian Baptists of Ontario and Quebec, 2017.

———. *This We Believe: Resources for Faith with Baptist Distinctives*. Etobicoke, ON: Canadian Baptists of Ontario and Quebec, 2016.

Canadian Baptists of Western Canada. "Identity Statement of the Canadian Baptists of Western Canada." https://cbwc.ca/wp-content/uploads/2023/02/FINAL-IDENTITY-STATEMENT-WITH-SCRIPTURE-REFERENCES-STATEMENT-OF-FAITH.pdf.

Canadian Institutes of Health Research, et al. *Tri-Council Policy Statement: Ethical Conduct for Research Involving Humans*. https://ethics.gc.ca/eng/documents/tcps2-2018-en-interactive-final.pdf.

Caputo, John D. *Deconstruction in a Nutshell: A Conversation with Jacque Derrida*. New York: Fordham University Press, 1997.

———. "Temporal Transcendence: The Very Idea of *à venir* in Derrida." In *Transcendence and Beyond: A Postmodern Inquiry*, edited by John D. Caputo and Michael J. Scanlon, 188–203. Bloomington: Indiana University Press, 2007.

Caputo, John D., and Michael J. Scanlon. "Introduction: Do We Need to Transcend Transcendence?" In *Transcendence and Beyond: A Postmodern Inquiry*, edited by John D. Caputo and Michael J. Scanlon, 1–16. Bloomington: Indiana University Press, 2007.

Carter, Craig A. *Interpreting Scripture with the Great Tradition: Recovering the Genius of Premodern Exegesis*. Grand Rapids: Baker Academic, 2018.

Cartledge, Mark J. *The Mediation of the Spirit: Interventions in Practical Theology*. Grand Rapids: Eerdmans, 2015.

———. "The Use of Scripture in Practical Theology: A Study of Academic Practice." *Practical Theology* 6 (2013) 271–83.

Clark, Elizabeth A. *History, Theory, Text: Historians and the Linguistic Turn*. Cambridge: Harvard University Press, 2004.

Clasquin-Johnson, Michel. "Towards a Metamodern Academic Study of Religion and a More Religiously Informed Metamodernism." *HTS Teologiese Studies/Theological Studies* 73 (2017) 1–11.

Collins, Helen. *Reordering Theological Reflection: Starting with Scripture*. London: SCM, 2020.

Corsa, Andrew J. "Grand Narratives, Metamodernism, and Global Ethics." *Cosmos and History* 14 (2018) 241–72.

Creedon, Anna Clare. *Do Small Groups Work? A Study of Biblical Engagement and Transformation*. London: SCM, 2021.

Day, Abby. *Believing in Belonging: Belief and Social Identity in the Modern World*. Oxford: Oxford University Press, 2011.

Dilthey, Wilhelm. "On Understanding and Hermeneutics: Student Lecture Notes (1867–68)." In *Wilhelm Dilthey: Selected Works*. Vol. 4, *Hermeneutics and the Study of History*, edited by Rudolf Makkreel and Frithjof Rodi, 229–34. Princeton: Princeton University Press, 1996.

Dulles, Avery R. *Models of Revelation*. Maryknoll, NY: Orbis, 1992.

Ehrensperger, Kathy. *Paul and the Dynamics of Power: Communication and Interaction in the Early Christ-Movement*. Library of New Testament Studies 325. New York: T. & T. Clark, 2007.

Erlingsson, Christen, and Petra Brysiewicz. "A Hands-On Guide to Doing Content Analysis." *African Journal of Emergency Medicine* 7 (2017) 93–99.

Espinoza, Benjamin D. Review of *Practical Theology: An Introduction*, by Richard Osmer. *Christian Education Journal* 10 (2013) 208–12.

Farley, Edward. "Interpreting Situations." In *Formation and Reflection: The Promise of Practical Theology*, edited by Lewis Seymour Mudge and James Poling, 1–26. Philadelphia: Fortress, 1987.

Faulkner, Peter. *Modernism*. 1977. Reprint, London: Routledge, 2013.

Feldman, Stephen Matthew. "Problem of Critique: Triangulating Habermas, Derrida, and Gadamer within Metamodernism." *Contemporary Political Theory* 4 (2005) 296–331.

Fish, Stanley E. *Is There a Text in This Class? The Authority of Interpretive Communities.* Cambridge: Harvard University Press, 1982.

Fortin, Ernest L. "Gadamer on Strauss: An Interview." *Interpretation* 12 (1984) 1–13.

Francis, Leslie J., et al., eds. *Empirical Theology in Texts and Tables: Qualitative, Quantitative, and Comparative Perspectives.* Leiden: Brill, 2009.

Fuyarchuk, Andrew. *Gadamer's Path to Plato: A Response to Heidegger and a Rejoinder by Stanley Rosen.* Eugene, OR: Wipf & Stock, 2010.

Gadamer, Hans-Georg. *The Gadamer Reader: A Bouquet of the Later Writings.* Edited by R. E. Palmer. Evanston, IL: Northwestern University Press, 2007.

———. *Truth and Method.* Translated by Joel Weinsheimer and Donald G. Marshall. Bloomsbury Revelations Series. London: Bloomsbury, 2013.

Gerrie, Vanessa. *Borderless Fashion Practice: Contemporary Fashion in the Metamodern Age.* Newark, NJ: Rutgers University Press, 2023.

Graham, Elaine L. Review of *Practical Theology: An Introduction*, by Richard Osmer. *Scottish Journal of Theology* 64 (2011) 493–94.

Graham, Elaine L., et al. *Theological Reflection: Methods.* 2nd ed. London: SCM, 2019.

Graves, Michael. *The Inspiration and Interpretation of Scripture: What the Early Church Can Teach Us.* Grand Rapids: Eerdmans, 2014.

Gray, Carole. "From the Ground Up: Encountering Theory in the Process of Practice-led Doctoral Research." Paper presented at Arts and Humanities Research Council Postgraduate Conference, Loughborough, UK, June 26, 2007.

———. "Inquiry through Practice: Developing Appropriate Research Strategies." http://carolegray.net/Papers%20PDFs/ngnm.pdf.

Green, Chris E. W. *Sanctifying Interpretation: Vocation, Holiness, and Scripture.* 2nd ed. Cleveland, TN: CPT, 2020.

Gregory, Jeremy. "The Long Eighteenth Century." In *The Cambridge Companion to John Wesley*, edited by Randy Maddox and Jason Vickers, 13–39. Cambridge: Cambridge University Press, 2010.

Grenz, Stanley J. *A Primer on Postmodernism.* Grand Rapids: Eerdmans, 1996.

Grenz, Stanley J., and John Franke. *Beyond Foundationalism: Shaping Theology in a Postmodern Context.* Louisville: Westminster John Knox, 2001.

Grondin, Jean. *Introduction to Philosophical Hermeneutics.* New Haven: Yale University Press, 1994.

Guest, Greg, et al. "How Many Interviews Are Enough? An Experiment with Data Saturation and Variability." *Field Methods* 18 (2006) 59–82.

Gunter, W. Stephen, et al., eds. *Wesley and the Quadrilateral: Renewing the Conversation.* Nashville: Abingdon, 1997.

# Bibliography

Han, Byung-Chul. *Hyperculture: Culture and Globalization*. Translated by Daniel Steuer. Cambridge: Polity, 2022.

Hanegraaff, Wouter J. "Provincializing American Theory." *Religious Studies Review* 48 (2022) 510–12.

Hastings, W. Ross. *Pastoral Ethics: Moral Formation as Life in the Trinity*. Bellingham, WA: Lexham Academic, 2022.

Heiser, Jörg. "Super-Hybridity: Non-Simultaneity, Myth-Making, and Multipolar Conflict." In *Metamodernism: Historicity, Affect, and Depth after Postmodernism*, edited by Robin van den Akker, et al., 55–68. London: Rowman and Littlefield International, 2017.

Hiemstra, Rick. *Confidence, Conversation, and Community: Bible Engagement in Canada, 2013*. Toronto: Faith Today, 2014.

Hirsch, E. D. *Validity in Interpretation*. New Haven: Yale University Press, 1967.

Hoffmeister, Andrew Charles. "Fundamentalism and Modernity: A Critique of the 'Anti-Modern' Conception of Fundamentalism." MA thesis, Georgia State University, 2006.

Holben, Lawrence. *What Christians Think about Homosexuality: Six Representative Views*. North Richland, TX: Bibal, 1999.

Hollinger, Dennis. *The Meaning of Sex: Christian Ethics and the Moral Life*. Grand Rapids: Baker Academic, 2009.

Holsinger, Bruce. *The Premodern Condition: Medievalism and the Making of Theory*. Chicago: University of Chicago Press, 2005.

Huber, Irmtraud, and Wolfgang Funk. "Reconstructing Depth: Authentic Fiction and Responsibility." In *Metamodernism: Historicity, Affect, and Depth after Postmodernism*, edited by Robin van den Akker, et al., 151–66. London: Rowman and Littlefield International, 2017.

Hughes, Glenn. *From Dickinson to Dylan: Visions of Transcendence in Modernist Literature*. Columbia, MO: University of Missouri Press, 2020.

Irenaeus. *Against Heresies*. In *Ante-Nicene Fathers*, edited by Alexander Roberts and James Donaldson, 1:315–567. 1885. Reprint, Peabody, MA: Hendrickson, 1994.

James, William. *The Varieties of Religious Experience: A Study in Human Nature*. New York: Longmans, Green, and Co., 1917.

Jensen, Peter. *The Revelation of God*. Contours of Christian Theology. Downers Grove, IL: InterVarsity, 2002.

Johnson, Keith. *Theology as Discipleship*. Downers Grove, IL: InterVarsity, 2015.

Judd, Andrew. *Playing with Scripture: Reading Contested Biblical Texts with Gadamer and Genre Theory*. London: Routledge, 2023.

Julien, Heidi. "Content Analysis." In *The Sage Encyclopedia of Qualitative Research Methods*, edited by Lisa Given, 120–21. Los Angeles: Sage, 2008.

Kirby, Alan. "The Death of Postmodernism and Beyond." *Philosophy Now* 58 (2006) 34–37.

———. *Digimodernism: How New Technologies Dismantle the Postmodern and Reconfigure Our Culture*. New York: Continuum, 2009.

Kochlefl, Mary Katherine. "From Modernist Transcendence to Postmodern Immanence: Redefining Divinity and Authority in 20th Century American Theology and Literature." PhD diss., Indiana University, 2003.

Krippendorff, Klaus. *Content Analysis: An Introduction to Its Methodology*. 2nd ed. Thousand Oaks, CA: Sage, 2004.

Lacoste, Jean-Yves. "More Haste, Less Speed in Theology." *International Journal of Systematic Theology* 9 (2007) 263–82.

Larkin, William. "Approaches to and Images of Biblical Authority for the Postmodern Mind." *Bulletin for Biblical Research* 8 (1998) 129–38.

Lawrence, Bruce B. *Defenders of God: The Fundamentalist Revolt against the Modern Age.* San Francisco: Harper and Row, 1989.

Lawson, Kevin. "Theological Reflection, Theological Method, and the Practice of Education Ministry: Exploring the Wesleyan Quadrilateral and Stackhouse's Tetralectic." *Christian Education Journal* 1 (1997) 49–64.

Leiviskä, Anniina. "The Revelation of Hans-Georg Gadamer's Concept of Tradition to the Philosophy of Education." *Educational Theory* 65 (2015) 581–600.

Lindbeck, George. A. *The Nature of Doctrine: Religion and Theology in a Postliberal Age.* Philadelphia: Westminster, 1984.

Lyotard, Jean-Francois. *The Postmodern Condition: A Report on Knowledge.* Minneapolis: University of Minnesota Press, 1984.

MacMillan, Ken. "John Wesley and the Enlightened Historians." *Methodist History* 38 (2000) 121–32.

Maddox, Randy L. *Responsible Grace: John Wesley's Practical Theology.* Nashville: Abingdon, 1994.

Makkreel, Rudolf A. "Dilthey: Hermeneutics and Neo-Kantianism." In *Routledge Companion to Hermeneutics,* edited by Jeff Malpas and Hans-Helmuth Gander, 74–85. Routledge Philosophy Companions. London: Routledge, 2015.

Malcolm, Matthew R. *From Hermeneutics to Exegesis: The Trajectory of Biblical Interpretation.* Nashville: B&H Academic, 2018.

McAdoo, Henry R. *The Spirit of Anglicanism: A Survey of Anglican Theological Method in the Seventeenth Century.* London: A. & C. Black, 1965.

McFarlane, Graham. *A Model for Evangelical Theology: Integrating Scripture, Tradition, Reason, Experience, and Community.* Grand Rapids: Baker Academic, 2020.

McGuire, Seán. "Being Equipped for Every Good Work: Scripture Study and the Missio Dei." In *Singing into Splintered Spaces: The Rhythms of Mission and Spiritual Discipline,* edited by E. Janet Warren, 44–58. Eugene, OR: Cascade, 2022.

McHale, Brian G. "Introduction: On or About the Year 1966." In *The Cambridge History of Postmodern Literature,* edited by Brian McHale and Len Platt, 85–94. Cambridge: Cambridge University Press, 2016.

McKnight, Edgar V. *Postmodern Use of the Bible: The Emergence of Reader-Oriented Criticism.* Eugene, OR: Wipf & Stock, 2005.

McLaren, Brian. *A New Kind of Christianity: Ten Questions That Are Transforming the Faith.* New York: HarperOne, 2011.

McNamara, Andrew. "Six Rules for Practice-Led Research." *TEXT: Journal of Writing and Writing Courses* 16 (2012) 1–15.

Merwe, Dirk van der. "Reading the Bible in the 21st Century: Some Hermeneutical Principles: Part 1." *Verbum et Ecclesia* 36 (2015) 1–8.

Miller-McLemore, Bonnie J. "Introduction: The Contributions of Practical Theology." In *The Wiley-Blackwell Companion to Practical Theology,* edited by Bonnie J. Miller-McLemore, 1–20. Chichester: Wiley-Blackwell, 2014.

Morris, Helen, and Helen Cameron, *Evangelicals Engaging in Practical Theology: Theology that Impacts the Church and World.* New York: Routledge, 2022.

Morris-Chapman, D. J. Pratt. "Beyond the Quadrilateral: The Place of Nature in John Wesley's Epistemology of Theology." *Theological Studies* 78 (2022) 1–8.

Motak, Dominika. "Postmodern Spirituality and the Culture of Individualism." *Scripta Instituti Donneriana Aboensis* 21 (2009) 149–61.

Moules, Nancy J., et al. *Conducting Hermeneutic Research: From Philosophy to Practice.* Critical Qualitative Research 19. New York: Lang, 2015.

Mul, Jos de. *Romantic Desire in (Post)modern Art and Philosophy.* Albany, NY: State University of Albany, 1999.

Murphy, John L. "Modernism and the Teaching of Schleiermacher, Part 1." *American Ecclesiastical Review* 116 (1962) 377–97.

O'Donovan, Oliver. *Church in Crisis: The Gay Controversy and the Anglican Communion.* Eugene, OR: Cascade, 2008.

Osborne, Grant R. *The Hermeneutical Spiral: A Comprehensive Introduction to Biblical Interpretation.* 2nd ed. Downers Grove, IL: InterVarsity, 2006.

Osmer, Richard R. *Practical Theology: An Introduction.* Grand Rapids: Eerdmans, 2008.

Outler, Albert C. "The Wesleyan Quadrilateral in John Wesley." *Wesleyan Theological Journal* 20 (1985) 7–18.

———. *The Wesleyan Theological Heritage: Essays of Albert C. Outler.* Edited by Thomas Oden and Leicester Longden. Grand Rapids: Zondervan, 1991.

Packiam, Glenn. *Worship and the World to Come: Exploring Christian Hope in Contemporary Worship.* Downers Grove, IL: InterVarsity, 2020.

Pattison, Stephen. "Some Straws for the Bricks: A Basic Introduction to Theological Reflection." *Contact* 99 (1989) 2–9.

Pattison, Stephen, and James Woodward. "An Introduction to Pastoral and Practical Theology." In *The Blackwell Reader in Pastoral and Practical Theology*, edited by James Woodward and Stephen Pattison, 1–19. Malden, MA: Blackwell, 2000.

Paver, John E. *Theological Reflection and Education for Ministry.* Explorations in Practical, Pastoral, and Empirical Theology. London: Routledge, 2021.

Peckham, John C. *Canonical Theology: The Biblical Canon, Sola Scriptura, and Theological Method.* Grand Rapids: Eerdmans, 2016.

Pius X. *Pascendi Dominici Gregis.* https://www.vatican.va/content/pius-x/en/encyclicals/documents/hf_p-x_enc_19070908_pascendi-dominici-gregis.html.

Pool, Jeff B. "Christ, Conscience, Canon, Community: Web of Authority in the Baptist Vision." *Perspectives in Religious Studies* 24 (1997) 417–45.

Porter, Stanley E. *Interpretation for Preaching and Teaching: An Introduction to Biblical Hermeneutics.* Grand Rapids: Baker Academic, 2023.

Porter, Stanley E., and Matthew R. Malcolm, eds. *The Future of Biblical Interpretation.* Milton Keynes: Paternoster, 2013.

Porter, Stanley E., and Jason C. Robinson. *Hermeneutics: An Introduction to Interpretive Theory.* Eerdmans: Grand Rapids, 2011.

Powell, Mark Allan. *What Do They Hear? Bridging the Gap between Pulpit and Pew.* Nashville: Abingdon, 2007.

Putman, Rhyne R. *The Method of Christian Theology: A Basic Introduction.* Nashville: B&H Academic, 2021.

———. *When Doctrine Divides the People of God: An Evangelical Approach to Theological Diversity.* Wheaton, IL: Crossway, 2020.

Ratté, John. "The Transcendence of God and the Modernist Crisis." *CTSA* 23 (2012) 221–44.

Reimer, Sam. *Caught in the Current: British and Canadian Evangelicals in an Age of Self-Spirituality.* Montreal: McGill-Queen's University Press, 2023.

# Bibliography

Roest, Hank de. *Collaborative Practical Theology: Engaging Practitioners in Research on Christian Practice*. Leiden: Brill, 2020.

Rogers, Andrew P. *Congregational Hermeneutics: How Do We Read?* Burlington, VT: Ashgate, 2015.

———. "Looking into the Mirror: The Bible, Normativity, and Reflexivity." *Practical Theology* 16 (2023) 462–88.

Root, Andrew. *Christopraxis: A Practical Theology of the Cross*. Minneapolis: Fortress, 2014.

Saldaña, Johnny. *The Coding Manual for Qualitative Researchers*. London: Sage, 2021.

Schleiermacher, Friedrich. *Hermeneutics: The Handwritten Manuscripts*. Edited by Heinz Kimmerle. AAR Texts and Translation 1. Missoula, MT: Scholars, 1977.

———. *Hermeneutics and Criticism and Other Writings*. Translated by Andrew Bowie. Cambridge Texts in the History of Philosophy. Cambridge: Cambridge University Press, 1998.

Schindler, D. C. "Metamodernism and Its Premodern Forebear." *Ad Fontes*, February 2022. https://adfontesjournal.com/member-exclusive/metamodernism-and-its-premodern-forebear.

Schreier, Margrit. *Qualitative Content Analysis in Practice*. Los Angeles: Sage, 2012.

Smith, Kevin G. Review of *Practical Theology: An Introduction*, by Richard Osmer. *Conspectus: The Journal of the South African Theological Seminary* 10 (2010) 99–113.

Sprinkle, Preston. *People to Be Loved: Why Homosexuality Is Not Just an Issue*. Grand Rapids: Zondervan, 2015.

Stackhouse, John G. *Making the Best of It: Following Jesus in the Real World*. Oxford: Oxford University Press, 2008.

Stein, Zachary. "Love in a Time between Worlds: On the Metamodern 'Return' to a Metaphysics of Eros." *Integral Review* 14 (2018) 187–221.

Steinmetz, David C. "The Superiority of Pre-critical Exegesis." *Theology Today* 37 (1980) 27–38.

Stone, Howard, and James Duke. *How to Think Theologically*. 3rd ed. Minneapolis: Fortress, 2013.

Storm, Jason Ānanda Josephson. *Metamodernism: The Future of Theory*. Chicago: University of Chicago Press, 2021.

Swinton, John, and Harriet Mowatt. *Practical Theology and Qualitative Research*. 2nd ed. London: SCM, 2016.

Tate, W. Randolph. *Biblical Interpretation: An Integrated Approach*. 3rd ed. Peabody, MA: Hendrickson, 2008.

Taylor, Charles. *Modern Social Imaginaries*. Durham, NC: Duke University Press, 2004.

———. *A Secular Age*. Cambridge: Harvard University Press, 2007.

Thiselton, Anthony C. *Hermeneutics: An Introduction*. Grand Rapids: Eerdmans, 2009.

———. *New Horizons in Hermeneutics: The Theory and Practice of Transforming Biblical Reading*. Grand Rapids: Zondervan, 1992.

Thorsen, Donald. *The Wesleyan Quadrilateral: Scripture, Tradition, Reason, & Experience as a Model of Evangelical Theology*. Lexington, KY: Emeth, 1990.

Tillich, Paul. *Perspectives on Nineteenth and Twentieth Century Protestant Theology*. London: SCM, 1967.

Timmer, Nicole. "Radical Defenselessness: A New Sense of Self in the Work of David Foster Wallace." In *Metamodernism: Historicity, Affect, and Depth after Postmodernism*, edited by Robin Van den Akker, et al., 103–16. London: Rowman and Littlefield International, 2017.

Toren, Benno van den, and Liz Hoare. "Evangelicals and Contextual Theology: Lessons from Missiology for Theological Reflection." *Practical Theology* 8 (2015) 77–98.

Tracy, David. *Blessed Rage of Order*. New York: Seabury, 1975.

Turner, Tom. *City as Landscape: A Post-Postmodern View of Design and Planning*. London: E. & FN. Spon, 1996.

Tyson, Paul G. *Returning to Reality: Christian Platonism for Our Times*. Cambridge: Lutterworth, 2015.

Van den Akker, Robin, and Timotheus Velmeulen. "Periodising the 2000s, or, the Emergence of Metamodernism." In *Metamodernism: Historicity, Affect, and Depth after Postmodernism*, edited by Robin Van den Akker, et al., 1–20. London: Rowman and Littlefield International, 2017.

VanderBerg, Kristen deRoo. "Synod 2022 Summary." *CRCNA News and Events*, June 22, 2022. https://www.crcna.org/news-and-events/news/synod-2022-summary.

Vanhoozer, Kevin. *Is There a Meaning in This Text? The Bible, the Reader, and the Morality of Literary Knowledge*. Grand Rapids: Zondervan, 2009.

Velmeulen, Timotheus. "Depth." In *Metamodernism: Historicity, Affect, and Depth after Postmodernism*, edited by Robin Van den Akker, et al., 147–50. London: Rowman and Littlefield International, 2017.

Velmeulen, Timotheus, and Robin van den Akker. "Notes on Metamodernism." *Journal of Aesthetics and Culture* 2 (2010). https://doi.org/10.3402/jac.v2i0.5677.

———. "Utopia, Sort of: A Case Study in Metamodernism." *Studia Neophilologica* 87 (2015) 55–67.

Ven, Johannes van der. *Practical Theology: An Empirical Approach*. Translated by Barbara Schultz. Leuven: Peeters, 1998.

Vilhauer, Monica. *Gadamer's Ethics of Play: Hermeneutics and the Other*. Plymouth: Lexington, 2010.

Village, Andrew. *The Bible and Lay People: An Empirical Approach to Ordinary Hermeneutics*. Burlington, VT: Ashgate, 2007.

Walton, Roger L. "The Teaching and Learning of Theological Reflection: Case Studies of Practice." PhD diss., Durham University, 2002.

———. "Using the Bible and Christian Tradition in Theological Reflection." *British Journal of Theological Education* 13 (2003) 133–51.

Ward, Pete. *Introducing Practical Theology: Mission, Ministry, and the Life of the Church*. Grand Rapids: Baker Academic, 2017.

Webster, John. *The Domain of the Word: Scripture and Theological Reason*. New York: T. & T. Clark, 2012.

———. *Holy Scripture: A Dogmatic Sketch*. Current Issues in Theology 1. New York: Cambridge University Press, 2003.

Westphal, Merold. *Whose Community? Which Interpretation? Philosophical Hermeneutics for the Church*. Grand Rapids: Baker, 2009.

Whitehead, James. "The Practical Play of Theology." In *Formation and Reflection: The Promise of Practical Theology*, edited by Lewis Seymour Mudge and James Poling, 36–54. Philadelphia: Fortress, 1987.

Whitehead, James, and Evelyn Eaton Whitehead. *Method in Ministry: Theological Reflection and Christian Ministry*. Oxford: Sheed & Ward, 1995.

# Bibliography

Wimsatt, William K., and Monroe C. Beardsley. "The Intentional Fallacy." *Sewanee Review* 54 (1946) 468–88.

Winterling, Aloys. *Caligula: A Biography*. Oakland: University of California Press, 2011.

Wit, Hans de. *Empirical Hermeneutics, Interculturality, and Holy Scripture*. Intercultural Biblical Hermeneutics Series 1. Elkhart, IN: Institute of Mennonite Studies, 2012.

Wright, N. T. *Galatians*. Commentaries for Christian Formation. Grand Rapids: Eerdmans, 2021.

# Index

# Index

theological interpretation of Scripture, 47–49, 100

theological reflection, 7–9, 20, 58, 60–61, 63, 68, 81–82, 91–92, 99; correlative, 63; integrative, 64, 64n.139, 66, 180; methods, 58–63, 77–79 (*see also* hermeneutics), method; source priority, 85, 87, 92–93, 100, 146, 171, 182

Thiselton, Anthony, 38–39

Thorsen, Donald, 22, 58, 66, 68–69, 78n.13, 84, 88

Tillich, Paul, 17, 63

Tracy, David, 63

tradition, 6, 24, 42–43, 60, 71, 144, 151–54, 162–64

traditional (theology of marriage), 2–3, 5, 31, 100, 121, 124, 129, 140–41, 149–50, 153, 166, 170, 178–79, 185–86, 188, 190

transcendence, 98–99, 105, 131, 145–46, 154, 156, 172

transformation, 12–13, 57, 62, 171, 174, 183–84

transformative reading paradigm, 175–77

Turner, Tom, 42n.41

universal truth, 97, 126–27

validity, 28–29, 107

Vanhoozer, Kevin, 45, 47, 57–58

Velmeulen, Timotheus, 15, 20, 76

Ven, Johannes van der, 10

Vilhauer, Monica, 44

Village, Andrew, 11–13, 183

Walton, Roger, 60–61, 62n.131

Ward, Pete, 62, 171, 179–80

Webster, John, 50, 55

Wesley, John, 66–68, 80, 84, 85, 86, 88,

Westphal, Merold, 163

Whitehead, Evelyn, 59–60, 65, 177

Whitehead, James, 59–60, 65, 177

Wimsatt, William, 37

Wolf, Freidrich August, 35n.9

Wolfe, Virginia, 17

Woodward, James, 60

www.ingramcontent.com/pod-product-compliance
Lightning Source LLC
Chambersburg PA
CBHW060336100426
42812CB00003B/1019